Advance Praise for

Lean Out

"*Lean Out* rang so true for me, and gave me the permission I needed to say no to two assignments that normally I would just say yes to—because I'm terrified of missing a single opportunity, of appearing ungrateful, and falling behind. Adrenaline can play a role in keeping us alive, but it's no way to live. Beautifully written, brimming with insight and reassurance—I'm so grateful for this book."

—Olivia Sudjic, author of *Exposure*

LEAN OUT

A MEDITATION ON
THE MADNESS OF MODERN LIFE

TARA HENLEY

appetite

Appetite by Random House® and colophon are registered
trademarks of Penguin Random House LLC.

Library and Archives of Canada Cataloguing in Publication
is available upon request.
ISBN: 978-0-52561-091-5
eBook ISBN: 978-0-52561-092-2

Cover images: (island) Olga Matveeva/Moment; (paper page)
MirageC/Moment; (city) rorat/IStock. All via Getty Images.
Printed and bound in the USA

Published in Canada by Appetite by Random House®,
a division of Penguin Random House Canada Limited.

www.penguinrandomhouse.ca

10 9 8 7 6 5 4 3 2 1

appetite   Penguin
by RANDOM HOUSE   Random House
                  Canada

This book is for my mother and my brother.

Why does anybody tell a story? It does indeed
have something to do with faith, faith that
the universe has meaning, that our little human
lives are not irrelevant, that what we choose or
say or do matters, matters cosmically.

—MADELEINE L'ENGLE

CONTENTS

"*What do you do when the work you love tastes like dust?*"
I first heard this question in an airy newsroom in Vancouver, during a downpour in February of 2016. TED was in town, and I was watching a YouTube talk on burnout from TV mogul Shonda Rhimes. I had pitched a segment on this phenomenon for our morning radio show the next day, and was busy trying to track down an expert to talk about the global epidemic of overwork.

Watching the video, it dawned on me that Rhimes's story was actually my own. And that her question couldn't have come at a better time.

I was forty years old, and had been working at breakneck speed for fifteen years. I had traveled the world, from Soweto to Bangkok and Paris to Brooklyn, interviewing authors and community leaders, rappers and philanthropists, politicians and Hollywood celebrities. I had trekked the jungles of Borneo. Visited Buckingham Palace. Experienced the thrill of sitting down with Beyoncé. And of debating with Kanye West.

But in that moment, none of it seemed to matter. I was hunched over my desk, holding my torso, racked by chest pains that I was trying—and failing—to ignore.

My drive, always my greatest asset, suddenly felt like a dangerous liability.

The Work World

One of the great challenges of my life is that I have never had the stamina to match my enthusiasm. In the beginning of things, the shiny and new stage, I'm like those motivational posters in corporate boardrooms, all triumphant hikers atop mountain peaks and eagles soaring through cloudless skies. Which is to say: I unleash my potential, I go above and beyond, I make things happen. And there's a real sense of satisfaction to be had in that. At least, there would be if I could ever get a moment to stop and catch my breath.

The thing is, I'm a sprinter, not a marathoner. And so, after hurling myself at a job for months or years, I inevitably get weary and worn out. I can't keep up the pace. And then I get a lung infection, or some other such ailment, and I can never quite seem to regain my momentum.

This is the story of my complicated relationship with modern life. I moved to a big city at the age of thirty, and stayed until I was weeks shy of my fortieth birthday. But if I had a stronger constitution, I would probably be there still, logging twelve-hour days and donning cocktail dresses well into my sixties.

When I arrived in Toronto, back in 2006, I had no idea I'd stay. Like many across the country, I thought it was too big, too ugly, too corporate, too cold. I figured there was a reason my hippie parents had fled the city when I was still an infant, driving a run-down camper across the States to the West Coast, stopping at folk festivals along the way.

So I can't say that I *wanted* to move to Toronto, per se. It was more that I needed to move, period.

In short: my hometown was suffocating me. I found Vancouver's scenic beauty oppressive, its inhabitants slow-moving and smug. I did not want to sit in coffee shops, waiting for friends to finally drift in, thirty minutes late. I did not want to check out *The Secret*. I did not want to quit eating refined sugar, or have my chakras read, or attend workshops to learn Lion's Breath. I did not want to do a master cleanse.

There were other problems, too. After completing a master's degree, I was $60,000 in debt. And trying to make my living as a freelance journalist. It was difficult to pay rent, and at times even to buy groceries.

I hadn't planned for this state of affairs. During grad school, studying English Lit, I had joined the staff at the student newspaper on a whim—largely because one of its editors, now an acclaimed essayist and stand-up comic, penned a weekly column called "Thank You/Screw You" that was so insanely smart and funny I felt compelled to get involved.

My first assignment was a news story on Disney and sweatshop labor, in the summer of 2001. Nobody in Canada was able to get a comment from the company. Late one night in the paper's cavernous basement office, I somehow got through to Disney's director of corporate relations and he gave me an interview. The next day, I went to see my favorite professor, and she told me I should call up our local independent newsweekly and offer to sell them the story.

I did, and they bought it, and then after it ran the news editor agreed to meet with me. "Do you want to do this?" he asked over coffee. It had never occurred to me that I could become a journalist. Without hesitating, I said yes. I was, by then, writing my master's thesis on hip-hop (a story for another day), and so the news editor referred me to the music editor, who started assigning me concert reviews and interviews.

I soon discovered one of the great joys of journalism: you could get curious about something, anything at all, and call up whoever was doing it and ask them about it. I loved this. And I loved doing things people in my sleepy West Coast town would never have imagined possible. Covering global hip-hop summits in Caracas or Johannesburg, say, or landing an online column with the American rap bible, *XXL*. I loved feeling like I was bang-smack in the middle of the action. Of life.

Of course, I knew absolutely nothing in those days, and was too scared to ask anyone, let alone my editor. I did not know, for instance, that it was not normal for a male recording artist you interviewed on the phone to invite you backstage after his show to say hello. (I learned fast.) I did not know that you weren't supposed to spend your own money chasing down stories, either, so I waitressed and sent myself to Manhattan to stand in the back of B.B. King's at two in the morning, surrounded by semi-famous rappers, and to share vegan meals in the East Village with radical rap duos who were unfailingly polite.

In the weeks leading up to the second Gulf War, I was in New York again, this time writing a story about anti-war hip-hop. One bitterly cold night, I took the train into Brooklyn, where a young artist met me at the Clinton–Washington Avenues station and walked me through his neighborhood to an apartment in an old brownstone that he shared with his entire rap group, where we all sat around and listened to Coltrane and drank herbal tea and talked politics. Later, I stood on an abandoned subway platform, listening to George W. Bush give his State of the Union address.

The morning papers screamed of war, and a sense of foreboding could be felt throughout the city, then still reeling from the trauma of 9/11. I recall one rapper telling me what it was like in the months after September 11, how haunted everyone was. How you would sit in bars and hear snippets of the same conversation, over and over again.

I was in the center of one of the biggest news stories in the world, and I didn't ever want to leave. But I was scheduled to travel to a Canadian university town to speak at a cultural studies conference that was expected to be cutting edge. I took a fifteen-hour train north. When I arrived, not one single professor mentioned Iraq. It was business as usual: long, tedious debates on postmodernism.

I gave the talk that I had prepared, to an audience of about eleven people. And then I went home to Vancouver and wrote my story on anti-war hip-hop for my newspaper's hundreds of thousands of readers. The next week when it came out, I was at a Starbucks on Main Street when I spotted a man my age who sat, engrossed, reading it. My decision to leave academia was so easy as to barely be a decision at all.

In the years after I became a full-time journalist, I scored bylines in newspapers like the *Globe and Mail* and *The Guardian*, in addition to my column at *XXL*. But I could not get enough assignments to pay the rent, and I could not get a staff job to move legally to New York. I sent wave after wave of pitches and job applications and query letters out into the abyss of the Internet.

The rest of the time, I watched *Sex and the City* reruns and pined for the life I felt I should be living. I walked Kits Beach every morning, blasting Alicia Keys in my headphones, sick with restlessness and longing. All I wanted was to write regularly, go out at night to interesting events and become friends with other people doing the same. Eventually, in July of 2006, bored and broke and thoroughly fed up, I packed up an enormous purple mountaineering backpack, took a $2,000 cash advance on my credit card and left town, frowning furiously over my shoulder.

I went to Toronto because it was the only big North American city that could offer me top media opportunities, legal employment and free healthcare. When I landed, the city came as a total surprise—a gift I wasn't expecting. Almost immediately, I got everything I wanted in life, and it was just as wondrous as I had imagined.

That first humid summer, moving into a shared loft in Kensington Market, I walked the area in a state of awe. The streets were full of punk rockers and their rescue dogs, Rastafarians playing bongo drums, Caribbean grandmothers, University of Toronto students comparing produce prices. Bay Street lawyers in tailored suits shopping for charcuterie. The air was a heady mix of incense, marijuana fumes and chili smoke.

I walked past dim sum restaurants on Dundas, slim brick Victorians in the Annex, markets on Baldwin, stands overflowing with durian and star fruit, okra and plantain. Past streetcars on Queen and lines of taxis, Somali drivers with their heads hung out the window, K'naan's "Soobax" blaring from the radio. I watched a black woman in her sixties cross the street, arms flung around a white woman her age, their heads thrown back in laughter. *This city is special*, I thought. *Where else could you have all this?*

Fall arrived, with its riot of red and orange and yellow leaves. I hurried down Spadina, my coat turned up against the wind, my life feeling like an early Margaret Atwood novel. I checked out books from the library, and counted coins for plates of fried noodles at King's, and walked up and down wooded ravines. I went on dates to documentaries at the Carlton, and attended potlucks at the Danforth homes of the magazine editors I was meeting. I worked catering gigs in Rosedale mansions, unable to tear my eyes away from the Attila Richard Lukacs paintings on the wall as I passed around canapés. In the mornings, I fried eggs and peameal bacon in a fog of contentment, as the chill of winter crept in.

Then the deep freeze arrived, and I didn't know anyone could get so cold, and I landed a staff writer job at a women's magazine. Just like that, I found myself walking into lavish galas, standing with microphones on red carpets. Wandering through parties in looming hillside castles, the terrace packed with people, faces illuminated by thousands of glimmering lights. Can you imagine?

Toronto was an enchanted wonderland I explored at night. It was a city where you might plausibly spot Matt Damon and his wife at a film screening, or find yourself in an elevator with Salman Rushdie, or wind up having drinks at a rooftop bar with Ken Taylor, the Canadian diplomat who helped Americans escape the Iran hostage crisis. A city where, of course, Drake appeared around every corner, speeding past in his SUV, eating dinner across from you in a discreet Italian restaurant, living in a penthouse in your friend's building.

Toronto was a city, too, with doors to other charmed places: London, New York, Hollywood. I soon found myself boarding planes for press conferences in British palaces, and ushered into midnight parties in Tribeca, hosted by iconic pop stars and their rapper husbands, the Notorious B.I.G.'s "Hypnotize" blasting from giant speakers, the pop star's sister in the DJ booth commanding us all to dance.

It was a strange and satisfying leap from the obscure bohemian poverty I'd grown up in to this, this glittering heart of Western culture. And I was always aware that it could not have happened in any other city in Canada, and, really, few others in the world. There are only a handful of places anywhere that hold out that level of promise. That sense of limitless possibility. That feeling that your life could be utterly transformed, simply because you wanted it badly enough and were willing to get on a plane and show up.

I flew to New York to interview the president's daughter, and then again to talk to a top fashion model. I flew to Vancouver to attend a rock star's wedding and to walk English Bay with a crooner. To Montreal to stand in the back of a church as a prime minister's son got married. I flew to a ski party fundraiser in Banff, to interview the man who is now Canada's prime minister. To Las Vegas to dine with celebrity chefs, and to Malibu for poolside photo shoots with hockey players. The feeling of jet lag was with me always, bleeding into my days and nights.

Many of you will know this: There is an electricity to that kind of busyness. A strange sort of comfort. Rootlessness, franticness—these are great distractions. In this vortex of activity, the mundaneness of life evaporates. Your blood is perpetually flooded with adrenaline, and you are gloriously in the moment. It feels so good, you start craving this heightened, ultra-alive feeling all the time.

But of course there is a price you pay.

The first time I got sick was a month before the Toronto International Film Festival. I had been at the magazine eight months. I was accustomed, now, to our three press days a week, nights when an editorial assistant would email around taking orders for soggy Thai food. We would crowd into the glass-walled boardroom at six o'clock, the city splayed out before us, the table laden with fragrant cartons of green curry and pad thai. After dinner, we'd go back to our desks, and to the pages.

I was used to doing my makeup in the women's washroom in the evening, and changing into synthetic H&M dresses and taking taxis to product launches and film screenings and charity galas where women wore couture. I liked the feeling of walking through these packed parties in towering heels, scanning the crowd. I liked plunging into conversations, finding out what was interesting about a person. I liked talking fast and laughing loud and swimming in a sea of sparkly people, all of whom seemed to be doing fascinating things with their lives. I liked sitting in the backs of cabs afterwards, watching the darkened city speed past.

The next morning, though, I would inevitably wake up dreading the day. I would be at my desk by nine-thirty, in a loud newsroom where I would be interrupted every few minutes, and would stay there for nine or ten or twelve hours, writing and editing under punishing deadlines.

All day, I would long to sit in a perfectly silent room, in comfortable clothing, with nothing but a book and a blank stretch of time. I wanted this so badly sometimes I wasn't sure how to cope.

In the case of my first lung infection, all that wanting kept building and building, and the smog and the long hours and the lack of exercise and the junk food were like a wave that crashed into my body. I woke up drenched in sweat, lungs afire, my mind racing with looming deadlines. Night after night I lay in bed willing my body to get better, dreading the morning call to my boss to tell her I wasn't coming in, certain that my entire world was just one more sick day away from imploding.

Three weeks passed like this, a truly staggering amount of time in magazine land. Eventually, I got a prescription for a steroid inhaler, which I stayed on for the next nine years. I made it back into the office in time for the film festival, twenty pounds lighter, greeted by an around-the-clock schedule of parties and celebrity interviews.

Miraculously, I was able to gear back up. But I was shaken. What if this happened again? What if my body refused to cooperate? It had begun to dawn on me that my life required me to operate at full steam, every single day. The lung infection had been a warning: *This is how fast it can all fall apart.* The cracks had begun forming.

One Sunday morning six years later, I was sitting on the couch in my pajamas, meditating, in the tiny one-bedroom condo I rented in Yorkville. I had forgotten to silence my cell phone. In the moments that I sat "contemplating the universe," it began pinging with texts, and then emails, and finally phone calls. I pulled myself up off the couch and crossed the room to check the device. Whitney Houston had died. I would need to go to the office immediately. I knew I would be there until midnight. I got dressed and went.

Generally, when news broke—Obama was elected, say, or Michael Jackson died—there was no place I'd rather be than the office. I wanted to be in the thick of things, working the phones as the story unfolded, at the center of the storm.

But that day, alone in the newsroom, making call after call, all I experienced was fatigue.

That was the year that I caught red-eye flights to arrive at the birth of treasured nieces, and donned saris for friends' spectacular, days-long Catholic-Hindu weddings in a blur of exhaustion. The year I slept for a full day on a bench at O'Hare airport in Chicago, en route to celebrate Christmas with my family in Ireland. The year I left work sick one day only to discover when I got home that I was not sick at all, just profoundly weary, and proceeded to spend the day baking lemon squares and watching the first snowfall of the season. The year I began to wonder if this 24/7 pace was even remotely sustainable.

Sometime around then, I went out for brunch with a TV-host friend. We were enjoying a rare moment of quiet in an empty, high-ceilinged restaurant on King Street.

We were in our mid-thirties. Both of us lived in compact, shiny apartments in downtown buildings with imposing foyers and gyms that were rarely used and doormen who stood in for family. I was single, and she lived with her entrepreneur boyfriend. We went to parties and got photographed. Posted these photos on social media. Met well-connected people. Got invited to more parties. Posted more photos on social media.

How long are we going to do this? my friend wondered. *How long do we live this downtown lifestyle for? Would we still be doing this when we were fifty? Should we be?*

I didn't have any answers to such questions. And it would still be years before the allure of this life wore thin.

But I was dimly aware, by then, that there were things being crowded out by work. Things being silenced by the deafening chorus of pop culture news, the relentless chatter of the Internet, the notion—singular, unquestioned—that the way to succeed in any industry, and especially mine, was to give it absolutely everything you had.

I did not, for instance, have time to draft online dating profiles. Nor embark on awkward coffee dates. I often did not have energy for friends who existed outside my media bubble. I didn't sleep well. I downed fistfuls of candy every afternoon to keep me going. I never exercised, beyond the mad dash to get to the office every morning. I had access to the best concerts and dance performances and exhibits Toronto had to offer, yet it had been years since I had truly lost myself in a piece of art. When had I last spent an unscheduled day with anyone? Been properly kissed? Woken up without an alarm?

These things—the things I was missing, the things that I couldn't fathom how to bring into being—became harder and harder to ignore.

But really, what was to be done about it? Who was I to turn down the opportunities I was getting? So I drank a lot of coffee, gulped back tears and pushed on.

The years passed, and I moved from women's magazines to serious current affairs TV and radio shows on our nation's public broadcaster, rushing through the heavy glass doors at the station on Front Street every morning, never once failing to feel chuffed. For someone who'd grown up listening to CBC Radio, there was nothing more satisfying than walking purposefully through its impressive atrium every morning, silently cheered on by posters of the late Barbara Frum (who managed to look both as glamorous as Mary Tyler Moore and as serious as Knowlton Nash).

Still, I found myself secretly looking around at my colleagues, trying to find someone who might understand the toll that this dizzying sprint through my thirties was taking on my mind, body, spirit. Someone who could point the way forward.

I recall interviewing a famed radio host. Slumped in my cubicle, I cradled the phone and listened as he confessed how tired he was. The pressure, the tremendously long hours, the always being on. It was a lot, he said.

Now, of course, I can't help but read into that interview, given how things turned out. But back then I thought: *I know what you mean. And you are a man, without a wife or children, without even obligatory baby showers to attend every weekend. And you have one of the best jobs in the country. And the money to hire someone to do your laundry and clean your bathroom and answer your email. And you are still exhausted by this life. And what does that mean?*

I don't remember when construction became a presence in my life, but I can tell you that during the period I worked in current affairs it began to feel like an actual person I knew and interacted with daily. I didn't like this person very much, and yet I couldn't for the life of me get them to go away.

Three in the morning would find me in bed in the Yorkville condo, covering my ears with a pillow, listening to a jackhammer penetrate concrete, counting down the hours until my alarm sounded. It would jolt me awake at six, I knew, and I would get up and put the espresso pot on the stove. Turn on the radio. Reluctantly step into the shower. Mainline two cups of coffee. Rush the five minutes to Yonge station, fight my way through crowds on the subway platform and, if there were no signal problems that day, squeeze myself into the crush of bodies on the train.

Until then, there was nothing to do but wait.

Outside my window, a construction crew drilled on and on. The city had dug up the concrete on Yonge Street, apparently for water and then hydro work, and then ripped up and paved Yorkville Avenue. And now, months later, was ripping it up and paving it again.

I knew I was doomed to many more sleepless nights, too. It was only a matter of time until construction crews broke ground for the fifty-eight-storey colossus planned across the street, tearing down the entire heritage brick block, saving only a slim facade. Triggering a fresh onslaught of chaos and noise and dust and debris. Punctuating my waking hours and my sleeping ones with the steady drumbeat of development. The heartbeat of the modern city.

It upset me, the inevitability of it. The clatter and crash of it all. I mourned each new closing of a shop in my neighborhood. The dry cleaners across the street, where the middle-aged owner liked to chat about the dresses I brought in. The Yorkville Espresso Bar, its light glowing warm against a dusk sky, a chef in the glass-walled kitchen churning out delicate almond muffins, the baristas remembering how I liked my cappuccino.

It troubled me—the loss, the change, the noise. The fact that I always found myself alone in the small hours of the morning. And that I could think of nothing to do about any of this except bide my time, waiting on dawn, staring out floor-to-ceiling windows at all the cranes in the air.

How do you measure the soul of a city? How do you quantify the health of its residents, the sanity of its communities, its collective well-being? These questions began to haunt me as I became more and more weary and the Toronto around me seemed to accelerate out of control, spinning off its axis.

Every day, I swam in the soup of the city, tracking every shooting, each new study on precarious work, every city council squabble and school board scandal and rental rights violation. Every last failure of transit and the police.

These were the days of rampant carding of young black men. The days of the Ashley Madison hack, and Tinder culture, and polar vortexes, and class-action suits over unpaid overtime. Of the populist mayor Rob Ford getting caught smoking crack, and making racist comments, and making sexist comments, and then getting caught smoking more drugs, this time with gangs in the city's Jane and Finch neighborhood, and somehow still managing to stay in office. Days well before Donald Trump.

These were the days when we started talking a lot about mental illness in the city, later found to afflict one in every two workers in our city.

One icy night, after drinks with friends at Soho House, I got on a train, headed home. Within seconds after it left the station, a man at the front of the car began screaming. Everyone on the train froze. Time slowed, senses heightened. That prickly feeling of anticipation—the feeling just before violence erupts—pervaded the car. People appeared afraid to move, afraid to even look, for fear of escalating the situation.

After making eye contact with several others, silently conferring, I pressed the emergency button as we sailed into the next station. We all sat there, stricken, for a full eleven minutes as the man became increasingly agitated, screaming and thrashing about in anguish. When the transit police finally arrived, he was removed without incident. Stunned, acting on instincts I did not then understand, I combed the car, interviewing people on my iPhone for what would later become a radio essay on public violence. I arrived home close to midnight, wide awake, the shock slow to leave my body, a feeling of safety slow to return.

I had no idea how to come to terms with what the city was becoming. This shimmering metropolis that had delivered all my dreams. That had made me feel, for a time, like I was in the right place at the right time, living the right kind of life. That I belonged. The city that was still, in spite of all, producing artist-run galleries like Younger

Than Beyoncé, and game-changing documentaries about domestic violence like *A Better Man*, and independent publishers like Book*hug, which hosted free public readings at its founders' house, complete with homemade pie.

How did one reconcile all this creative energy with the bleakness of cold and sleet, the daily battle to navigate the crumbling subway system, the struggle to find ways to connect in spite of long, grueling days in the newsroom?

That summer, I returned home to B.C., seeking solace. I took a ferry to Vancouver Island and then a long bus ride to the coastal outpost of Tofino to walk its windy beaches. A friend joined me, fresh from a burnout crisis overseas, having worked fourteen hours a day until she finally collapsed and an ambulance had to be called.

A shift seemed to be taking place. A couple of years before, I couldn't find anyone who could relate to the fatigue I felt. But now it was all anyone talked about.

For the first time, I looked squarely at what the always-on work world was taking from me and so many others. And I became convinced that I had to make a radical change, for my health and well-being first and foremost, but if I wanted any chance of having a home life, too.

So I did something drastic. Something that would change my entire life, and not necessarily in the ways I'd hoped. Right before my fortieth birthday, I gave notice on my apartment, quit my job and sold most of my possessions to move back across the country, to the Lotus Land I'd grown up in.

At the time, I was reading, not surprisingly, Joan Didion's farewell to New York City, "Goodbye to All That," and imagining writing my own melancholic love letter to big-city life. Which is of course exactly what I have done.

By now, you will understand that this is a bittersweet love story—about a city, and also a profession. You will see that this is about health, and how fragile that can be. But what this story is really, truly about is work, and the way we all work now. It just happens these things are all related.

❯

CHAPTER ONE

The Modern City

I soon found myself standing in Pearson Airport, before six on a dark November morning. Terminal 3 was packed. Businessmen in overcoats plunged impatiently through the crowds. Couples in light jackets, catching connecting flights from warmer climes, blinked back exhaustion. Suburban women in parkas gripped Tim Hortons cups with one hand and toddlers with another, somehow managing to find a free hand to steer luggage carts.

And there I was, struggling to navigate my own cart, which my driver had helped me pile with a hulking hockey bag, a carry-on suitcase and that mountaineering backpack that had been my sole piece of luggage when I moved to Toronto a decade ago. At 5 a.m., I'd walked through the marble-floored lobby in Yorkville, my home for the past five years, and had been ushered by an overnight doorman into a waiting town car and chauffeured through the sleeping city. Now all my worldly possessions—save a few boxes at my mother's apartment in London, Ontario— were being lifted onto a squeaky conveyer belt, bound for the belly of the plane.

I landed in Vancouver early on a Sunday morning, greeted at the airport by my new roommate, a friend of a friend. By nine Pacific time, I was standing in the living room of my sublet, a dingy two-bedroom apartment with creaky floors and wood-paneled walls in a Kitsilano heritage house. The furniture sagged; dust covered every surface. Wind howled through a hole in one of the stained-glass windows in the bedroom. There was a fruit fly infestation in the kitchen that rendered it unusable. The rent was $1,100 a month. Each.

The heat soon went out for a week, and it was so cold that I had to stay with friends, displacing their seven-year-old from her single bed. Back at the apartment, I discovered dark, suspicious-looking mold over the kitchen sink, which the owner was adamant was not black mold but which was nevertheless removed the same day.

I could hardly comprehend what I had done.

Stunned, I walked the rainy streets, the air smelling of damp leaves, unsure what to do next. Had I really given up a fantastic gig at the heart of Canadian media, inspiring colleagues, a solid social circle and an upscale apartment for *this*? For fruit flies and financial instability? Had I traded security, success—glamour, even—for fresh air and some vague suggestion of work/life balance?

Could this ever be seen as a fair trade?

The move west had, in a single day, transported me back to the struggles of my twenties. It was as if those ten years in Toronto had never happened. The shock I felt was profound.

It took me seven weeks to find a decent place to live. Every day, after I finished my shift in the local newsroom, I would trudge through the rain to view apartments. I was shown a tiny one-bedroom in a building undergoing renovations, inhabited by heavy smokers. Stepping through the dust and debris, jackhammers pummeled the floors above and the stench of nicotine mingled with off-gassing from the new flooring. I toured a filthy luxury studio, too, accompanied by a bored real estate agent who refused to confirm it was bug-free. I saw a one-bedroom-and-den that reeked of marijuana smoke from a dispensary below, and a cramped, unremarkable basement suite with a line of potential tenants so long the owner did not bother to make eye contact when she handed me an application. Every week, my budget inched up, until I found myself viewing an apartment for $1,885.

After what felt like an eternity of searching, I hit the rental jackpot: a quiet, clean 1940s walk-up in a treed West Side neighborhood, priced (then) at $1,350 a month, sans washer, dryer, dishwasher or permission to have pets. In Toronto, for slightly more, I had had all those things, plus a gym, sauna and twenty-four-hour concierge. Even so, I was obscenely grateful.

Housing secured, I flew to Ireland for Christmas, and then on to Paris on assignment for a travel story, where I camped out at the Plaza Athénée in a sprawling suite with a grand piano, overlooking the Eiffel Tower. I walked Montmartre's winding streets at sunset, gazing out over the city from the Sacré-Coeur. Window-shopped at the chic boutiques on the tree-lined Avenue Montaigne, took my tea in the Plaza's La Galerie surrounded by impeccably dressed French women, biting into the most delicate-tasting of *financiers*. I slept late and lounged on the sofa in my robe and took long baths in the enormous tub. The contrast between this indulgent interlude and the grim reality that awaited me at home could not have been starker.

I returned to Canada determined to make Vancouver work, determined to find the promised land of nine-to-five workdays, weekend hikes in old-growth forests, leisurely coffees with friends. By New Year's Eve I was in bed by nine, already exhausted by the effort.

In Toronto, pretty much everyone I associated with led a middle-class existence. People earned decent salaries and, if they had spouses, bought East End bungalows for reasonable prices. They could afford vacations, and in very rare cases, cottages. It's true they were harried, working and parenting long hours, grappling with day-care costs that threatened to overwhelm. It's also true that huge portions of the city enjoyed nothing close to this lifestyle. I regularly met and interviewed people living in priority neighborhoods who made long daily commutes on broken-down buses to low-paying, precarious jobs, and could still barely afford to feed themselves. But for all the city's staggering inequality, there was still a semblance of a middle class. And I was part of it.

In Vancouver, on the other hand, the gap between the haves and the have-nots felt absolute—and I immediately found myself on the wrong side of the equation.

The class disparity in Vancouver was enough to make one's head spin. Worse yet, nobody seemed to notice. It was as if all the city's decision-makers were those famous frogs—forever referenced in politicians' and environmentalists' speeches—whose water temperature was turned up one degree at a time until they were boiling, utterly unaware.

A handful of friends, mainly ones who'd had family money for down payments way back when, were living in West Side (or, increasingly, East Vancouver) homes now valued at two or three million dollars. They drove SUVs, and went away most weekends in the summer. You might see them at the latest farm-to-table bistro, sampling the tasting menu, or at the local yoga studio, sinking into Shavasana. They were far busier than they wanted to be, too, and spending massive amounts on childcare. But their home equity cast a golden glow over the landscape.

Meanwhile, the rest of my friends lived in run-down basement suites and poorly maintained mid-century apartment blocks, shelling out the bulk of their take-home pay on rent, which continually increased. (To give you an idea how much: in one case, a friend had rented a South Granville heritage one-bedroom for $1,250 a month; within four years, similar apartments on her floor were renting for $1,850.)

Those who'd been lucky enough to find flats before rents soared were forced to stay put, raising children in the same dwellings they'd launched their adult lives in, often in spite of double incomes. Many threw their hands up in disgust and moved to the outer suburbs, or Bowen Island, or the Sunshine Coast, reluctantly cutting long-standing ties and making epic commutes to downtown jobs. "Dear Vancouver" breakup letters circulated regularly on social media. The rage was tremendous.

At the same time, the global elite driving the housing crisis could be spotted all over town, behind the wheels of Lamborghinis and Maseratis, toting Hermès handbags, emerging from tony Alberni Street boutiques, arms laden with purchases. They were in Thomas Haas ordering box upon box of confections, and in Holt Renfrew emptying out the shoe department.

The offshore capital that had transformed the city was visible elsewhere, too. Whole neighborhoods sat empty, converted from housing stock to investment properties. Downtown apartment towers remained resolutely dark at night. Pre-war character homes were torn down with dizzying speed, sending dump trucks of debris to landfill—the city's goal of being the greenest city in the world by 2020 be damned. These homes were then rebuilt as mega-mansions, stretching to the very edges of property lines.

Anyone could see that much of the money was coming from China. Many restaurant signs were now in Chinese; ATMs offered Mandarin options. Apartment listings on Craigslist sometimes cited a preference for Mandarin speakers. The "for sale" signs that littered lawns frequently were written in Chinese characters. Friends who tried to view new condo developments were told units had been sold overseas before breaking ground. At the café I wrote in every day, it was not uncommon for a group of Chinese speculators to come in, dump a stack of real estate listings on the table and hold animated debates. Sometimes English-speaking realtors would join them, and I would be privy to the details of the deals.

Vancouverites who protested the influx of Chinese capital were considered culturally insensitive at best, racist at worst. Developers accused local residents of jealousy;

the mayor objected to housing crisis research, claiming it had "racist tones." At the height of the public outcry over the housing crisis, then premier Christy Clark insisted foreign investment was playing a negligible role—just around the same time, it was later discovered, that she flew overseas with the express purpose of courting more Chinese investment, telling investors that Chinese money played a huge role in our real estate industry. In the years to come, we'd learn, too, the part that money-laundering schemes played in exploding the housing market and making the city so unaffordable (with one report finding that $5 billion had been laundered in B.C.'s real estate sector in a single year).

In 2016, government data showed that in one five-week period, close to $1 billion in foreign money had poured into Metro Vancouver's real estate market.

Unpacking all of this seemed to overwhelm all but the most courageous and determined of civic leaders, some of whom were Asian Canadian, like Simon Fraser University's Andy Yan, who maintained that speaking out against the destructive impact of foreign capital was not synonymous with anti-immigrant bigotry, and that that charge was, in fact, being used to silence the conversation around housing affordability.

Social tensions were perilously high. Between races. Between income brackets. And, crucially, between generations.

Those who owned property made up roughly half the population, and if they were not millionaire migrants, they were often baby boomers. The city's aging residents had become rich—at least on paper—and were understandably giddy. In one case I heard of, a family had watched their property value jump $5 million in a single year.

Many of these boomer homeowners were sympathetic to renters, in theory. But dig a little deeper and you'd find they were increasingly exasperated with the constant talk of the housing crisis. They didn't want to appear uncaring, but it was all getting a bit tedious. And perhaps a little overblown? A young friend of a friend had just bought a house in East Vancouver, after all, so it must still be possible with a little budgeting and hard work, no?

At a press event at a lavish hotel, a journalist I'd never met approached, curious to hear my impressions of the city after being away for so long. I started to tell her how surreal I found the housing situation, but she waved me away. "Everyone says that," she said. My comment was cliché, tired. Old hat.

Meanwhile, I heard the same arguments again and again. *Not everyone is going to be able to own, and not everyone is going to be able to live downtown,* many insisted. *Some people are going to have to be lifelong renters, or else buy condos in nearby suburban communities like Port Moody.* Never mind that the average one-bedroom in Vancouver rented for more than $2,000 a month, and that an acquaintance had told me her condo in Port Moody was now valued at half a million dollars. Or that the tiny coastal communities I visited for travel stories, like Galiano Island and Quadra Island and Gibsons, had no affordable housing either, with local workers forced to live in tents or on houseboats. Remote mountain towns like Nelson didn't seem to have any affordable housing either. Where, exactly, was everybody supposed to go?

Another common line from those defending the status quo was that Vancouver had become a world-class city, on par with New York and London. The difference, of course, was that these cities had jobs, industry, opportunities, salaries (not to mention subways and independent bookstores). Meanwhile, Hootsuite's CEO, Ryan Holmes, penned an impassioned op-ed in the paper saying he couldn't recruit, or retain, talent in a city where nobody could afford to rent, let alone own. Even on tech salaries.

And there just weren't that many decent-paying jobs to go around, anyway. The city's median income for a single person hovered stubbornly around $35,000 a year. For a single woman, the median income clocked in even lower, at an incomprehensible $29,820 a year. As writer Michael Kluckner put it in Caroline Adderson's edited collection *Vancouver Vanishes*, the city had the economy of Honolulu, the wages of Halifax and the cost of living of San Francisco. *Globe and Mail* real estate reporter Kerry Gold's *Walrus* cover story featured a photo of a tear-down with these words above it: "This Vancouver house: $2,198,000. Average income: $43,000. Something's got to give."

Vancouver Sun investigative journalist Sam Cooper went even further, arguing that the social contract in the city had been broken. And that's certainly what it felt like. Those of us who'd grown up here had been raised to think that if we went to school, worked hard, contributed to society and respected the law, we could expect to build a decent life for ourselves, and have a family if we chose. Clearly, this was no longer the case.

I had been a journalist for fifteen years by then, work-ing at some of the top outlets in the country. I then made an income above the Canadian average, and certainly above the Vancouver average. I was good with money, too, track-ing every penny and drafting budgets and weighing every purchase. Within a year of returning home, I made my last student loan payment. I had no debt and no dependents—not even a dog. Still, in this city, I couldn't conceivably own a car, let alone a condo. I could get by, but I couldn't save for dental emergencies or Christmas or retirement.

Meanwhile, rents continued to skyrocket. Renovictions were common. Many who rented condos were displaced every time units changed hands in the frenzy of specula-tion. Airbnb further limited housing stock. Sam Cooper told the makers of the documentary film *Vancouver: No Fixed Address* that a former city planner had told him 90 percent of all the city's condos were purchased by investors.

A church in Kitsilano was put up for sale, evicting doz-ens of community groups and shuttering an emergency cold shelter for homeless men, the last remaining one on the West Side. After forty years, a meditation center was forced to find a new venue when its building was sold and converted to luxury condos. A family-owned restaurant lost lifelong regulars to the mass exodus to rural B.C. Meanwhile, gas stations and grocery stores everywhere evaporated, the land simply too valuable to not be condos. Crushed by soaring property taxes, small businesses closed their doors. The ones that were left struggled to find minimum-wage staff, who could no longer afford to rent apartments here, roommates or no.

Even in ultra-wealthy neighborhoods like Shaughnessy, all was not well. I walked its streets regularly. During the day, the area was swarmed with landscapers and handymen and construction workers. But come nightfall, you could often walk a mile in total darkness without seeing a single other human being. In some cases, the windows of these stately homes were boarded up with planks, front lawns overgrown with weeds, moss spreading across roofs. These crumbling compounds gave the appearance of neglect, abandonment. Shaughnessy now felt like a weird, rich Detroit.

I went for a walk with a friend who lived in another old-money neighborhood, Kerrisdale. She mourned the demolitions of the old houses, with their cheap basement suites, and the lack of economic diversity that followed. She said she'd gladly give back a huge portion of her home equity just to have a community again. Another friend, who lived in affluent Dunbar, was afraid to walk her dog at night—her block had become that deserted.

Everywhere in the city, fury seethed below the surface, frequently erupting in traffic. One day I was on a public bus driven by a transit worker in her thirties. Next to the bus, a twentysomething couple pulled up in a flashy SUV, not quite in their lane. A shouting match ensued, feeling like it was more about economic inequality than it was about the rules of the road. A friend who'd recently returned to the city after years abroad wanted to know what was up with all the road rage. And, not unrelated:

"Why can't anyone go more than a few hours without talking about the housing crisis?"

A few months before I'd arrived home, data had been published revealing that Shaughnessy was one of the lowest-income neighborhoods in the city. More than 30 percent of residents in Shaughnessy declared poverty-level incomes, underscoring the problem of millionaire migrants with "satellite families," whose breadwinners stayed in China while their spouses or children came to the city, purchased property and went to school here, but did not earn income or pay income taxes. The federal government had released studies to show that refugees earned more income than those who arrived through Canada's controversial investor immigration program, which had essentially created a pipeline for wealthy migrants who traded five-year interest-free loans of $800,000 for citizenship and then continued earning their income abroad—without paying taxes on it. In an opinion piece for the *Vancouver Sun*, SFU professor Josh Gordon pointed out that in order to purchase a two-million-dollar home in a premium Vancouver neighborhood, your household income would need to be about $300,000 per year (at current interest rates, with a 20-percent down payment). This would mean that your household would pay between $90,000 and $110,000 a year in income tax, plus about $6,000 in property tax and more in sales taxes. But if you earned, or accumulated, your income elsewhere, you would only be paying the property and sales taxes. In this scenario, Gordon wrote, the tax subsidy these rich residents received amounted to about $100,000 per year, every year. Essentially, they got to enjoy all the services offered in Vancouver—without paying for them. "Is it any wonder that vast numbers of wealthy foreign individuals want to buy property in Vancouver?" he asked. "Is it any wonder that we can't build enough to meet that global elite demand?"

The problem, he wrote, was that government had allowed this to happen on a mass scale. "Ultimately, young working Vancouverites are subsidizing the global elite that is pushing them out of their childhood city—an incredibly toxic dynamic," he concluded.

It was painful confronting what my city had become—how divided it was, how wide the chasm between rich and poor.

I walked the streets day after day, in a state of shock, unclear how to proceed. What does it mean if a place becomes the sole domain of the one percent? Who will serve the coffee and teach the kids and nurse the sick and collect the trash? Is it reasonable to expect workers to commute hours a day to jobs? And: What does it mean when a community shatters apart?

I thought of a friend and her husband, who'd lived in the basement suite of a house for twenty years before the owner sold and forced them to relocate. The family who'd rented the main floor had children who'd grown up visiting my friend. She had not had children, and had poured so much love and care into these young neighbors. When the family upstairs moved to the suburbs, a long drive from my friend's new place, she mourned the loss for months.

Should we be forced to leave friends, family, neighbors, the streetscapes that are imprinted on our psyches—all those things that anchor us to who we are? That make life worth living? If so, what does that do to our souls?

After I read William Gibson's brilliant novel *Pattern Recognition*, I started to believe that our souls are rooted in a specific time and place. In the novel, Gibson coins a term, "soul lag," for the surreal sensation that accompanies international jet travel. That feeling that although our feet are standing on foreign ground, some fundamental part of our being has yet to show up. And we must wait for it in order to feel whole again.

I suspect some parts never catch up. Strictly speaking, of course, my soul is always with me. But when I fly to the other side of the world and visit another corner of the planet, I think a little fragment of my soul lingers on there. As I march through life, I leave pieces of myself in the places that have changed me.

And so if you charted my soul's movement around the globe, I think you would find a good-sized portion of it with my body, walking the rainy beaches of my hometown, breathing in the salty sea air. You'd also probably find a fragment of it racing around downtown Toronto, humming Usher ballads. And another piece on the Upper West Side of Manhattan eating bagels and lox. And yet another in a longhouse in Borneo, waking at dawn and watching the mist rise off the jungle canopy (a story I'll get to shortly). But I think you would find the most sizable piece of my soul in a burnt-out plot of land on 4th Avenue in Vancouver, in what was once the kitchen of the Topanga Café.

The forty-seat eatery has been home for as long as I can remember. When I close my eyes, I can transport myself back there in an instant. There I am, sitting at a table gazing out the front window, waiting for my shift to begin, eating hot tortilla chips and homemade salsa. It's fall in Vancouver, at once extravagantly lush and green and gloomy with rain. The light outside is violet. Cars swoosh past and their headlights look like fireflies in an enchanted forest.

This is how it happened: When I was eight years old, my mother enrolled in art school. Overnight, she became cool. Or rather, she began expressing her inherent cool. She dressed all in black and wore red lipstick. She bought a thrift-store fedora, and Clemente art books. She played Leonard Cohen records.

Until then, we had been living in Penticton, a dry, arid town in the interior of B.C., where my dad ran a group home for troubled teen girls who wore caked-on blue eye shadow and went AWOL all the time. My mum stayed at home to take care of me and my baby brother. When she put my brother down for a nap, she would get out her easel and canvases and brushes, and paint clowns. Not the kind of clowns that entertain children at birthday parties, but the stylish, sophisticated ones that always look depressed. They have chalky white faces and maroon lips and a tear on each cheek. They wear black caps on their heads and frilly white collars on their smocks. Pierrot, I think they are called.

My mother painted them all the time. And when she wasn't doing that—or driving me to soccer or ballet— she was bemoaning the lack of culture in our town. The only paintings you could find in galleries were of horses grazing in fields. Or else windmills, sailboats, farmhouses.

It was a nice, quiet life for us kids, but it really was very suburban, and alas, my parents simply were not suburban people. So my mother applied to art school, and she got in. The August I was eight, we drove a U-Haul through the mountains to Vancouver. When we arrived, renting a run-down two-bedroom apartment in Kitsilano that was not without its charms, I was introduced to city life and my mother was introduced to her calling.

By the time I was fourteen, my parents had endured a nasty divorce, and my father was largely absent. He remarried, set up a private practice as a therapist and moved to a beach town an hour away. My mother worked countless jobs, cleaning houses and manning tills at department stores. Now she painted giant canvases with haunting, ethereal faces. My life was unrecognizable to myself.

The upshot of that painful period was that my mother's friends were always around. One of them, a painter, had a boyfriend, Iain, in a punk rock band called Curious George. One night I got to pile into the back of a rusty van with the band and all the gear and then stand backstage at their show and watch the skateboarders in the front row mosh.

Iain worked at the Topanga Café, and he got me a gig in the kitchen for the summer between grades nine and ten. It was my job to take the steaming plates out of the oven and decorate them with lettuce, tomato and shredded cheese. I also made nachos and blended margaritas and opened cold cans of Coke for the waitresses. The walls were adorned with hundreds of framed menus that patrons had colored with crayons. The Cole Porter tribute *Red Hot + Blue* always seemed to be playing on the stereo. That or the dreaded, ubiquitous Gipsy Kings.

The most soothing thing about Topanga, I think, was its predictability. Things were in the same places that they'd been in since the restaurant opened in the late 1970s, when I first visited as a toddler. The broom was always in the staff washroom behind the door and the chopped tomatoes were always in the back fridge, on the second shelf next to the avocado sauce. In between unloading all the condiments at 4 p.m. and scraping the vinegar off the wooden island to clean it at ten-thirty, you could be assured a mad, adrenaline-filled evening, during which the only thing you thought about was the enchiladas in front of you. Your mind would go blissfully blank. For years afterwards, I was tempted to pick up a shift just for the comfort of it all being exactly the same.

For thirty years, Tom Zallen owned the Topanga, until my dear friend Andrew bought it. Tom was from California and had a PhD in psychology, but he left academia to run the family business. (Though, when I ran into Iain recently, I learned Tom had quietly served as a police psychologist for the Vancouver Police Department the entire time I'd known him.)

Tom oversaw Topanga's daily operations with a blend of dogged hard work, biting sarcasm and unprecedented kindness.

He expected us to work hard. But food was always free to the staff. And when one of the waitresses developed a heroin addiction, he did not fire her. Another staff member's

friend was in a car accident, and Tom opened the restaurant on a Sunday and held a fundraiser to help her parents,
who'd flown into town and were staying at a motel on a
very limited budget. Tom had never met this girl. "I felt
she needed a boost," he explained to a local newspaper.

I, too, was often the recipient of Tom's generosity. He
allowed me to come and go over the years. He hired my
brother during his troubled teen years, and was very good
to him. One time, when a customer complained that I
worked at a Mexican restaurant and didn't even speak
Spanish, Tom replied, deadpan, "Right, because minimum-
wage workers should always be required to be bilingual."

He once made a donation to a writing project, backed
by the government-funded Canada Council for the Arts,
that I had undertaken. In true Tom fashion, he sent me the
check with a note wryly pointing out that the sum was in
addition to the amount he'd already contributed through
his taxpayer dollars.

We shared a love of food and good books. He loaned
me Anthony Bourdain's *Kitchen Confidential*. I loaned him
a morose memoir from an Irish novelist about her tortured
childhood. He cheerfully refused to read it.

When I was in my mid-twenties and taking a break
from the restaurant, Tom fell ill and had a major opera-
tion. I wrote him a card telling him how much Topanga
had meant to me, how it had been an anchor in my life.

I'm very glad I did. Shortly afterward, he passed away.
He was 59 years old. I could not attend his memorial, held
at Jericho Beach, where we had our staff picnic every year,

because I was in New York City and could not afford to fly home. More to the point, I could not bring myself to say goodbye.

For many years, every time I burst in the door of that tiny restaurant, inhaling the pungent fragrance of cilantro and garlic and craving a prawn burrito, I would expect to see Tom holed up at the corner table, painstakingly poring over bills. I never stopped hoping that he'd be there, and that he'd look up and smile, mutter something sarcastic and pull out a chair for me.

And then, one day as I was drinking my morning coffee on my couch in Vancouver, I got a dozen texts from friends, at home and all over the world, informing me that Topanga was on fire. It burned to the ground. I wept much of that day as the building smoldered, mourning the loss as if it were a cherished friend. Which, in many ways, it was.

In those early months back in Vancouver, I thought a lot about home, and what it meant. What it felt like, after a decade in a big, anonymous city, to run into a friend's mother, whom I'd known for thirty years, on the street. Or to take a yoga class from someone I'd gone to high school with. Or have a coffee with the friend I'd back-packed Thailand with. What this complex web of connections was worth. What happened in its absence. What remained.

I thought, too, about how I'd longed for mountains and ocean and forests when I was away. How I'd pined for the sound of rain hitting the leaves on the maple trees on West Side boulevards. And the dampness when autumn arrived and darkness fell early and the air smelled of earth.

How hearing U2 or Naughty by Nature instantly transported me back to the intoxication of high school dances, the sweetness of midnight kisses outside the planetarium at Vanier Park, the heady abandon of sprinting down a West Side soccer field, chasing the ball, a summer sun slipping behind the trees.

Or August afternoons, walking through Dunbar, listening to the chorus of wind chimes, all the front doors thrown open to the breeze. Sitting on the deck of a BC Ferry in early July, surrounded by aging boomers with their flowing tunics and *New Yorker* canvas tote bags. Catching snippets of conversations in 4th Avenue cafés, the characteristically slow drawl of West Side residents espousing the city's weird philosophy—a bizarre brew of self-help books, ancient yoga practices and Silicon Valley exceptionalism.

I thought about all of this as I worked in the Vancouver newsroom, forever on the phone, probing residents to tell me their stories, to share their perspectives, to try and articulate what it was that we were all living through. As I did, the despair of the city seeped in through my pores, rearranging the molecules in my body and plunging me into darkness.

In Toronto, covering a story about health and income inequality, I had once interviewed a doctor who served the homeless population. He pointed to a research study that had demonstrated that in societies with a massive gap between the rich and the poor, everyone's physical health suffers, even that of the rich. I wanted to know why. It was obvious why poverty made people unwell, but what was making everyone else sick?

Nobody knew for sure, he told me, but it was believed to come down to stress. Likely caused by a lack of social cohesion. A result of severed connections.

The day that I broke was a rainy Thursday in Vancouver, in February of 2016. I was sitting in CBC's newsroom, hunched over, racked by intense chest pains that had started shortly after I arrived back in town.

I'd hoped the cross-country move would cure my burnout, but it had only amplified it. I loved my job, loved my colleagues, loved, above all else, my profession. But I didn't like my life very much. And the fight had seeped out of me.

In the end, my surrender was a quiet one. Soundless and sad. After filing scripts for my segments, I sighed, packed up my things, and left.

In his essay collection *The Horrors*, Vancouver writer Charles Demers writes about our need for narrative arcs, for imposing narrative structure on our lives, and quotes Douglas Coupland, that as the twenty-first century unspools, "it will become harder to view your life as 'a story.'"

We can no longer kid ourselves that we are living out our own narrative, I thought, reading that. *Now there is really only the narrative of our time.*

I saw, then, that I was indeed not living out my own story. I was not even really living out the story of Vancouver or Toronto. I was living the story of the modern city. And it left no room for the stories of individual people to unfold.

CHAPTER TWO

The Woods

A few months later, I found myself seated in a small float plane suspended above Jervis Inlet on the Sunshine Coast of B.C., drinking in the looming mountains just beyond the cloudscape and the dense rainforests and vast ocean below. Swirling mists lent a mystical quality to the scene, a feeling of being transported back in time. A time before smartphones and social media and smog. Before endless emails and packed public transit. Before Netflix and takeout, even.

My shoulders unclenched. My breath slowed and deepened. My mind cleared.

Our small group of travel journalists landed on the sheltered Princess Louisa Inlet and scrambled out onto the dock just as the clouds cracked open and rain thundered down.

Seeking refuge from the deluge, we made our way through the moss-covered, enchanted pathways, emerging beside the granite cliffs of Chatterbox Falls, allowing the awe and wonder of forty meters of cascading water to wash over us.

Taking shelter under a wooden hut in the forest, we drank the hot coffee that our guide had packed for us and warmed ourselves by a smoky bonfire. Listened to the rain and meditated on the history of this magical spot, likely named after Princess Louise, Queen Victoria's fourth daughter, whose husband, the ninth Duke of Argyll, was governor general of Canada in the late 1800s.

The region was, of course, home to First Nations before that, and was still rich in Coast Salish lore. We heard stories of the mountains young men climbed with heavy rocks as rites of passage. And were later taken by boat to the rock faces where Early Peoples' art survived: haunting, rust-colored pictographs of what looked like fish chasing a whale.

There were tales of the American adventurer James F. MacDonald, who founded the Princess Louisa International Society in 1953, and donated land back to the commons, stating that "it should never have belonged to one individual."

Stories, too, of the dashing aviation executive Thomas Hamilton, who purchased part of the area for $500 and founded the Malibu Club in Canada (now a Christian youth camp). The resort entertained the likes of John F. Kennedy, Bing Crosby and Bob Hope—until a polio outbreak ended all the fun.

The area was also home to trappers, loggers, and squatters.

Now luxury yachts dotted the harbor. And explorers in their kayaks, braving the wind and wet. Nature-starved adventurers, eager to escape the city.

All of whom we encountered on the way out of Princess Louisa. Zipped up in orange jumpsuits, we sped through the ocean on a Zodiac. Rain needled our faces, a barrage of determined little icicles jolting us from reverie. We clung to the side of the inflatable boat, scanning the water for whales.

That night, at a remote wilderness lodge in Egmont, we tucked ourselves into pillow-soft beds and allowed the healing power of nature to soak through our skin. The release from care and worry. The pitch-black darkness of night. The deep dreams. The strong feelings of wellness, of aliveness. Of everything-is-all-right-ness.

Early the next morning, we hit the water in kayaks, paddling the placid, glassy waters as the sun rose in the sky. Communed with seals and seagulls. Willed whales to appear. Forgave them when they didn't. Retired to the wisteria-drenched deck with our coffees.

Then set off again. A quick ferry from Earls Cove to the northern Sunshine Coast followed by a winding coastal drive, and we arrived at Penrose Bay, in Okeover Inlet, at a kayak company run out of nineteenth-century log buildings.

After loading our bags onto a tiny boat, we were shepherded through the haunting beauty of Desolation Sound, striking for its isolation. We docked on the rocks of Kinghorn, an uninhabited island in close proximity to the high-society outpost Savary Island and the boomer-hippie hub of Cortes Island.

Time took on a dreamlike quality as we passed a contented couple of days at this secluded outpost. We slept in luxe open-air cabanas with no electricity. Dined in a solar-powered communal kitchen complex. Kayaked the length of the island. Unplugged in a way we hadn't imagined possible.

I had no idea how much I'd been craving this state of being until it arrived.

It was so still, so silent, that you could hear the wings of a raven flap as it flew by. The snorts and sighs of passing sea lions. The splash of seals slipping from rock to water.

I felt my entire being uncoil. The helix of tension at my core eased into a straight, liquid line, quiet and calm radiating out into every cell.

Every few hours, staff and guests alike circled a long table and sampled the exquisite cuisine dreamed up by the island's resident cooks. Buckwheat pancakes drenched in sweet maple syrup and tart berries. Wild salmon soaked in basil pesto. Salty oysters, tasting of the sea, grilled fresh on the beach. Coconut crème brulée. Spicy ginger cookies. Thick, rich chocolate avocado pudding.

While we ate, we told each other stories of adventure. South Africa, Greece, Chile. Borneo.

Every once in a while, one of us would jump up, imagining we'd heard a telltale spray of water. We'd race to the bluffs, hoping to spot a whale. Once, we heard a humpback's spout. But he refused to show himself, remaining hidden, submerged below the ocean.

Come nightfall, I retired to bed with a hot-water bottle and read books from the resort's lending library, by the light of a hiking headlamp. I disappeared into Grant Lawrence's *Adventures in Solitude: What Not to Wear to a Nude Potluck and Other Stories from Desolation Sound*. Absorbed the rich historical tapestry of the region—tales that stretched back hundreds of years. Marveled at how much this area had changed, yet how much it had stayed the same. How wild it still was.

Flashes of my West Coast youth flooded me: eating steamed crab dipped in garlic butter, fresh from traps, at a friend's wood cabin on Lasqueti Island; hiking Mount Garibaldi with my high school French class; standing atop a peak in the Stein Valley; sleeping in tents in the snowy alpine terrain below, dreaming of grizzly bears. Staying at a waterfront cabin somewhere on the Gulf Islands, eating berry crumble from a cast-iron stove and telling stories around the campfire.

The next morning, I awoke to a knock: a French press of coffee delivered to my door. I rose and made my way out to the point, settled into a wooden Adirondack chair. Relished the silence, the stillness. The gentleness of the wind in the trees. The quiet calm of the water.

If city stress was a sickness, I realized, wilderness was the medicine.

My parents met in Toronto, in high school, back when it was a town awash with beehive hairdos and letterman jackets. My dad was a track star living in a rambling old house near the top of Avenue Road, with a Canadian veteran father who taught shop at high school and an English homemaker mother who was far more interested in history books than vacuuming or baking casseroles.

My mother, the child of a Welsh sailor and an English factory worker, lived in Rexdale and dropped out of school on her sixteenth birthday to clerk at Woolworths and save her earnings for cashmere sweater sets and Italian shoes. My mum and dad dated for a while, until she stood him up one night when he had a party in his basement and she had nothing to wear.

There's a photo of my mother around that time, seated at a table in a restaurant. She's wearing a cream sleeveless dress à la Jacqueline Kennedy and her hair is piled in tresses on her head. It looks like she's wearing false eyelashes. Her lips are painted a frosty hue. If the photo weren't black and white, you would marvel at how her pale Welsh skin was offset by her black hair and hazel eyes. She's smiling, but there's a part of herself she is holding back. She could be a young Elizabeth Taylor.

After my mother stood my father up, they broke up, and then became fast friends. He often went over to her house for sandwiches. What kind, I wonder. Tuna? Egg salad? Bacon, lettuce and tomato? You can see there are a lot of unanswered questions.

My parents remained close as my dad graduated and backpacked through Europe. In London, he had an Indian roommate who taught him how to make curry, which he proceeded to make, quite well, for decades after.

Somehow, my mother and father reunited, and then they were married for twenty years. Until they were not.

You can't talk about my parents' marriage, though, without talking about the sixties. Their union was built on a foundation of brown rice, vinyl rock records, peace marches, homemade yogurt, fern plants, Nag Champa incense, herbal tinctures, poetry readings and—in deference to their scandalized British parents—lots of strong black tea.

Divorced people don't tend to wax poetic about their

lives together, so I've been forced to invent most of the details. But here's what I know for sure: my parents lived in Project One, an intentional community in San Francisco located in an abandoned candy factory, where my mother baked fresh baguettes and cooked multi-course meals for sixty or so people every night (including, possibly, Steve Jobs?). Before that, they went to Pittsburgh for my dad to do a master's degree in psychology, and lived in the inner city, watching a generation of young men ship off to Vietnam. They lost an acquaintance's sister in the anti-war protest at Kent State.

They camped on the Russian River, which I've come to find out is located in the redwood forests of California. And, before I was born, they lived on a commune, the secluded Primal Point on Galiano Island, in a chicken coop they had scrubbed down, painted and decorated with pillows my mother had woven.

Then they returned to Toronto, and I arrived, sighing in contentment as I peered out at the world. I proceeded to keep the household up all night, already worried I was going to miss something.

In the coming months, my mother and I settled into a routine. She would take me for a walk in the park, settling us beneath the weeping willows, and, after returning home, put me down for a nap while she taught weaving classes out of their tiny living room. In the meantime, both sets of grandparents embarked on anguished divorces, wartime unions collapsing in the new country at long last, a victim to alcoholism and poverty in one case, infidelity in the other.

So it's probably not surprising that my father's restlessness kicked in before my first birthday, and the clarion call of the West Coast rang out, and the three of us were soon driving a homemade camper truck across America. My earliest memory is of being curled up on the mattress in the back, the rain lashing the roof, a pot of my mother's borscht bubbling on the stove. And of dancing with a hippie woman in a sunny field at a folk music festival.

We lived for a few years in Vancouver, in a chaotic communal house in Kitsilano with organic vegetable gardens and consensus decision-making and a crew of dumpster-diving grownups who felt entitled to tell me what to do.

Eventually, we moved to the Gulf Islands, to the draft-dodger haven of Salt Spring.

I have dedicated great swaths of my life to mocking this sort of existence, but the truth is it was really quite idyllic.

Picture this: A ramshackle 1800s farmhouse with hardwood floors and an ancient wood-burning stove. (It once almost burned the place down, but never mind that.) A sun-dappled backyard with a claw-foot bathtub my mother and I planted with nasturtiums. Apple orchards in one direction; miles of meadows in another. To the north, dense forest. To the south, the Pacific Ocean, regal-looking ferries floating slowly through the inlet.

I spent whole days outdoors, making art installations with the fruit that was ripe for the picking. I would cut crab apples into interesting shapes and lay them out on plates, garnishing them with flowers and leaves and tree bark before presenting them proudly to my mother.

My father often took me on long walks. We would climb the steep bluffs at the point, me kicking up the moss on the rocks with the toes of my red gum boots, sunlight illuminating the rust-colored arbutus trees. Or else we'd amble through the forest to Fulford Harbour, where my mother waited tables at the local diner. In the summer, the bay would be lit up, the maple trees golden. In the winter, the trail would be transformed into a magical kingdom of snowflakes and dripping icicles.

When it was cold, I would spend hours at the dining room table drawing paper dolls, our dog Georgia (named after Georgia O'Keeffe, naturally) galloping around in the background as the stray notes of Pachelbel's Canon wafted from the turntable. At night, the whole family, including my brand-new baby brother, would curl up in lawn chairs in the kitchen as my mother read aloud from *Anne of Green Gables*, a loaf of her caraway rye in the oven.

Every Saturday at dawn, we went to the farmer's market to trade the apples my father picked and the herbs my mother dried for necessities. Notably: a feathered hair clip from one of the jewelry vendors, which I absolutely adored. It was the late seventies, after all.

Sunday mornings, we'd eat store-bought lemon Danishes and my parents would give me presents. One week, a ladybug fridge magnet, the next a pack of pink Trident gum. They left these treasures out for me to find, pretending they were from fairies.

What stands out most from that time is the air, so fragrant and fresh. And the feeling of open space: endless sky, vast ocean. Also, the fact that we ate a lot of vegetables.

Naturally, I got the hell out of Dodge the instant I could swing it. By the time I was in my late twenties, I was thoroughly appalled by this sleepy, stifling corner of the world and all its inhabitants, who loped down 4th Avenue in nearby Vancouver, chai soy lattes in hand, gazing dreamily at the mountains as if there were nowhere in the world they needed to be. I left, and never even considered going back.

But in my late thirties, drowning in stress in downtown Toronto, what do you think I found myself aching for? A farmhouse on the Gulf Islands. The ocean. The woods. If only just for a few weeks a year.

What I wouldn't have given to sit on a porch and look out at the fir trees swaying in the damp West Coast rain, breathing in that cold, clean air.

When I returned to the West Coast from Toronto, retracing my parents' pilgrimage from decades before, I did not find the oasis of calm they'd discovered. Instead, a hectic newsroom, a frazzled city, a fraying society. Fear, frustration, jagged chest pains.

In the months after I stepped away from work, my nerves were jangled. I felt raw and utterly defenseless. I couldn't socialize or even make passable small talk. My whole being felt like it was teetering on a precipice. Like my skin was on backwards. Like I was perpetually in danger of bumping into something. Like one awkward interaction could gut me.

My life was an abyss I had fallen into. I did not know how to climb out.

All I could manage was sleeping and reading. Day in and day out, I lay on the couch.

Meanwhile, wave after wave of text messages flooded my phone. Could I babysit on Wednesday night? Since I was off work, did I have time to read this person's book proposal and offer some feedback? Could I give that person's nephew some career advice? Did I know someone on this or that radio show, and would I make an intro? Today? Was I around to talk through this person's looming family crisis? And, hey, remember that book I mentioned a few months ago, what was it again? Would I mind sending a link to my review?

When you've been hyper-competent—a giver of all things to all people—it's hard for others to comprehend that you are down for the count. Since everybody needed something from me, I couldn't ask anybody for help. So I stopped responding. What I did instead was walk.

I walked the woods of Queen Elizabeth Park, and the trails of Pacific Spirit Park and Stanley Park. I did the loop in Lynn Headwaters Regional Park, over and over again. I walked in rainstorms and windstorms. On clear, cloudless days, and ones so cold I needed to wear three layers beneath my coat. I walked and walked and walked.

There, in the woods, I began to see and feel and experience the gaping holes in my life. The spaces where support, security, comfort, companionship might have resided. Joy, even. I grieved these absences, along with new losses—the loss of career, of financial stability, of my identity as a journalist. Of community, and a structured life. Of my place in society, in the mainstream, in the middle class. Of my sense of belonging, however precarious that had turned out to be.

As I spent time exploring the wilderness outside my door, then, I started also contemplating the wilderness within.

Waiting for the cardiac tests to come back, I walked slowly, out of breath, anxious, holding a hand over my heart, praying the chest pains would subside.

Every outing in the forest felt like a balm for my soul. I breathed in the clean air, and my fluttering heart calmed, and I felt less afraid. I walked until I was satiated by the green, and somehow set right.

As the months progressed—and the tests came back normal, one after another—I walked more and more. Summer arrived and I joined a hiking club, taking midnight excursions to Buntzen Lake with a crew of friendly strangers, stumbling through the pitch-black trail, arriving at water's edge to lie on the dock and watch stars explode in the sky.

I hiked Mount Maxwell on Salt Spring Island, alone, singing loudly to myself as I summited, lungs screaming, heart full. I took a trip to the Sunshine Coast, again with my club, climbing local mountains and traversing lakeside forest paths, sleeping in a tent in the pounding rain, ecstatic to be one with the night air. I hiked Mount Seymour at dusk, and the grueling Grouse Grind first thing in the morning, and then three sections of the densely wooded Baden-Powell Trail. And then came Kinghorn

Island. And the uncoiling I'd been waiting for, without knowing it.

After that, as I put one foot in front of the other, everything in my life started to feel just a little bit better. I outwalked grief, anger, confusion. I outwalked old conceptions of myself.

Heeding my craving for nature, I returned to the woods again and again and again. Every rain-soaked leaf, every slug on the trail, every single moment of stillness and silence changed me.

Given my Birkenstock-filled childhood, it's probably no surprise that my response to a dark night of the soul was to withdraw to the woods. Before I could even talk, I looked to the trees for comfort. My earliest memories, playing in Tatlow Park or climbing logs on Kits Beach, are a kaleidoscope of fir, cedar, oak, spruce, juniper. Ocean waves, ravensong and wind rustling in the branches above. I was primed to seek my solace here, among the trees.

After I left the newsroom, I began to see the wisdom in this. The Japanese practice of *shinrin-yoku*, or forest bathing—essentially meditation in wooded settings—has been shown to have many benefits, including significantly decreasing stress hormones like cortisol.

Other data-driven findings include decreased blood pressure, a sharper ability to focus and increased energy. Researchers at Stanford even found that participants who took a ninety-minute walk in nature experienced decreased rumination, negative emotions and anxiety, and increased memory function. Japanese teams, meanwhile, discovered that those who spent time in nature inhaled aromatic plant-based compounds that increased their natural killer white blood cell counts, which support immune function, are linked to a lower risk of cancer and help fight inflammation and infection.

Add to that, forest walks have been proven to relieve confusion. And Korean researchers have determined that study participants who so much as just look at pictures of natural settings have increased brain activity for altruism and empathy.

Another study, published in *Nature*, established a direct link between city living and sensitivity to stress. MRI scans determined that urban environments could increase activity in the amygdala, the brain center in charge of fear and emergencies. City dwellers, the research report noted, had a 21 percent increased risk for developing anxiety disorders, and a 39 percent increased likelihood of suffering from mood disorders.

And yet, as Dr. Qing Li, the world's leading expert in *shinrin-yoku*, points out in his book *Forest Bathing: How Trees Can Help You Find Health and Happiness*, the average American now spends 93 percent of her time indoors.

Which is, not for nothing, roughly the amount of time I'd spent inside when I lived in Toronto.

Modern society is insanely stressful—of course it is. The work world especially. We all know this. I knew this. But

I had little idea what that meant. I had, after all, spent the better part of two decades ignoring my basic needs. Pushing through hunger, exhaustion, illness.

Ignoring my bladder. Ignoring my gut instincts—siren screams that went off when stretch deadlines were announced, or lineups changed at the last minute, or emails sent informing us that we'd be working the weekend. To live that life, I had to disconnect from my body.

There were a lot of other things I had to disconnect from, too, including common sense. Any thinking person could see that open-floorplan offices were a disaster for productivity, and indeed for sanity. The cheery collaboration promised by sneaker-wearing tech futurists had, in fact, resulted in bedlam. Working in an open office environment essentially meant enduring an around-the-clock assault on the senses—idle chatter, noisy jokes, overheard phone calls, cell phone alerts, spontaneous shoulder-tap queries, deskside chinwags, tantalizing smells from a dozen desk lunches. Focus was elusive, the effort to accomplish concrete tasks made futile by the constant cacophony.

Add to that the endless meetings. And the buffet of digital distractions, which all were expected to respond to instantaneously, further chipping away at our window for actual work. None of this made any sense.

What I intuited back then has since been confirmed by fact. We now know that every interruption requires time to recover from, as the brain switches gears. A study at the University of California, Irvine, found that the average office worker was interrupted every eleven minutes, and it took people an average of twenty-five minutes to refocus after every interruption. Try living that math day in and day out, and you'll see what an impossible position we're putting our workers in. It's little wonder, then, that the study's lead researcher, Gloria Mark, wrote in the *New York Times* that attention distraction can lead to high stress and bad moods, as well as the obvious low productivity.

This wasn't the only source of tension my white-collar peers were grappling with, either. There was a lingering feeling of injustice eating away at many I knew. Companies now routinely ignored labor laws, particularly when it came to overtime. An overwhelming majority now worked that last ten or twenty hours a week for free. (In light of this epidemic of unpaid overtime, the most radical thing our society could do to curb income inequality may not be implementing a Universal Basic Income but simply enforcing existing labor laws.)

Either way, it was pretty clear that the nine-to-five was officially a thing of the past, the act of clocking in and out over, lunch breaks obsolete. The average worker now checked email for the first time just after seven in the morning, and finally logged off around seven in the evening. For professionals (and those in the gig economy, or stringing together contracts, or working several part-time jobs), twelve-hour days were now business as usual. For some, a badge of honor, even. So much so, in fact, that boasting about the "996"—working nine to nine, six days a week— had become practically a religion online.

Still, public conversations about the pitfalls of marathon work hours, when we even acknowledged this reality at all, tended to focus on individual responsibility, sidestepping systemic pressures. *We're doing this to ourselves*, the line went. *We all need to get better at putting down our devices, and/or setting boundaries.*

Meanwhile, there was a treasure trove of data amassing, and the news was far from good. Working long hours was terrible by pretty much any metric imaginable: productivity, accuracy, creativity, morale, team cohesion, turnover. It was horrible for individual health and well-being, but also for families and community life. There was really no good reason to work this way. Yet try convincing your average corporate manager of that fact.

As my thirties came to a close, my health problems ramped up, from headaches to asthma, as if to underline all I was learning. Working in high-stakes TV production, I filled the toilet bowl daily with blood, my bowels screaming in outrage. Then came radio, and the chronic lung infections. No new diet, no amount of vacations or massages or meditation, could restore my equilibrium.

The first inkling of my come-to-Jesus moment came while I was seated at my desk in Toronto, months before my fortieth birthday in late 2015, perusing photos of the Sunshine Coast Trail on my old Vancouver newspaper's website. A friend from the student press (now the author of popular hiking books) had trekked the route, snapping pics along the way.

There was a moody blue-tinged photo, taken at sunrise from the summit of Tin Hat. A shot of Fiddlehead Landing Hut, located in dense forest, laundry hung out on a line. An image taken from behind Tin Hat, the valley below ensconced in thick fog.

I read my friend's piece about the North Coast Trail on Vancouver Island next, pining for the rainy beaches, humpback whales, and fern-dotted forest ravines I saw in his images.

Sitting there at my computer, I felt such an intense, visceral longing for the forest, it was akin to being desperately thirsty, and urgently in need of a glass of water. Outside the newsroom window was the smog, the packed subways, the sirens and the construction, the street people experiencing psychotic breaks. The stress, the aggression, the suffering. The unraveling of society. But in these photos, there was green, quiet, calm, adventure. A different kind of life. Two months later, I moved home to Vancouver.

Shortly after arriving, in early 2016, I left the newsroom for good. Walking away from screens, and off into the woods.

Everything you need to know about stress and its impact on the body, you can learn from a Scottish rapper named Loki, a.k.a. Darren McGarvey. During the months that I grappled with chest pains that would not let up, I read a whole stack of books by medical experts on the subject of stress, and what happens when the central nervous system's stress response can't calm down.

But all you really need to know—the emotional and physical and psychological impact of this over weeks and months and a lifetime—you can find in the pages of McGarvey's prize-winning book *Poverty Safari*.

McGarvey grew up in the community of Pollok, in

Glasgow, Scotland, surrounded by poverty, addiction and violence. Drawn by his book's descriptions of chronic stress and brilliant class analysis, I tracked him down. On the phone, he described how the hostile environment he'd grown up in had impacted his body as a child, flooding him with adrenaline and, due to the ongoing physical threats against him, locking him into hyper-arousal and hyper-vigilance. All the while, due to the mechanics of the stress response, suppressing his reasoning faculties.

This chronically agitated, fight-or-flight state was so difficult to come down from, it felt natural to crave relief in the form of alcohol, drugs, junk food. Anything to get a break from the charged anxiety, the sense of impending calamity, the feeling that danger lurked around every corner.

In his book, McGarvey points to an *aha* moment around all this: a 2010 study of Glasgow's physical health that found a link between early brain development in the city's low-income children and poor health outcomes and troubled circumstances later in life. The report, he notes, found that "chronically activated stress responses, especially in children, affect the structure of parts of the frontal lobes of the brain, and these determine the physical reaction to stress, which could result in chronic ill health."

Much of the research around all of this, I discovered, centers on what's called the ACE questionnaire—a list of ten "adverse childhood experiences," or traumas, from divorce and living with a parent with mental illness to abuse and neglect—with higher scores being correlated with higher levels of not just mental illness but also physical illness throughout life.

These poor health outcomes were attributed to toxic stress syndrome. Once the body is highly stressed and stuck in fight-or-flight, it's very difficult for it to calm down. And the body needs to be calm for the immune system to fight disease.

"For those of us affected by this phenomenon, the Glasgow Effect [report] was proof that we were not insane or paranoid—at least not completely," McGarvey writes. "Proof that while we must take personal responsibility for our actions, that the social conditions we are exposed to have a lot to answer for. The Glasgow Effect eloquently described, in scientific terms, the reality of our existence; going about our days, oblivious to the social and psychological disadvantages that define our chaotic and abbreviated lives." It explained, McGarvey adds, how living in stressful conditions inhibited, impaired and even deformed people.

Not all of us live with the extreme levels of stress—the devastating violence, the heartbreaking addiction, the crippling financial strain—found in Glasgow's poorest postal codes, of course. But increasing numbers are nevertheless living with untenable levels of it.

A recent study commissioned by a think tank in Britain, the Mental Health Foundation, found that in the previous year 74 percent of adults had felt so overwhelmed by stress that they were unable to cope. Even more alarming, one in three felt suicidal as a result.

In the U.S., three out of four people report having experienced at least one stress symptom in the past month, with 45 percent unable to sleep, 36 percent feeling anxious or nervous and 34 percent feeling fatigue as a result of stress. Workplace stress costs the economy upwards of $300 billion a year, with 190 billion being spent in healthcare dollars. And three in four Americans suffer from lifestyle-related chronic diseases like obesity, heart disease and diabetes.

Meanwhile, in Canada, 73 percent of adults report feeling stressed. And what do they list as the top cause of that stress? You guessed it: work.

Despair. It's not something we talk about much. But it's the logical result of chronic stress, and it's all around us. It is the homeless person on the street corner. It is the commuter stuck in gridlock. It is the single mother struggling to piece together housecleaning jobs and patchy childcare and still pay the rent. It is a million people alone in front of computer screens, searching for something they will never find.

To unearth this sorrow—to allow it to surface—one really only need ask a question or two. Over my years interviewing people, I would often feel the conversation drop into the realm of intimacy, that suspended space of connection, and then the other person would begin to share their despair. It happened over coffees with friends a lot, too, and sometimes at work lunches. I would feel myself slip into a sort of meditative state, actively listening, and then the energy would shift and the other person would begin to voice their unhappiness.

Single, childless women devastated by how out of reach family felt; working mothers crushed by too many responsibilities; single men ashamed by their loneliness; men and women alike baffled by how much gender roles had changed, unsure how to communicate with each other, unsure how to bridge the gap; young people in agony over global warming; older people baffled by technological innovations that had sped up the pace of the world and relegated everyone to separate silos of flashing screens. The working classes stretched thinner and thinner, blaming themselves for it. The middle classes drowning in debt. The rich more and more alone. Everyone, everywhere, scrambling to find some small scrap of community, some semblance of connection, of love. All of us struggling to comprehend polarized politics, precarious work, rising inequality, racism, violence. Our pain anesthetized only by bad food and good TV.

It always felt, in those moments of listening, that the opposite of this vast, collective sadness would not, in fact, be happiness. It would be hope. Hope for a different future, one in which we were all less alone.

But such hope was hard to come by in this day and age. Hope could not spring forth in an atmosphere of stress, exhaustion. Depleted soil could not birth new shoots.

In the months after I left the newsroom, all the sorrow I'd heard, absorbed, lived, bore down on me. It weighed on my spirit, dragging my energy downwards and making my limbs unbearably heavy. Much of the time, I could not get off my couch.

The only way I could think to return to the green of growth—of hope—was to seek it out on a literal level. To nudge myself out my door, and head off into the woods.

To allow the forest itself to nourish me, infusing my soul with a kind of emerald optimism.

As I walked and walked, I began to wonder about other ways one might approach life. What exactly would life look like if it was not lived in fast-forward? What would it mean to live simply, slowly, in harmony with the natural world? Was there anyone out there dreaming up new models? Was there anyone who was leaning out?

There was, it turned out. And, lucky for me, many of them had even written about it. Library shelves were now practically groaning from the weight of all these books. I read every last one.

There was Kristin Kimball, a Manhattan writer who, after a fortuitous interview with a handsome farmer, ditched city living to marry him and run an organic acreage in rural New York.

There was the Hollywood film executive Gesine Bullock-Prado, sister of the actress Sandra Bullock, who traded L.A. glamour (and a grueling schedule) to make pretty pastries for her own bakery in small-town Vermont.

Then there was the *Marie Claire* editor Helen Russell, who left a harried life in London to move to the stress-free Danish seaside with her husband, resolving years of fertility problems in the process. There was the Canadian journalist Naomi Klein, who noted in her book on climate change that she'd moved to the Sunshine Coast of B.C. with her husband, Avi Lewis, a change of pace that had similarly allowed her to conceive a child. ("I was probably pushing myself way too hard," she told the *Vancouver Sun* of the years leading up to this, during which she had been constantly on the road. "We sort of hit a wall with a certain kind of lifestyle. It was too crazy.")

There was Dee Williams, too, whose heart problems had forced her to retire from full-time employment. She streamlined her finances, and her life, by building a tiny house on wheels and parking it in her friends' backyard—kicking off the small-living craze as she did so. One of her fans, Tammy Strobel, wrote her own book after trading the rat race (and $30,000 of debt) for a tiny house and a relaxed life writing and cycling, experiencing the seasons up close.

Then there were the Minimalists, a pair of male bloggers who'd published a book about divesting themselves of their possessions, and subsequently their jobs, addictions and debts, and for a time moving into a communal house in Montana to pursue passion projects. And Ken Ilgunas with his book *Walden on Wheels*, living in a van on his Duke University campus, getting out of student debt and freeing himself up to later walk across America.

Also: the adventurer Joanna Streetly, writing books from a homemade houseboat in the waters off Tofino, B.C., kayaking through impenetrable fog, weathering lightning storms, encountering wolves and bears, and braving ocean swells.

And the academic Kate Harris, who took ten months out to cycle 10,000 miles and ten countries of the Silk Road. "Every day on a bike trip is like the one before—but it is also completely different, or perhaps you are different, woken up in new ways by the mile," she writes in her award-winning travelogue, *Lands of Lost Borders*. "The less focused I was on the brute mechanics of pedaling—aching legs and lungs, kilometres covered and kilometres to come—the more awake I could be to the world around me, its ordinary wonders."

"On a bike, you're so exposed to the world around you," Harris told me when I called her up to talk about it. "Every bump in the road, every change in the wind or change in the weather, you feel it in this really intimate—maybe too intimate—way. I love that about bicycle travel."

The author, who now lived off-grid in a cabin in Atlin, B.C., with her wife, told me that as a child she was "deeply inspired by the literature of exploration, and the spirit of it . . . this idea of deliberately setting off toward the unknown, into risk. And the idea that you can discover incredible things about yourself, and the world, and your relationship to it, through that."

There was so much to be gained from exposing oneself to this, she said, including empathy, since it invariably meant encountering people from all walks of life. Empathy, she stressed, was something that the world was direly in need of at the moment.

The radicals I was reading about had all traded stress for adventure. In this parallel track I was uncovering, ordinary people were dropping out of mainstream culture and reclaiming their lives in all kinds of weird and wonderful ways. Underlying all these disparate approaches was a rejection of consumerism, and a growing appetite for social contribution and meaningful, face-to-face connection in this age of loneliness and isolation.

It was a bright spot in the bleak landscape of contemporary culture. And I thought about it all the time, mulling over how I might make that leap myself. Breathing in that fresh West Coast air, and returning to the woods again and again and again.

These books all captured, in their own way, a fantasy that was wedged deep in the psyche of every professional woman I'd ever met or spoken with. Every single one of us, at one point or another, had harbored a secret desire to up stakes, ditch the condo and the cubicle, and head for the hills, forging a slower, more rural and—let's face it—more domestic life.

The details of the Great Escape varied from woman to woman; one might be keen to take up beekeeping, while another may long to learn canning and preserving. Others still may fancy quilting. Or growing vegetables. Or sewing clothes, or baking bread from scratch, or raising chickens, or making soap. Homemade granola seemed to loom pretty large in the collective imagination, too; that, and luxuriously cooking one's way through cherished cookbooks.

Here we were, twenty-first-century women racing around big, congested cities, designing advertising campaigns and fashioning PR strategies and building tech start-ups. Yet in our heart of hearts lurked some version of Laura Ingalls Wilder.

The earth-mama Instagrammers often exploited this impulse, manipulating us into purchasing overpriced floral aprons and organic soy candles, poor substitutes for the homemade bumbleberry pie and breezy afternoon walks in cornfields we all craved—but ones we grudgingly accepted, since work deadlines prohibited taking actual nature walks or baking literal pies.

There's no doubt the impulse was a sincere one, though, and a powerful one at that. And one increasingly felt by men, who started dropping out of accounting and finance to open artisanal ice cream shops and spend Sundays making sausage.

Still, to understand why so many women in particular were so attracted to this throwback existence, one had to understand the alternative—which is, it turns out, exquisitely articulated by the *New Yorker*'s Jia Tolentino in her recent book *Trick Mirror*.

In the essay "Always Be Optimizing," Tolentino mulls over the model for the modern cosmopolitan woman, whose lifestyle is now as oppressive as her job. She works until 1 a.m. and is so harried she barely has time to chew the twelve-dollar chopped salad she buys every day at Sweetgreen (served up in record time by fevered clerks, "as if it were *their* purpose in life to do so and their *customers'* purpose in life to send emails for sixteen hours a day with a brief break to snort down a bowl of nutrients that ward off the unhealthfulness of urban professional living").

"It was just a long-simmering discomfort I would have when I would get a Sweetgreen every day for lunch," Tolentino said with a laugh when I called her up to talk about it. The salad, she explained, represented a kind of ideal for the creative class. It was a symbol of a certain kind of life, "which is, you just work all fucking day and you just do everything as efficiently as possible, including your lunch."

You order your salad online, and then you go pick it up, and send emails the entire time you are in line and the entire time you are eating. The chopped-salad spot itself functions like a factory. Every transaction, at every stage, is striking for its inhumane efficiency, she said, with the workers handling order tickets as furiously as if they were stockbrokers.

"This is just so fucking people like me don't have to wait fifteen seconds longer than they want to for their chopped salad!" Tolentino said. "There was just this monstrous efficiency that struck me as so upsetting. At the same time that part of me partook in it happily and eagerly, because it did in fact fit into the way I was working, and the way I was living. And the way that the world encourages you to work and live."

What she was writing at, she said, was that feeling of *What am I doing? What are we doing?*

The dwindling hours off the clock, of course, are no more a woman's own these days. As Tolentino points out in that same essay, after work we all now routinely subject ourselves to torturous forty-dollar barre classes in order to keep our bodies as efficient, as maximized, as our workflow. Able to withstand the daily onslaught.

For what barre is truly good at, Tolentino writes, is "getting you in shape for a hyper-accelerated capitalist life." These classes prepare you "less for a half marathon than for a twelve-hour workday, or a week alone with a kid and no childcare, or an evening commute on an underfunded train."

All this terrifying efficiency that we women must now cultivate—firing off emails from the backs of cabs and arranging play dates at office meetings while simultaneously easing tensions between coworkers and paying bills and ordering groceries online and preparing ourselves mentally for a grueling after-work spin class—is obviously exhausting. Relentless.

But it's not even enough to perform all of this for survival's sake. No, now we are all expected to embrace this ferocious productivity as self-improvement. As work/life balance. As a "healthy lifestyle."

Of course, it feels like anything but.

So it's probably no surprise, then, that when I mentioned at dinner with a bunch of high-flying professional women the other night that I was about to interview a "radical homemaker" who lived on a farm in upstate New York—just those few brief words alone were enough to capture the attention of everyone at the table, all of whom immediately confessed that this was, in fact, their dream. All of whom became instantly, utterly rapturous.

"I could be fucking it up just as much as the next person," Shannon Hayes said with a laugh when I reached her on the phone in West Fulton, New York.

Like so many of us, Hayes started out sold on the idea that education and achievement would enable her to create a fulfilling life and make a contribution.

But when she graduated with a PhD from Cornell University and a 3.9 GPA, having studied sustainable agriculture and community development, she found that the economy did not deliver on this promise. After spending hours completing the university's online graduate placement questionnaire to determine her skills, talents, employability, the results came back with a single job posting. Hayes was, it turned out, uniquely qualified to write scripts for the World Wrestling Federation.

Hayes laughed remembering that. "What was really clear is there is no path," she told me, more seriously. "There is *no path*. You have to cut your own path."

At the same time as she had that realization, her then fiancé, now husband, was fired from his job. The young couple had just bought a cabin on the edge of a five-thousand-acre state forest in the hills of Schoharie County, down the road from Hayes's parents' farm, and they did not want to leave the mountains that sustained their souls. So they ran the numbers. If they were forced to relocate to a big city to find work, they'd need to pay an exorbitant mortgage as well as fund two cars, two professional wardrobes, plenty of takeout dinners and, eventually, daycare.

But if they stayed at home in West Fulton and forged a different kind of life, rejecting the modern economy and remaining in their own community, they'd need way less.

The system, they felt, was totally broken. So they decided to try and build a new one. A life-serving economy in which, as Hayes puts it in her book of essays, *Homespun Mom Comes Unraveled*, "everyone is able to earn a living wage, where ecological resources are sustained, where community life is vibrant, and where relationships are easily nurtured."

Hayes came to see the home as a response to a lot of the structural problems facing our generation, from income inequality to industrialized healthcare (particularly when it comes to lifestyle diseases), poor education, industrialized food, the destruction of the environment, the fragmentation of families. For Hayes and her husband—who also identifies as a "radical homemaker"—focusing one's energies on the home as a center of production, as opposed to consumption, came to constitute a radical political act.

So the couple made a life for themselves working on Hayes's family's grassfed livestock farm. As she writes in her book, they planted vegetable gardens, split firewood, canned peaches, wove baskets, sold meat at the farmer's market, made soap, knit sweaters and baked wholesome, sugar-free cookies (and pretended they were delicious). They homeschooled their daughters. They spent little. Hayes penned cookbooks and nonfiction titles about their movement, along with a popular blog. The entire family became passionately involved in their local community and politics. They now also run a farm store and restaurant, feeding the surrounding area.

There is the fantasy of this folksy, rural kind of life, and then, of course, there is the reality. It's worth pointing out that a lot of Hayes's life would not Instagram well. She describes her house as messy and chaotic; reading her essays, one can picture the clutter and dust bunnies, the piled dishes and sticky counters and overgrown yard. She wears thrift store clothes—and probably not the sort that sell for $200 a pop in vintage shops in the city. It's highly unlikely that her hair looks camera-ready at all times.

But her life does seem to epitomize the relaxed pace, close community and connection to nature that so many women I know are so desperately seeking.

Take Hayes's schedule, for instance. When we chatted on the phone, she walked me through her day. She had risen well before dawn and had sat outside alone, watching the lightning bugs as the sun slowly rose in the sky, relishing the stillness and silence. Then she'd spent some hours writing. Around seven, she and her husband made coffee and ventured out for a few hours, hiking in the woods and connecting, taking in the beauty of local waterfalls. (This two-and-a-half-hour retreat to the woods took place every single day. Every day!)

After she hung up with me, Hayes said, she might do some bookkeeping before the whole family sat down for lunch together (today was leftovers, tomorrow a pot roast). And then later, they'd all work down at their café in the hamlet for the afternoon, prepping food, as it was only open on weekends. That evening, she'd perhaps hit a yoga class in a local barn, steps from the farm café, and catch up with her neighbors. And then maybe listen to her husband play guitar, go to bed.

It was a universe away from the alienation of barre classes and Sweetgreen salads.

There was, in fact, no fast food in Hayes's life. The clock didn't seem to figure prominently in her psyche. Her family spent a lot of time together, and always had. And they didn't experience financial stress, despite earning poverty-level incomes.

Add to that, Hayes's marriage was a strong one—in

part, she thought, because they'd had the luxury of putting each other first and of nurturing their relationship as best friends, business partners and intellectual companions.

"I think what my life represents to the people who crave it is balance," she reflected. "[That's] what I am trying to achieve and I'm always trying to be transparent about it, because I'm always struggling. But I might get a little bit farther than some people do.

"I am employing myself to the highest levels of my intellect," she went on. "At the same time, finding the time to restore my body and my spirit. And to find time for those things that really matter most to me, which is family and community. I feel like I get to apply myself as a whole person to building the world that I want, *fully*. And to taking the benefit from the world that I am trying to build. I'm trying to create a more environmentally sustainable, balanced and kind world. At the same time that I am trying to create it, I am benefiting from that world I am creating.

"Just because we care about our children, and our parents, and the environment, doesn't mean we don't want to make our mark on the world and bring our creative magic to the fore," she stressed. "And I feel like I get to do that. I don't have to choose between being a career woman and a parent and a child and a neighbor. Or someone who just likes to hang out by waterfalls."

CHAPTER THREE

The Plate

If there's one thing you can count on in life, it's karma. Time and time again, I've found that whenever I'm judgmental about something, chances are good that I'll eventually do it.

I spent decades rolling my eyes at the Gwyneth Paltrows of the world, who inconvenienced everyone around them with their elaborate dietary restrictions. So naturally during my first year of leaning out, I found myself regaling a patient waitress at Salt Spring Island's Tree House Cafe—named for a plum tree that sits in the middle of the eatery—with a laundry list of foods that must not pass my lips. The naturopath-recommended elimination diet I was on banned gluten, dairy, soy, corn, eggs, refined sugar, every fat except cold-pressed extra-virgin olive oil, most meats, fish, chocolate, coffee, citrus, nuts and most seeds, plus nightshade vegetables. I woke up mid-list and cringed. What the hell was I doing?

Raised a reluctant hippie child, I had of course rebelled in the only way possible: moving across the country, donning stilettos and getting a job at a women's magazine. As we've seen, I logged marathon hours at the office, went out every night to cocktail parties and—until the chefs I interviewed harangued me into learning to cook—existed mainly on Starbucks and Purdy's chocolates. But, as we've also seen, that lifestyle takes its toll.

In addition to the headaches and gastro issues and chronic asthma, I had eczema on one of my hands for close to a decade. When my hand wasn't inflamed and itchy, it was covered with microscopic cuts that stung whenever I washed the dishes, and made shaking hands a painful trial. The eczema bothered me more than the other three issues combined, because it was a constant, daily agony, and because over the years I had exhausted every option available in mainstream medicine.

So when the dust settled and my doctor informed me that the chest pains were, in fact, anxiety, and it became obvious that I wasn't going back to the newsroom any-time soon, I decided to focus on my health in earnest. What would happen if I made that my top priority?

Around that time, my naturopath informed me—no surprise—that my central nervous system was stuck in the fight-or-flight stress response. So I began, in addition to the forest walks, to attend meditation groups and restor-ative yoga classes, lying on the floor in darkness, wrapped in blankets, allowing my parasympathetic system to find its footing.

I also underwent the aforementioned elimination diet, which lasted a few months and essentially meant I couldn't eat out at any restaurant in my city, or in fact anywhere at all that was not my own kitchen. (But which, amazingly, got my asthma under control to the point that I no longer required daily doses of steroids, or even an inhaler. And still don't, three years later.)

In the midst of this useful but extremely inconvenient phase, I found myself returning to Salt Spring, the island of my youth, famous for its natural West Coast beauty, counterculture residents, thriving wellness centers and decades-long tradition of local, organic food.

Here's the thing: if you are nutty enough to travel while on an elimination diet, Salt Spring is the place to go.

I say this because all the restaurants in town easily and cheerfully accommodated my dietary demands, serving me delicious meals that catered to the long and crazy list of banned substances. But I also say this because one morning, my friends and I stumbled into Morningside Organic Bakery Café and Bookstore in Fulford Village, the charming South End harbor near the cabin we'd rented in the woods.

Morningside was tailor-made for my extreme diet, and was a massive relief to find, although one could never describe its customer service in such terms. Its owner was a curt, eco-chic French woman. Online reviews of her customer service lean toward moral outrage; one poster refers to her as "the angry vegan." A blog on the café's website broke down her ethos: "If you are bringing your snooty consumer 'me first' attitude, I suggest you move along. If you want to stay in your monocultured, supersized, Starbuckified box, then you will be sorely disappointed."

Not having read any of this, I didn't exactly get off on the right foot with the place. The café keeps random hours, and my blood sugar was dangerously low when its doors finally swung open. As a result, I sent back the rice bowl I ordered, though in fairness it was meant to be a noodle bowl, and did not contain a single ingredient listed on the menu. (The bearded male server shrugged and said sometimes they cooked with whatever was in the fridge.)

As it happens, I myself am prone to moral outrage, particularly when I'm hungry, and so I was decidedly nonplussed. But then I took a sip of the owner's famous chai.

Gorgeously spiced with a hint of heat, made with coconut milk and served at the perfect temperature—it was so ridiculously good I was determined to persevere. Anyone who could make chai with this much heart and soul was clearly worth knowing.

And so I returned the next morning. The owner and I then bonded over our shared aversion to canola oil, and I told her that her chai was the most magnificent I'd ever tasted. In the end, I enjoyed her gruff, no-nonsense manner. And anyway, the chai.

I bought a steaming cup of it, along with several rice flour, pumpkin seed and anise cookies, and met my friends down by the wharf. On the dock, a barefoot concert pianist was playing an ancient piano. The smell of the sea wafted up to us, mingling with the scent of ginger and chili from the tea. There was blue water for as far as the eye could see. Seagulls circled overhead. We sat, rapt, as the music washed over us. And gave silent thanks for the island's strange magic.

"Is the tea any good?" my friend asked, hugging a cup of coffee. "The best," I replied.

My friends had been good-natured about my food restrictions. Which was lucky, because after that I went on the Spleen Qi Deficiency Diet, a regimen based in traditional Chinese medicine that was even more limited (if that's possible) and bizarre-sounding to outside ears.

These naturopath-inspired diets, it must be said, were not my first experiences experimenting with food, and surely would not be the last. To live in twenty-first-century North America is to live with the knowledge that our food is making us sick. And to have not the slightest clue what to do about it.

"Fruit is highly toxic," a Toronto media acquaintance once felt the need to warn me, after I bumped into her in the company cafeteria while eating a banana. "The sugars trigger massive spikes in your insulin. And then there's all those carbs. What a nightmare!" What did she suggest I eat instead? A giant hunk of salami. "Protein is the breakfast of champions," she insisted.

Days after that, I was out shopping with a friend. As we stopped for burgers and fries, my friend explained that she'd embarked on a new dietary regime. Her naturopath had informed her she was allergic to a whole host of foods, and so she was cutting out numerous things and switching from dairy to soy products. "The only thing is, I've heard the hormones in soy aren't good for you," she said. "Something about early-onset menopause? I'm not sure. I'm thinking I'll just do a juice cleanse every month to reduce the risk."

Such admittedly amusing conversations pointed to an alarming reality: the majority of us were utterly baffled by food. What exactly constituted a healthy diet? We had no idea.

And the media wasn't helping. One year we were advised to eat low-fat; the next, nutritional experts were telling us that carbs were the problem. One report said to increase intake of omega-3s by eating fish; the next screamed of high mercury levels in seafood. Some health gurus suggested going Paleo; others advised veganism. And if Gwyneth Paltrow had her way, we'd all be on a steady diet of kale and quinoa. Not that there's anything wrong with kale and quinoa.

In an attempt to simplify this confusing, and often quite silly, conversation around food, journalist Michael Pollan spent years unpacking the forces that have led to our anxiety. In a 2008 talk at UC Santa Barbara about his bestselling book *In Defense of Food*, he describes how he tracked the rise of "nutritionism," defined as the widespread belief that people require expert advice to eat properly.

Nutritionism maintains that food is the sum of its scientifically measured parts, or nutrients. It follows, then, that there are good nutrients and bad nutrients; the bad are to be avoided at all costs and the good are to be consumed religiously. The trouble is that nutritional science—so new a discipline that Pollan quips it's essentially where surgery was in 1650—continually discovers new information. And so nutrients that were once demonized are, a handful of years later, zealously promoted.

Food is in fact incredibly complex, Pollan points out, and it may take decades for scientists to fully comprehend how an apple or carrot works, and how it interacts with the human body. In the meantime, since nutritional science is still in its infancy, maybe we don't change our diets every time nutrition experts change their tune?

The second problem with the "nutritionism" movement is interference from the industrialized food industry. It throws billions at lobbying government and favors processed foods, which are easier to sell than, say, potatoes or broccoli. Grocery stores are now packed with highly processed foods claiming all kinds of health benefits, whereas whole foods have no such ad budgets to recommend them.

The third problem is that we all now believe that the sole purpose of eating is to promote bodily health. There are, of course, lots of other reasons to eat, from pleasure and identity to ritual and community, Pollan notes. And many of them are richer and more rewarding. And more balanced than scrutinizing every last mouthful.

The net effect of all this is that many of us are now suffering from orthorexia, or an unhealthy obsession with healthy eating. In his talk, Pollan says this disorder is an "American paradox"—that people who are so concerned with nutrition have such poor dietary health.

Clearly, I was suffering from this affliction. I agonized about my dietary choices, read nutrition articles online, plowed through all manner of books, listened to podcasts, rode wave after wave of food trends. Subscribed, without knowing it, to the idea that healthy eating was an extremely complex puzzle to be solved.

Over the years, I tried being vegan. I tried being gluten-free. I tried Paleo, albeit for just a week. I tried avoiding just dairy. And then just meat. I quit sugar. And then caffeine.

(Truly awful, if you're wondering.) And then sugar again. All of this required a ton of effort and energy. And was not social, not by any stretch of the imagination.

I was relieved to discover from Pollan, then, that in reality, the Standard American Diet is one of the only human diets in history that can reliably be counted on to cause disease and death. The Standard American Diet (or SAD) is basically the fast-food diet: refined grains, processed foods, red meat, processed meat and very few fruits, vegetables and whole grains. The SAD is now responsible for the top four causes of death in the United States. This was the very diet I always fell back on whenever I got bored, or fed up, or busy. It's the diet modern society pushes us toward in a thousand ways every day: long working hours that leave us no time to prepare fresh food, the mind-boggling ubiquity of grab-and-go snack food, the redirecting of social life from the home to restaurants.

The big question, as Pollan sees it, is how to escape this Western diet without having to flee Western civilization.

If we can all agree that nutritional science should not be dictating our food choices, who do we look to for answers? Culture, Pollan says. Or, put another way: our mothers. And our mothers' mothers. Food traditions have always been passed down from mother to daughter, and if we want to establish sane eating practices again, that is what we must return to.

I was incredibly lucky in this respect. My mother and my grandmother didn't eat anything our current generation survives on. They didn't eat half their meals from packages, and the other half at insanely overpriced hipster hotspots. And they certainly didn't hold up sushi and Starbucks as the gold standard for a healthy dinner.

What they did was eat whole foods. And cook. Every night, month in and month out, year after year. Something that until I was in my early thirties, I had no idea how to do.

On my tenth birthday, my grandmother gave me the *Better Homes and Gardens New Junior Cook Book*. I can't say that I remember cooking from it, though there are grease stains on some of the pages, so I must have.

If there's anyone in my family that I aspired to take after, it was my Nan. She adored food and family in equal measure, and she gave her whole heart to both. Working-class as she was—she toiled in factories in England, fashioning chocolates and later airplane parts on an assembly line—my Nan was as refined a woman as any could hope to be.

Her hair was always set in curls. She never left the house without a full face of makeup. She wouldn't dream of cursing. She wore sparkling rings on her fingers and smelled faintly of pressed powder and lilies and roses. She was warm and gracious, always ready with a kind word. She cared very much for her family, and her neighbors, and strangers on the street who appeared to be having a difficult time. Also, she adored small dogs.

When my mother was five and her family finally moved out of my great-grandmother's cramped row house and into their own council flat, Nan got the 1953 edition of the *Good Housekeeping Cookery Compendium* and worked her way through its pages.

The results were spectacular. My mother and uncle tell me that Nan's food was always fresh and wholesome, delicious and perfectly executed. She made everything from scratch, even bread. Nan and Grandad had a kitchen garden in London, so there were always piles of greens at every meal to balance out the mouthwatering dessert that was the *pièce de résistance*. Even after they immigrated to Canada and fell on particularly hard times, Nan always managed to make meals a festive occasion.

Her specialty was Sunday dinner. Her roasts were tender and juicy; her Yorkshire pudding melted in your mouth. Her mashed potatoes were whipped to perfection and buttery smooth. And she could make a mean dessert from nothing: rice pudding, bread pudding, macaroni pudding—you name it. Plus, on special occasions: Queen Victoria sponge cake with layers of jam, marzipan-topped Christmas cake, treacle pie.

Nan drank her weight in tea every day, and lived for sweets. There were times in my childhood when my parents refused to let me eat anything that contained refined sugar. It was all honey and carob and maple syrup for me. And halva—those chalky bars of sweet sesame paste that haunt health food stores everywhere—if my parents were feeling extremely generous.

But they knew better than to press the issue with Nan. And so my memories of her are drenched in chocolate and marzipan, buttery frosting and powdered sugar and sticky, saccharine jam.

Her blue eyes shining, she would tell me about her first husband, a fighter pilot who died in the war. Or her second husband, my grandfather, a dashing Welshman whose picture she had first seen on her brother's wife's mantelpiece. Grandad was this sister-in-law's cousin, and when Nan laid eyes on his photo, she thought, *That is the man I am going to marry.* She used to call him her Mantelpiece Romeo, and when he returned from the war after serving in the navy, they wed within two weeks.

I loved Nan's stories. Late at night, lying across the room from me in the single bed that my parents had rented for one of her visits, she whispered about the dances during the war. All the windows were painted black and the German planes flew low overhead as the teenagers danced with the kind of giddy abandon that can only come from imminent danger. Only recently did I realize she must have been telling me about the Blitz.

She told me, too, about the day of the Queen's coronation, when the masses flooded into the streets. The atmosphere was jubilant, and the people cheered and welcomed their new sovereign with fistfuls of flowers. Commemorative silver spoons, teacups and saucers were given out. Cake and ice cream were delivered to every British subject, much to the glee of my mother, who inherited Nan's sweet tooth. My mother was then almost five, and spent the day atop Nan's shoulders in downtown London, craning her neck to catch a glimpse of the young monarch. Nan's tale wove together gilded carriages and marching soldiers and trumpeting horns, and Queen Elizabeth II, in her calm, steady voice, promising to serve the Commonwealth for the rest of her days.

Such stories would often be accompanied by a chocolate macaroon. A humble factory worker, Nan gave the only thing she had to give: food. And I lapped it up gratefully, licking chocolate from my fingers and holding out my hands for more.

By the time I was old enough to fly alone from Vancouver to Toronto to visit her—eight, according to the hilariously lax parenting standards of the day—my grandmother's hands were so gnarled from arthritis that it was difficult for her to zip up her own dress, let alone cook a proper supper. But family stories of Nan's culinary gifts make me wish that I could have cooked with her.

Nan died when I was thirteen years old. The night that she passed away, I dreamt of her, sensed her presence in my bedroom, felt her being wrenched away. I woke up, startled, at 4 a.m., and understood that she'd made her exit from this world.

In the morning when I got up, my father confirmed that she was gone. I knew what I had lost. We went to the aquarium that day; I had by then read Madeleine L'Engle's magical marine tale *A Ring of Endless Light*, and sought solace among the dolphins and whales.

I wept for days, inconsolable. I wrote a poem that was read at her funeral, likening her to a ballerina from *Swan Lake*, the most beautiful thing I could think of at the time.

There have been many times that I felt her absence over the years, but I feel it most keenly in the kitchen. Sometimes, standing there at an open fridge, trying to figure out what to feed myself, I am hit with a deep ache.

A yearning for my Nan. For her stories, her love and care. For her recipes. For her food.

In spite of the rich culinary tradition I come from, I was in my thirties when I finally learned to cook properly. For years, I walked around bereft, longing to put on a Sunday supper and not having the slightest clue where to start. The story of my relationship with food, as with the broader story of my leaning out, involves dozens of false starts, dozens of detours. And so much casting about, trying to find a different way.

In the end, though, my dream was Nan's dream: a house full of family and friends, a table laden with good, nourishing food, an evening of entertaining stories and a ridiculously decadent dessert—served up with a shot of glamour (in my case, candy-colored lipstick; in her case, pearls and Chanel No. 5). All inevitably followed by a steaming pot of tea.

My mother's favorite cookbook is *The Cooking of Provincial France*. Before I had ever heard of its Francophile authors, M.F.K. Fisher and Julia Child, I knew about the pretty amber book with the soufflé on the cover. It was jammed in a cupboard above the fridge, and my mum would stand on her tip-toes to pull it down whenever she was in the mood to make something special.

For reasons best known to my mother, she has always been enamored of France. Something about the country's language and philosophers and music and love of life— the savoring of every moment of pleasure, every hunk of baguette, every last square of dark chocolate—has always spoken to her. I gather that it all began with this volume of the famed Time-Life Foods of the World series, *The Cooking of Provincial France*, which my mother was given by an Italian friend who knew enough about food to know what she was giving.

My mother hasn't been to France yet. The closest she's gotten, I imagine, was during one of her trips to visit me in Toronto. I took her to a Parisian creperie in Yorkville, where airy batter was tenderly smoothed onto griddles, cooked, topped with homemade tartinade and fresh strawberries, and carefully folded onto plates. It was a breezy summer day and we sat in chairs out on the sidewalk and sipped our café au laits without speaking. The servers drifted in and out of the shop, delivering orders in lyrical bursts of French, and an accordion player planted himself near us and began to play. I looked over and saw that tears were rolling down my mother's cheeks.

My mother discovered French food at a dinner party in the 1960s, when she sampled a heavenly fish recipe from *The Cooking of Provincial France*. Concetta, her Italian film-professor friend, happened to have the book and was generous enough to give it to her.

It wasn't an easy time in my parents' life. They were living in inner-city Pittsburgh while my father pursued his graduate degree in psychology at Duquesne. They often had no money for food, and had to wash all their clothes by hand. The apartment they lived in was so dilapidated, it once filled with clouds of soot—one hundred years of grime that had built up in the vents and were released when the heating system was replaced—which left a black film on all of their belongings that lasted for days.

They eventually moved on to the famed Project One in San Francisco, where my mother became its head cook. Every night she made a soup, a salad, a main and a dessert for sixty or so people, all from her cherished book.

When my brother and I were growing up, my mum supplemented the hippie macrobiotic cuisine of the time—and the hearty shepherd's-pie fare she herself was brought up on—with the best of rustic French country cooking. Chunky vegetable soups garnished with thin trails of pesto; cream of carrot or cauliflower purees; delicate, buttery quiches with cheese; simple seasonal salads; flaky tomato pies; glazed strawberry tarts bursting with summer sweetness.

I took these delights for granted. I took it for granted that my mother went to the trouble of creating such beautiful food, particularly in the era of the boxed macaroni and cheese and Fruit Roll-Ups that I so coveted. I couldn't comprehend that her passion was anything unusual, anything out of the ordinary.

So I didn't understand what she was entrusting me with one day in grade nine when she handed over her prized cookbook to take to my French class for show-and-tell. I carted the book to school. I unpacked it and made some random remarks, possibly about cassoulets. And then I left it in the chilly classroom, abandoned, never to be found again. My mother was devastated. I felt terrible.

But then I forgot all about the slim tome. And if my mother had mournful cravings for the *pâte brisée* recipe contained within it, she didn't mention it.

Many years later, I myself fell in love with cooking. It started with Weight Watchers. Admittedly, this is not the most poetic beginning to a love affair with food, but it is my beginning and it is the truth.

I was thirty-one years old. My diet was appalling. It consisted mainly of soggy Asian takeout, Tim Hortons bagels, coffee and absurd amounts of drugstore chocolate. Unsurprisingly, I was overweight.

The problem was that I found myself working in quite possibly the most glamorous office in all of Canada. My coworkers were willowy reeds with supermodel hair and manicured nails and closets full of stylish clothes. One of the interns wore Louboutins to work, for goodness' sake. When I left the office, it was to interview celebrities or attend cocktail parties peopled by similarly skinny sylphs. All day long, I looked at layouts of celebrities (an exercise in boosting self-esteem, as you would expect). I did not like how frumpy I felt, how unpolished. I did not like fussing over clothes that didn't fit right. I did not like how I appeared in photos. Plus, as I've said, I was pretty unhealthy.

Clearly something had to be done. But what?

I had absolutely no idea. So I started going to Weight Watchers meetings, where I sat among a motley crew of Torontonians and heard, for what felt like the first time, that it was not a good idea to eat processed foods if you wanted to lose weight. (How I had missed this message in my counterculture childhood is beyond me.) The program advised me to eat mainly fresh fruits, vegetables, whole grains and, in much smaller quantities, high-quality meat and dairy. These simple guidelines were a revelation.

Next, I landed on the book *French Women Don't Get Fat*. The tone was instantly appealing—all pleasure, no pointless deprivation. Its author, Mireille Guiliano, whom I later tracked down, suggests in the book that women cut out nasty processed foods and takeout; drink lots of water; walk everywhere (thankfully eschewing the gym); enjoy bread, chocolate and cheese in moderation; eat slowly, in courses; and plan one's daily meals around a variety of fresh, seasonal, local fruits and vegetables. She maintains the secret to a fit figure is to redefine your relationship to food—to find joy in eating—and to simply use your head about how and when to indulge. It was another revelation. Here was the cultural wisdom that Michael Pollan had been talking about. The French had honed their eating habits over centuries, and they were more than happy to pass along their formula.

The more I read, the more it became obvious that I was going to need to learn how to cook. And Guiliano made it all seem so easy. Throw together a little grated-carrot salad or a beautiful mixed vegetable soup. Cook up a piece of fish with olive oil and lemon. Enjoy a single piece of dark chocolate for dessert, or perhaps some perfectly ripe cherries. Suddenly, eating well didn't seem so difficult. So I started to try a few recipes. To eat actual, full meals. And enjoy them, guilt-free.

And here is the French paradox that everyone marvels at: I did not starve myself to slim down. Far from it. The more I ate—good food, real food—the more weight I lost. First five, then fifteen, and finally twenty pounds. Food became less of a mystery, and I began to feel connected to what was on my plate in a way that I hadn't when I was absentmindedly scarfing down fast food. I felt alive. And I liked the way my little black dresses fit.

Next, I signed up for cooking classes at the local college. I made lasagnas and sole bonne femme, roasted whole chickens and baked pork chops with prune stuffing. To be honest, I didn't have much natural ability. But people had been cooking every night for centuries. Surely I didn't have to be gifted to make a decent dinner?

At the magazine, after I took over as editor of the food pages, I conferred with chefs, asking them over and over again if culinary skill came down to talent, or if passion and practice could get you there. I asked until I got the answer I was looking for. Over a cup of tea, Jamie Oliver gave me a playful piece of advice that's held me in good stead: "Just do what you're fucking told." As in: Just follow recipes, already—it's not rocket science.

And so, down long-distance lines, my mother read me her recipes. Bran muffins, banana bread, lemon yogurt salad dressing. Every week, we would detail the dishes that we had cooked the previous week. At the time, we favored Molly Wizenberg's *A Homemade Life*. On opposite coasts, we slow-roasted tomatoes and ate them on hunks of baguette slathered with triple-cream Brie.

After having roommates for years, I moved into my own apartment and filled the tiny space with cookbooks. I spent hours in my galley kitchen stirring soups and sauces, rolling out dough for tourtières, baking brownies. I discovered that I could cook just fine, thank you very much. Once in a while I could even be great. Also, happily, my friends' standards were spectacularly low. As it turns out, most people these days are accustomed to eating greasy takeout. A homemade meal—however basic—beats eating out of Styrofoam any day of the week.

Every now and then I would scour the Internet looking for that book that I had lost all that time ago. I couldn't seem to get the title right; lots of books came up in my search, but none of them had that familiar golden cover. Once I even found photocopies of some of the recipes and sent them to my mother. But it wasn't the same.

And then one day, I was sitting at my desk at work. It was a press day, and I was editing a cover story on Prince William and Kate Middleton. It seemed obvious that they would get engaged soon, which made me pleased. I wanted a coffee, and so I decided to venture out for a latte at the dreary mini-mall next door to our office tower. Please know that I almost never left my desk, and especially not on a press day. But I had to have a shot of caffeine to heighten the surge of contentment that I was experiencing.

Once the pages had been filed, I pulled on my enormous sunglasses and grabbed my oversized handbag and slipped out of the building. As I crossed the street, I was suddenly hit with an overwhelming urge to visit the Goodwill store in the mall and peruse their cookbooks. It was hot and humid, and when I entered the cool mall I walked right past the coffee shop and into the thrift store. I made a beeline for the cookbook section, heeding some strange magnetic pull.

There, on the first shelf that I looked at, was a familiar amber cover. I felt a jolt of recognition seeing that soufflé.

It was *The Cooking of Provincial France*. I lifted the beautiful book off the shelf and flipped through its immaculate pages full of photos of markets and fish and flowers and cakes. I could have cried. It was $3.49.

I left the mall and called my mother. Two decades later, I told her that I could return French country cooking to her, a lost sliver of her soul.

I recently found journals from the months I spent backpacking through Thailand at twenty-five, after the surgery that removed part of my colon. Rereading these notebooks, I see that they are filled with descriptions of food. Pho soup with rice noodles, cilantro, sliced chilis, mint leaves; plates of stir-fried pork with basil; sweet pineapple from street vendors; bamboo tubes filled with sweet sticky rice, fresh from the morning markets; jackfruit popsicles; cup after cup of spicy lemon ginger tea.

I remember stumbling onto a cart in a darkened alley in Chiang Mai, smelling the rich chicken broth, the lemongrass and kaffir lime leaves, sitting at a plastic table and slurping up the most flavorful soup I'd ever tasted, the old woman who had spooned it out smiling a toothless smile at me. I recall eating a delicate pomelo salad in a posh eatery near the Mandarin Oriental, the flakes of fruit seasoned with fish sauce, chilis, fresh-shaved coconut. Devouring a whole fish at an open-air restaurant on the Chao Phraya River in Bangkok, gazing out at the wooden boats lit against the dusk sky, sucking the flesh from bones, my mouth afire with the sweet-sour sublime of lime, sugar, chili.

The diet in Thailand suited me in a way that the Standard American Diet never had. The traditional Thai diet is rich in fresh fruits and vegetables and almost totally lacking in processed foods. There are very few dairy products and little refined sugar or flour. And, because much of the country is Buddhist and vegetarian, not much meat. Traveling the country, I dined on fragrant vegetable curries, snacked on the most divine rose apples from stands, lunched on tart green mango salads. The food on my plate felt alive.

Mealtimes became events. I was never in a rush, and I never ate alone. I'd spend hours dining with fellow travelers from hostels or trains. Or else I'd sit at stalls on the street and chat with vendors and customers. We would all invariably marvel at the food. These meals were so spicy and fragrant and fresh, they brought tremendous joy to my day-to-day life. And that joy spread through my entire body, lighting up every last cell.

My body came into harmony, regulating itself. I felt a new energy and vitality. I lost weight. I knew this way of eating suited me. So much so, in fact, that when I returned to Canada I cooked Thai curries every night for weeks, trying to keep it up.

All these years later, I realized that the diet I had stumbled upon in Southeast Asia was the very whole foods–oriented, fruit-and-veg-heavy diet that Pollan suggested, along with Guiliano. And my own mother, too.

This all came flooding back when I stepped away from the daily grind and began contemplating the madness of how we were all living. I had discovered the pleasures of home-cooked food in my thirties—and of whole, fresh, mainly plant-based eating in my twenties before that—and then lost it again to the maelstrom of modern life.

And really, who could blame me? For all our obsession with celebrity chefs, twenty-first-century North American culture totally disregards food. Mealtimes have ceased to exist. People eat on subways and in cars and on buses. Occasionally, even while rushing down the street. Work meetings are regularly scheduled during lunchtime and, increasingly, dinnertime. Exercise classes, events, cock-tail parties—everything exists in opposition to the body clock. There's no longer any hour of the day that's set aside to slow down, eat, socialize. No time that's consid-ered sacred, protected from the relentless, never-ending demands of work.

And yet, I promptly got hungry, starving even, three times a day. Eight. Noon. Six. I hated postponing meals, working through them, my stomach growling in protest. I got irritable. I wanted food. And not just salty or sugary snacks at my desk, either.

After I left the newsroom and my time was my own, I was finally able to heed my body's natural rhythms. For the first time in my adult life, I could eat when I was hungry. Every meal, every single day.

I began to revisit my early food inspirations, including the French model. I dug up my copy of Vancouver profes-sor Karen Le Billon's book *French Kids Eat Everything* and modeled my life after her suggestions, feeding myself as I would a small child. I gave myself vegetables first, when

I was most hungry, arranged in smart little salads. I limited desserts to once a week. (Or tried to, anyway.) I gave up snacks. I began eating at the table again, instead of on the couch, and setting it beautifully, sometimes even with flowers.

I invited friends over regularly, serving carrot parsnip soup, and salads with yeast dressing from the famed *Hollyhock Cooks* cookbook. Or the hilariously named vegan "Glory Bowls" with beets and carrots and microgreens, from the *Whitewater Cooks* recipe collection. I baked lasagna with grassfed beef and local, organic cheese. I visited Granville Island and bought fresh gnocchi, and topped it with a simple tomato sauce from David Rocco's first cookbook. I arranged artful salads, laid out crusty loaves of artisan bread, roasted stone fruit in simple crumbles.

I began inching back toward the Thai model, too, increasing fruits, vegetables, herbs and spices, and limiting sugar, meat, dairy and processed foods.

What I liked about this way of eating was that it avoided the extremes of the various healthy-eating subcultures, which of course dominated the scene in Lotus Land.

Veganism was too restrictive for me, and too reliant on processed foods like fake cheese and almond milk (and also upset my sensitive digestive tract with all its nuts and seeds and raw veggies).

Paleo did not make sense, either, given the fact that my gastroenterologist had advised me to limit meat, especially red meat. I loved the barbecue pork buns at dim sum way too much to go 100 percent vegetarian. The gluten-free fad passed me by, too, since its baked goods tasted like some combination of sawdust and cardboard. Raw food held little appeal, as I didn't relish the thought of spending roughly half my waking hours juicing and chopping vegetables. Keto was out; after the restrictive elimination diets I'd undergone, I wasn't into eating in a way that severely limited my social life. I still wanted to be able to go to people's houses for dinner.

Plus, I wanted to sidestep the near-religious promises that the health and wellness evangelicals made. Many implied that if one were only to align one's diet in a certain way—some mystical combination of non-nightshade vegetables and superfoods like acai—it would solve literally all problems in life, from infertility to anxiety.

I never understood how much of this thinking I had absorbed from my seventies childhood until I read the book *Hippie Food*, which traces the origins of many of today's food fads. Who knew, for example, that the macrobiotic diet (brown rice, soba noodles, miso, cooked veg) originated with a charismatic Japanese cult leader who essentially formed his own weirdo brand of spirituality around it? Some macrobiotic adherents, who stopped eating anything but brown rice, suffered from scurvy.

Since I wasn't interested in developing obscure nineteenth-century diseases, I decided to let common sense win out. That, and my mother, and my mother's mother.

The key for me, it turned out, was consistency. With the exception of a dinner out here or there, I cooked and ate all three meals a day at home. Most of the time, the groceries I bought were fruits, vegetables and organic dairy. Most of the time, I didn't buy meat. I mostly always served myself—and my frequent guests—meals at the table, with napkins and plates. And mostly always at regular, predictable intervals.

I shopped at farmer's markets and bought high-quality, seasonal food: spicy organic greens; salty sea beans; earthy, foraged morels; hazelnuts straight off the tree; fresh-baked, dense sourdough; nettle tea; tart rhubarb; dried cherries and peaches; flowering broccoli shoots.

For me, the healthy-eating riddle was solved, at least a little bit, with fresh food, tall glasses of water and time to digest. May I never have to go back to scarfing down takeout at my desk.

Of all the aspects of modern life that baffled me during those long months convalescing on the couch, I think the one that upset me the most was food. How had we let our mealtimes be taken from us?

CHAPTER FOUR

The Pocketbook

You probably won't be surprised to hear that after I left the newsroom, I thought about money all the time. In fact, I was never not thinking about money. It was as if there was a ledger in my brain, a workbook that was perpetually open. In it sat spreadsheets with dwindling income and growing expenses neatly recorded in categories, tallied up to the exact penny, indicating just how much cash I had on any given day. These numbers were not neutral, not simply marks on a page. They were charged, kinetic, frenzied. They wouldn't stay put, and they wouldn't go away. They were like a CNN ticker, on an endless loop running across the screen of my mind. Flashing an angry neon red, always and forever.

There was no debt on this loop, I was always delighted to discover. But there were almost no savings there either. So my relief was fleeting and my anxiety always resurfaced. Calculating, I wondered: How much money would it take to buy some peace of mind? Would $20,000 do the trick? Would $100,000? Would a house? A condo? I was never quite sure.

Growing up, my parents never had any money. At the time, this didn't seem like a big deal. They didn't appear overly stressed, and I felt like we had most things we needed. Plus, as I've said, my mother was a terrific cook, and so we always ate well.

But there were definite signs of poverty that I can recognize now, looking back. Our furniture was all hand-me-downs from relatives, or else rescued from the trash in the alley. Dentist trips were infrequent. I don't think we took one single vacation as a family. I can only recall a handful of times being taken to the mall to buy new clothes.

The thing is, you can't miss what you never had. I never pined for a life other than the bare-bones bohemian one we lived. Until I went to high school. At which point my father left, our scarcity came into sharp focus, and I woke up to the wealth all around me.

My first year of high school, in Kerrisdale, my peers lived in mansions and had second homes at Whistler and collections of Roots sweatshirts in every color. I recall, right before my parents' divorce, my dad taking me to a flea market and buying me secondhand canvas shoes that I tried to pass off to classmates as new. I remember, too, him picking me up at a party at the sprawling home of a real estate baron whose son I was dating, and feeling embarrassed by our beat-up Hyundai.

As the year progressed, I took to being deliberately vague about my address. My neighborhood, False Creek, was mixed housing, with low-income nonprofit units sitting directly across the street from luxury townhomes. It was easy enough to let people assume I lived on the good side. The handful of times my wealthy friends actually came over, I felt ashamed as we drank orange juice in chipped earthenware mugs around our battered wooden table.

After my father left, I observed my mother's increasing

dread at the end of the month. She juggled work as a secretary, store clerk and housecleaner, and taught at a community arts center so that I could get dance classes for free. She paid for my brother's hockey for as long as she could, before finally having to pull him out.

Eventually, she went back to school, getting a BA, then an MA and finally a PhD, becoming a professor after my brother and I became adults. Until then, we lived on her student loans, scholarships and bursaries, along with my father's child support and whatever jobs my mother could pick up. The effort that it took her to lift us out of poverty was near herculean.

Meanwhile, starting at age thirteen, when I enrolled in my second affluent West Side high school—often likened to that in the show *Beverly Hills, 90210*—I got a string of part-time jobs, which allowed me to buy the clothes I needed to feel comfortable. To belong.

I had long ago left all of this behind, of course. In Toronto, I'd lived in an upscale condo tower and rarely worried about bills, in spite of massive student loans. I didn't earn that much, really, but I was thrifty and had a regular paycheck and, when I was at the magazine, access to a life of fancy parties and high-end restaurants.

Because of that job, I felt at ease around the wealthiest of the wealthy—equally comfortable making small talk with CEOs as with the man who panhandled on my block. This I counted as one of the great blessings of my life: this ability to move between disparate worlds, and to appreciate the goodness in anyone and everyone I met along the way. I knew this might not be the case if I had been raised in privilege, so I did not resent the deprivation of my past. In some ways, I felt grateful for it.

But back in Vancouver, confronted with a class war and suddenly scraping by, I lost that feeling. And I wanted it back.

At the same time, I could no longer physically tolerate the long hours that had afforded me financial security. After I was cleared by my doctor to return to full-time work (though not to the newsroom), I spent a good year and a half sitting in job interviews for a range of fields, from communications to the nonprofit sector, as employers stressed the unpaid overtime required, labor laws be damned. If I so much as asked a single question about how the organization approached work/life balance, it would throw the interview. I once even received a rejection email spelling out as much. *We hope you find the balanced lifestyle you are looking for*, it read.

It was clear that if I wanted to land another full-time professional job, I would have to agree to a boundaryless life in which I would be available to work evenings and weekends, forever at the beck and call of my smartphone. Worse yet, I would need to buy in. I would need to be convinced that this was what it took to be successful, to contribute. I would need to be fully invested in my job, as much as if it were my own personal dream, my own private salvation. Punching a clock was never going to cut it. And I couldn't work like that anymore. The chest pains simply would not allow it.

The point turned out to be moot anyway, because I did not get any of these jobs.

During the many months I spent searching for work, my bank balance plunged and my savings dissolved, and it dawned on me that I had always expected to one day be wealthy. I had grown up around, and then worked around, so much wealth, I had always assumed that I would one day share in it. When I was still on the media treadmill, I was able to preserve this fantasy, thinking a high-profile hosting gig was just around the corner. But as soon as I stepped off, the illusion evaporated.

I was forty years old, without property, investments, savings or steady income. The chances were good that I was never going to be well-off. Maybe—probably—not even comfortable.

It's difficult to overstate just how shocking this realization was, how devastating a blow. The level of disbelief, and distress, and panic, and then ultimately rage that I felt. I had done everything right, had followed every one of society's rules to the letter. And I had still come up short.

With every year that passed—as Vancouver real estate prices ballooned, rents soared and salaries continued to flatline—it was less and less likely that I would end up in the Kits heritage house that I'd always envisioned living out my adult life in.

I was going to need to find another way to think about my life. And about money.

As I mulled this all over, the two obvious career options for me as a writer—journalism and book publishing—fell apart around me. Staff jobs in newsrooms and at magazines were increasingly hard to find and increasingly hectic, as small teams did double and triple duty. In book publishing, advances shrunk, lax copyright laws clawed back licensing fees and royalties declined.

Meanwhile, the digital revolution hogged ad revenue, robbed newspapers and magazines of subscribers and drove down writing rates dramatically by providing an army of young hopefuls willing to write for free. In Canada, magazine rates were one dollar a word, and newspaper rates around fifty cents a word. Web rates, meanwhile, were often ten cents a word. Or lower. You could do a travel piece for as little as thirty dollars. In the United States, meanwhile, long-form online essays that took months to write and would, in the past, have yielded thousands, now paid fifty to a hundred dollars.

As a freelance writer, my income was now fully half what it had been in the newsroom. And I was in the very top percentile of freelancers.

By 2017, most of us understood that it wasn't just us.

Late that year on Twitter, Toronto author Soraya Roberts polled long-form journalists to see how many were supporting themselves with this work. Only 15 percent were. Fifty-four percent had day jobs and 31 percent were subsidized by parents or partners. And according to the Writers' Union of Canada, the average Canadian writer earned less than $10,000 a year. (And in America? Authors earned a middling $6,080.)

The writing life, of course, has never been easy, but even a generation ago, authors could still picture one day supporting themselves with their craft. Even a few decades ago, an upward trajectory wasn't unheard of. Big breaks were still, if not probable, at least possible. Stateside, this dynamic was even more pronounced.

Consider this: In 1992, David Sedaris was working as a Christmas elf at Macy's in New York City, and performed a piece about this at an open mic night. He caught the attention of NPR producer Ira Glass, of *This American Life* fame, who commissioned it for an on-air essay. As Sedaris told me when we met for coffee in Vancouver, "Santaland Diaries" provided him with an overnight audience, regular radio work and, not long after, a book deal.

This is significant for several reasons. First, it's astonishing that a person was once able to support themselves in New York City doing seasonal work at a department store and other odd jobs. Second, NPR paid $500 for "Santaland Diaries," more than an unknown writer would now earn for a similar radio segment, twenty-five years later. And third, Sedaris was thirty-six years old when all this happened. Until then, he'd been traveling, doing odd jobs, attending art school and, in his ample spare time, doing crystal meth and hanging out at IHOP. Sedaris, of course, went on to become a bestselling author and one of America's most respected humorists.

His is a story from another time—all but impossible for the current generation of writers.

Take the case of another boomer luminary, Amy Tan, whose memoir *Where the Past Begins* details her trajectory. Tan also came to publishing late, picking up the pen at thirty-three. She was at the time earning a comfortable living as a freelance business writer and already owned her own home. Her first short story appeared in 1986 in the literary magazine *FM Five*, catching the eye of an agent who offered to represent her despite the fact that she had no intention of writing a book. In 1989, at the age of thirty-seven, Tan's *The Joy Luck Club* was published. She, too, went on to become a bestselling author—one who can afford to live between New York and California, devoted to writing so completely that she does not attend events, or blurb books, when she's working on a project.

Fast-forward two decades, to the next generation's "big breaks." In a 2014 online essay, Emily Gould, blogger and former *Gawker* editor, recalls selling her debut essay collection, *And the Heart Says Whatever*, in 2008 for $200,000, on the strength of her online buzz. By 2012, it had flopped, she'd spent her advance on splurges like rent, taxes and health insurance, and she was earning $7,000 a year doing freelance writing and teaching yoga. She sold her next book, 2014's *Friendship: A Novel*, for just $30,000, and promptly got a full-time job to "slowly repay the debts I incurred by imagining that writing was my livelihood."

Merritt Tierce—author of *Love Me Back*, a 2014 novel that the *New York Times* praised as "brilliant" and "devastating"—wrote a similar piece for *Marie Claire*, sharing her journey from literary darling to broke postal worker. Despite widespread recognition, her book sold 12,000 copies, not even enough to earn back her advance. And so she began pounding the pavement delivering mail.

This is a state of affairs that writers the world over are grappling with, including a leading literary critic, John Freeman, editor of the anthology *Tales of Two Americas*:

Stories of Inequality in a Divided Nation. His book includes stories of people selling blood plasma to pay off student loans, living above homeless shelters, earning income mowing the lawns of foreclosed homes, and watching young neighbors with no options join the military and ship off to conflict zones.

"It wasn't a surprise what came in, but it was still a bit clobbering to read those pieces, one after another— to realize how precarious much of life in the United States feels," Freeman told me, seated in the lounge of the Granville Island Hotel during the annual Vancouver Writers Festival.

Social mobility is deeply unlikely these days, he said, and everyone—including writers—is suffering for it. "The typical writer journey of having a big break is less and less happening, because culture in the age of the Internet is assumed to be free," he added. "So the big breaks you get are visibility breaks. You can have an essay that gets lots of traffic, but you don't get paid for that. The company that posts the piece gets paid for that. So we have a serious issue about how we're going to nurture our writers."

Freeman pointed to numerous other factors jeopardizing the writing life, including the cost of real estate. "The idea that we can live in the center cities of the world now, and write, is becoming increasingly a fantasy. Whether it's Vancouver or New York, it's just too expensive to do that unless you have a private income, or you work your butt off doing something else."

And this points to another problem: the fact that stable day jobs are a thing of the past.

Another anthology editor, Manjula Martin, addresses this in *Scratch: Writers, Money, and the Art of Making a Living*. She notes that the culture of overwork has accelerated so much in our lifetime that nine-to-five jobs no longer exist. In their place? Staff jobs with marathon hours, or precarious gigs and contracts that take a tremendous amount of time and energy to manage.

"If the act of being a writer is continually set up as a hobby, then that drastically narrows the breadth and diversity of the stories that are being written," Martin told me when I reached her on the phone. "That goes across the board, whether you are talking about journalism or literature. If only people who don't have to get paid are writing, only certain types of people are writing stories, and only certain types of stories are getting written.

"I think that's really dangerous," she said. "It's dangerous for our culture, our society. As well as for writers."

In Toronto, there's an organization called the Centre for Social Innovation. One of its locations is on Bathurst, in a five-storey, hundred-year-old brick building. The center often hosts workshops; its army of volunteers are into things like social ventures and co-working and the sharing economy. Back when I lived in Toronto, before I made the jump to current affairs radio, I went to a session that it helped put on, mostly because I was unemployed and a bit bored, and I liked the idea of free breakfast and somewhere to go early in the morning.

CreativeMornings Toronto was held in a hall, also on

Bathurst, filled with bearded millennials and smiling cyclists. The keynote speaker that day was a guy called Ryan Dyment, co-founder of a new organization called the Toronto Tool Library.

He'd gone to university, Dyment told us, and gotten a job as an accountant. He bought a car and a condo (this was before real estate went bananas) and lived in his shoebox, alone. He worked long hours and felt pretty depleted most of the time. His stress levels crept up and his joy steadily plummeted, until finally he felt like he had to make a change.

Drinking my coffee and picking at a gluten-free muffin, I identified. Of course I did. But I didn't see any solution to this quagmire, and I certainly didn't expect him to offer one.

He did, though. He said his ticket out of the rat race was to give up consumerism. He was working all the time, isolated from friends and family, to pay for a bunch of stuff that was not making him happy. He could give up that stuff, and take back his time.

So he sold his condo and moved into a cheap communal house, where he suddenly had company all the time. He got rid of his car and started biking, which did wonders for his pocketbook, not to mention his mental and physical health. He sold or gave away most of his possessions, which he found freeing, since he no longer had to maintain or store or repair any of them—a concept known in these circles as "the burden of ownership." He quit his accounting job.

With this newfound bonanza of time and energy, he was able to connect on a deep level with friends, family and community. In doing so, he could see that many were experiencing what he'd just been through, and there was huge value in providing an alternative model. His way of life itself now constituted a powerful contribution, and it began to build on itself.

He and his friends came together to found the Toronto Tool Library, a sharing economy venture that offers tools, woodworking equipment and 3-D printing as well as the Sharing Depot, "Canada's first library of things," which loans camping and sporting equipment, board games and even children's toys. A community sprang up around them, with people living in shared houses and growing vegetables and biking and baking bread and hosting free markets and bartering for the things they needed.

I found all of this intriguing. I had spent years at the center of our culture, interviewing people with inconceivable levels of wealth. And it didn't seem to be making any of them all that happy. Their lives were scheduled from sunup to sundown, a blur of activity, completely and utterly isolated from the most basic of human interactions. The deeper I'd gotten into this world, the more my life had mirrored theirs. (Minus the wealth, obviously.)

To be honest, if I could have had designer handbags *and* time to eat, sleep and see my friends, I probably never would have contemplated Dyment's model. But it was swiftly becoming clear that in the era of stagnant salaries and runaway real estate and a shrinking middle class—in other words, late-stage corporate capitalism—there was always going to be a fundamental tension between time and money. And after years on the clock, time was starting to look really, really good.

———

This feeling only intensified after I moved back to Vancouver and left the newsroom, and tracked down more of these simple-living radicals. Lawrence Alvarez, for instance, had grown up in Zimbabwe and immigrated to Canada, merging his and Dyment's communities of environmental activists and co-founding the Toronto Tool Library. When I called him up, he told me that he lived debt-free in a communal house on Toronto's east side, with six adults and one toddler. He biked everywhere, bought little, rarely ate out and kept his monthly budget under $1,600, which he earned at his part-time job in student services at a local college.

He'd been offered full-time jobs—four that year alone—but he wasn't interested. "I have so many colleagues who are totally burned out," he told me. "They work all day at these salaried jobs that have no defined hours."

Alvarez said he preferred to get proper sleep, see friends, read books and head off on two-hour bike rides through the city. And be available to work on his passion projects, for free. "It's extremely difficult to make money saving the world," he said with a laugh. "It's pretty easy to make it by destroying it.

"I think we should really not be focusing on everyone having a job," he added. "We should be focusing on everyone being able to survive with the bare necessities, and then allowing human creativity to emerge from that."

He thought his generation was waking up to the lie of advertising—the "manufactured inadequacy" that made people believe they were not complete, and that drinking a specific drink or buying a specific car would fill that void. That we could all consume this stuff indefinitely. "It's so decoupled from the physical realities of the planet," he said.

"I look at the earth and I think this is the largest crisis we've faced as a civilization," he continued. "I don't feel like luxury is important. Or buying something is important. I think that those things are very superfluous to what it really means to live on Earth as a human, together with other humans.

"The purpose of life is not to pay bills and then die," he said. "Life is so beautiful and so brief."

I agreed, but such lessons were easily lost in the urgency of Vancouver's housing crisis. Everyone just seemed so incredibly stressed out all the time. I remember an acquaintance once casually telling me he felt like a guillotine was hanging over him. It was hard for me to think of something as big as giving up consumerism when the more pressing issue was simply getting through the day.

And I was not alone. Were we really going to suggest to people working twelve hours a day and sleeping six hours a night that they should now stop buying their afternoon coffee, too? When such moments of relief were this few and far between, this fleeting, were we really going to propose scrapping them? Were we really going to make a stressful life even more stressful by introducing extreme frugality into the mix?

Despite such reservations, though, the lure of alternative

lifestyles was impossible for me to resist. Mainly because there were literally no other workable models out there.

So I continued to follow my curiosity, and soon found myself standing outside a Gastown building located in the middle of the besieged Downtown Eastside of Vancouver.

I was buzzed in to an institutional-looking co-op housing complex, on a street filled with strung-out addicts and newly minted hipster coffee bars. Stephanie Williams and Celestian Rince greeted me at the door to their apartment. It was a large studio with a spacious balcony and more than enough room for a bed, a kitchen table and a desk. Their cat circled, sniffing me out.

The first thing that struck me about this couple, then twenty-eight and thirty, was how relaxed they were. It had been a long time since I'd met anyone in Vancouver who looked this fresh-faced and, well, zen. Even the yogis had permanently furrowed brows, looking like they were constantly running numbers in their head. Which they probably were.

But not these two. As we unpacked the box of vegan cupcakes I'd brought along, Williams and Rince told me about their lives, and how they had deliberately arranged them so as to experience as little stress as possible.

They lived in cheap accommodation, they said, in this gentrifying neighborhood just blocks from their downtown jobs. Since they walked or cycled almost everywhere, they didn't need a car, nor did they have to use the sardine-can-packed public transit system. They planned their weekly menus meticulously, comparison-shopped in their area to find the best prices and ate all of their meals at home.

These two didn't frequent the local hipster coffee bars, eat meat or dairy, smoke or drink alcohol, or—gasp—own smartphones. They spent little on household items and clothing. For fun, they attended free lectures, borrowed books and video games from the library, scored deeply discounted "under thirty-five" tickets to the Vancouver Symphony Orchestra, hiked free trails and hosted dinner parties. Twice a year, they splashed out on big trips to places like Guatemala, France, China and Thailand.

It cost the two of them less than $1,500 a month total to live ($750 each!), and that number included the $787 rent on the four-hundred-square-foot apartment. Their combined income, meanwhile, was just under $90,000 a year. They saved roughly 60 percent of it. When their investment income hit a point where it could pay the bills, they'd bid their jobs as receptionist and administrative assistant adieu. Their savings then amounted to about $260,000.

They didn't have a whole lot of cash to burn every month, it's true, but they had time. Good lord, they had time.

I'll never forget the blissful look on Rince's face when he talked about what it was like to come home every night. Their bachelor apartment felt impossibly warm and cozy to him after the enormous, under-heated house he'd grown up in in Kerrisdale. He loved returning to this little nest knowing that the whole evening stretched ahead of him, with nothing to do but eat a home-cooked meal and enjoy his girlfriend's company.

There were no pressing after-hours emails to respond to at their low-level office jobs, no extra hours to put in. They weren't anxious about rent increases, or about getting renovicted. There was no looming financial crisis to contend with, no sleepless nights. No added stresses on their relationship.

Williams and Rince weren't worried about getting outsourced, or laid off, or having their jobs automated. When I asked what they would do if their employers pressured them to work unpaid overtime, they laughed. They'd quit, they said, or else complain. Let the chips fall where they may.

The only thing on their minds the night I met them, in fact, was which country they were going to retire to when they had enough money saved up. And, in the shorter term, when Williams was next going to bake an apple pie.

Much of the thinking behind this couple's lifestyle, it turned out, originated with a decades-old personal finance book, *Your Money or Your Life*, co-written by Vicki Robin— whom I visited on Whidbey Island in Washington, passing a delightful afternoon drinking tea and talking—and, more recently, with the blockbuster blogger known as Mr. Money Mustache. Originally from Caledonia, Ontario, Mr. Money Mustache (a.k.a. Pete Adeney) launched a popular personal-finance website of the same name after retiring at age thirty. He lived with his wife and son outside Boulder, Colorado, on as little as $24,000 a year.

As the *New Yorker* reported in a 2016 profile, he was so frugal he once refused to buy a mop, since washing the kitchen floor with a sponge worked just fine. His spending was so finely calibrated that he was still kind of pissed about a Rubik's Cube he bought for his son in 2015 that broke.

Needless to say, to those unfamiliar with the early-retirement movement, Mr. Money Mustache often came off as a bit extreme. But watching a talk of his online, I found him surprisingly convincing.

So I reached out to him, and we chatted over email. Adeney told me that one of the biggest misconceptions about early retirement was that it involved deprivation. "Most people assume that more spending is always better, which means that any reduction in your expenses will come with some pain," he wrote. "I have always looked for only win-win situations: places where you can redesign your life to spend less money, but live a happier life at the same time."

One such example was biking, he said, which gave him tremendous joy. "At least 95 percent of my errands are done on two wheels or on foot, which keeps me happier and in better shape while saving a lot of money as well," he noted. "But we have also consciously designed our family lifestyle with a smaller radius than most people. We prioritize making friends in the immediate neighborhood, attending the schools closest to us and finding fun right within our own city rather than always leaving on the weekend to seek out more expensive options in faraway places."

The first thing to do was to set your standards, he advised. As long as you had enough food and shelter to remain energetic and healthy, you were not experiencing poverty or deprivation. And, he pointed out, we had "a form of poverty even in rich countries: a poverty of free time and physical exercise, and too much stress."

Reducing spending on optional items like restaurants could actually give us back free time, "which allows you to build up your life in more important areas, like friendships and mental and physical health."

And while many critics claimed this lifestyle was impossible with kids, Adeney said that was nonsense. "Kids cost very little to keep around," he stressed in an email. "They only need a few sandwiches, a cozy bed and lots of attention. It's the optional activities that we pack into their lives that rack up the big bills: private schools and lessons, vacations to distant places, and the transportation costs of shuttling them around between all of these things. It's all optional. You can scale it all way back and focus your living in a much smaller, bikeable radius and your kids will still prosper. And the lower costs will allow you to work much less and be a better, more attentive parent because of it."

Back in uber-expensive Vancouver, the Mr. Money Mustache Meetup group that Stephanie Williams had cofounded did indeed include parents. Including Trevor van Hemert, whom I visited at the co-op housing apartment in Burnaby he shared with his wife Brittany and their then two-year-old son. Van Hemert hadn't "worked" in the traditional sense—i.e., for someone else—in seven years.

A tight job market in Victoria had once pushed him to take a $12,000-a-year position managing a composting company called Pedal to Petal. The urban-agriculture collective picked up residential and commercial kitchen scraps and biked them, in five-gallon plastic buckets, to urban farms and composting facilities in the area. Van Hemert soon realized that the buckets themselves could have further uses to DIY culture, which was on the rise. He founded a website, *Five Gallon Ideas*, and filled it with articles on wine- and sauerkraut-making, beehives, bird-houses and as many other conceivable uses as he could think of. It drew DIY fans from all over the world. Van Hemert told me that *Five Gallon Ideas* had up to two million readers a year, and its advertising and affiliate revenue constituted the bulk of his $2,500 monthly income. (He had several other revenue streams, including freelance website design and sales of an e-book he'd authored.)

When he last worked an office job, van Hemert told me, he suffered back problems from sitting for long hours, and found it depressing to leave for work before dawn and return home after dark. "What was most important to me was not *having* to work for somebody," he said. In order to accomplish this, he had to be pragmatic. "It is almost like this guaranteed base income that everybody is talking about," he told me. "I just made a guaranteed base income for myself." His spending level was in line with living on the poverty line. "But that didn't matter to me," he said. "Because I'm still living better than the vast majority of people in history."

Most importantly, he said, this modest lifestyle allowed him to be an involved father. He stayed home with his son while his wife worked full time. He grew food in community plots, was planning a garden for his co-op and volunteered for Car Free Day. He also ran a blog and contributed to the website *Early Retirement Extreme*.

The writing of Neil Howe—one of the co-authors of the 2000 book *Millennials Rising*, which likens millennials to the GI generation that rebuilt society from the ashes of the Second World War—had caused van Hemert to think a lot about the role that he and his peers would play in shaping human history.

Thrift alone couldn't solve the crises millennials were facing, "a fever pitch of problems" which included everything from climate change and political gridlock to the astronomical cost of living.

"The criticism from baby boomers is that millennials don't know how to handle their money," he said, citing the wry logic of a recent *Guardian* article that demonstrated that even someone who sacrificed their twenty-two-dollar avocado-toast brunch every week would need to save for 175 years to make a down payment on a house. People his age were starting urban farms and camping illegally in vans. Van Hemert and his wife lived in an RV before having their son, and he himself once lived in a sailboat.

For millennials like him, alternative business models, unorthodox living arrangements, close-knit digital communities and old-world skills were filling the void left by the disappearance of affordable housing, stable jobs, decent incomes and benefits.

"We're the ones making the creative solutions—not necessarily because we want to, but because we have to," he said. "That's our destiny as a generation."

———

I could get on board with eating at home most of the time, and forgoing working extra hours to fund pointless purchases, and enjoying cheap and nature-friendly pastimes like hiking. And I definitely wanted to take these folks' lead and start biking (which I did shortly after, discovering new friends and a new passion in the process). I admired their ingenuity, their resourcefulness, their warmth as a community. And I could see that they had come up with a possible solution to the stress problem.

But I wasn't keen to give up little luxuries, like cappuccinos. Or lipstick, for that matter, as the early-retirement blogger Elizabeth Willard Thames had done, chronicling her journey from stressed-out big city wage slave to makeup-free Vermont homesteader in her memoir *Meet the Frugalwoods*.

And hyper-frugality still seemed like a colossal ask. What we were basically expecting people to do was step outside their own culture. With roughly half of the adult population now single and the majority of them seriously overworked, asking people to forgo restaurant meals was tantamount to asking them to opt out of mainstream social life. A few decades ago when most people were part of nuclear families, extended families and active communities, and dinner parties were common, it made sense to say that we could all socialize without spending (much) money. But that was simply not the reality anymore. Many of the early-retirement folks I spoke to insisted that there were lots of other ways to connect—potlucks and hikes and beach barbecues—and I could see this was true for them, and even for me at times. But often, they had spouses with the same lifestyle and were embedded within communities who all lived the same way. In my own life, though, spurning restaurants would have meant constantly having to take the initiative to organize my circle's activities (exhausting), and frequently declining fun invitations from my professional, restaurant-loving friends in favor of sitting alone at home.

Any realistic analysis of hyper-frugality, then, had to acknowledge that it required a radical departure from our current culture. Which, of course, implied that the culture was so broken that the only way to survive it was to reject it entirely.

Perhaps, instead of scrutinizing each other's finances endlessly and asking how we could further economize, we should be asking why we lived in a society that we couldn't comfortably participate in. Why performing the basic functions of life in North America—eating, working, socializing—had become so difficult, stressful and out of reach.

Indeed, stress defined my generation's existence. We vaulted out of bed every morning in a state of panic, making hurried stops at coffee shops—either to stave off despair or for the adrenaline needed to face the day—only to slog for ten or twelve hours at "prestige" jobs that didn't pay overtime. Those of us who had children struggled to slip away from the office at five ("Leaving so early?"), rushing to daycares that ate up half our salaries. In spite of such heroic efforts, we often found ourselves scraping by, struggling to keep up with rising rents or runaway real estate markets, a mere paycheck away from calamity.

In light of all this, I had to admit that the early-retirement lifestyle—extreme as it might seem—was still far less extreme than the one we were already living.

Probably the most convincing argument I heard from anyone in this subculture finally came from Kristy Shen and Bryce Leung, a Toronto couple who saved a million dollars and retired in 2015, traveling the globe on $40,000 a year of investment income. When I FaceTimed the young couple in Germany, they were about to head to Singapore to go lie on the beach.

As chilled out as their tone was, though, this pair of computer engineers were deadly serious about their motivation. Before they retired, Shen had become so tense in the work world that she was vomiting regularly. A friend of a friend had had a heart attack on the job and passed away. He was in his early thirties. A coworker in his fifties, too, had collapsed at work and almost died. The doctor said if he'd gotten to the hospital thirty minutes later, it would have been too late.

This stress thing had the potential to be life or death.

Not just for us all as individuals, but for the planet too, as Mr. Money Mustache reminded me. "The most obvious way [early retirement helps the planet] is that it gets the fortunate people of rich countries like Canada and the U.S. to consume less fossil fuel and fewer natural resources," Adeney noted. "Every dollar you spend leaves a corresponding hole in the earth somewhere.

"Even more important, I find that getting a comfortable

nest egg can make us better people. Once you realize you no longer need to work for money, you are forced to reevaluate why you are doing it. At this point, you might make a point of prioritizing work that benefits other people, instead of taking shortcuts to pad your own pocket."

All of this brought to mind a travel blogger, Ayngelina Brogan, whom I'd met back when I was in Toronto. She'd left behind a well-paying advertising job and a swank downtown Toronto life, buying a one-way ticket to Mexico and carving out a new existence as a digital nomad, writing and roaming the globe.

To gain this freedom, she'd had to sacrifice the trappings of a traditional middle-class life. She'd had to give up North American consumer culture. In return, though, she'd gotten health, happiness, creativity, meaningful work and community. Last I checked online, she was living in Havana, writing a travel guide to Cuba.

"I keep a small apartment," she'd told me back then, "and try to live a big life."

And so, with a mix of enthusiasm, reluctance and resignation, I began incorporating elements of this movement into my daily life, dropping out of mainstream culture in ways big and small.

I surrendered the dream of home ownership. I committed to car sharing. I stopped shopping and instead adopted a French approach to fashion, maintaining a minimalist wardrobe that relied heavily on scarves for variety. I biked for transportation and for adventure, exploring my city on two wheels. I bought furniture secondhand. I cooked from scratch. I listened to the radio and read books and walked. I relished my small carbon footprint.

But for me, frugality didn't quite deliver the promised land. I wasn't earning much, so I could not build a nest egg—a key element of this lifestyle—to guard against uncertainty and stress. And despite applying for co-op housing and exploring local communal houses, I was not able to find a satisfactory solution to the problem of high rent.

Add to that, I'd already been broke for a good part of my life. This new thriftiness, forced as it was, often felt indistinguishable from the poverty of my past. What did it matter if I told myself that I was counterculture when the result was the same? When I still had to budget every penny, and agonize over every coffee I bought?

Plus, the arguments I heard from the early-retirement folks often focused on individual solutions to complex structural problems, and this felt like a blind spot. *This was easy*, they argued. *Why didn't everyone do it?* Of course, it wasn't easy at all, otherwise everyone would do it. Though certainly not intended this way, the personal-responsibility tone sometimes sounded strikingly similar to right-wing politics.

Still, what this new mode of being *did* give me was just enough financial breathing room to slow down. To rest and recover my health, and to try to find a way forward. And that was not nothing.

CHAPTER FIVE

The Internet

As I eased into this slower pace of life, I realized something. I did not like the Internet. In fact, I wished it had never been invented. Obviously, I didn't feel this way when I was using a car-sharing app, or FaceTiming with my niece and nephew in Ireland, or finding out about some awesome new book on Twitter. But the rest of the time—around twenty-three and a half hours a day, I figured—I wanted nothing to do with it.

Like many Gen-Xers who came of age before the Internet, I missed the way time used to feel. The vast expanse that was the weekend, with its stretches of uninterrupted hours. The deep contemplation of staring out a window, or sitting on a bus. The luxuriousness of being out in the world for hours, days even, untethered from work, unimpeded by the pressure to respond to texts and emails and social media. Free to think, and be, and focus on what was in front of you. Which was, generally, other people. People who were similarly focused, similarly engaged.

There were other things I missed, too. Phone calls, neighbors, walking down the street without people steering into me absentmindedly, engrossed in their phones. The whole character of public space, really. What it felt like to sit in a café before we all had to listen to each other's work calls, made in that exaggerated professional voice everyone uses. Eye contact and casual conversation; not sitting in isolated islands, hunched over devices, in thrall to flickering lights. What friendship felt like before social media, and dating before texting and apps. Punctuality. Privacy. Newspapers, long attention spans, foldout maps. The experience of being lost in a city, unaccounted for. Boredom, even.

Truth be told, if I could have reversed the whole world-changing ordeal and gone back to the peace and quiet of landlines and libraries, I probably would have.

I thought about this a lot during that first year of leaning out. And especially on one holiday weekend in Squamish, British Columbia, as friends and I hiked the Chief, officially known as Stawamus Chief Provincial Park. If you've hiked anywhere lately that's popular on Instagram, you know what's coming.

Picture this: a five-hour trek comprised of wooden staircases that lead straight up a mountain, eventually giving way to jagged, steep rock faces that can only be scaled with ladders, ropes, chains and scrambling. And then massive, seven-hundred-meter granite cliffs that offer sweeping vistas of the turquoise waters of Howe Sound below and the snow-capped mountain ranges of nearby Garibaldi Provincial Park.

The way up to the Chief's three peaks is grueling. The way down? Downright terrifying. As the signs at the foot of the trail remind you, this is no walk in the park.

I had my anti-technology awakening as we summited the second peak. We were lined up in single file at a narrow rock traverse with one chain. Finding one's footing was a precise exercise that required both total concentration and massive amounts of courage. (Evidenced by two women—one weeping, the other frozen in fear—at a similar point on the first peak.)

As my friends and I awaited our turn, practicing deep breathing, each and every member of a large group in front of us stopped on the chain to pose for Facebook action shots. A chorus of status updates, messages and incoming emails pinged loudly. Somewhere behind me, a young woman blared bhangra from her smartphone, oblivious to the task at hand. As the line grew, other phones competed for air space, blasting various upbeat playlists (and likely impeding birds' and insects' navigation with all the radiation). All of this was beyond annoying; it was downright dangerous. Also, it was hard to understand the logic. Why come all the way up here just to reproduce the noise and stress of the city?

The American essayist Meghan Daum has written that there's a moment at which it dawns on us Gen-Xers that we actually have everything in common with the oft-maligned baby boomers. "At least," she explains, "just about everything that means anything, like reading actual books and enjoying face-to-face contact with friends and not necessarily wanting to watch a movie on a three-and-a-half-inch screen.

"The vagaries of the digital revolution," she adds, "mean that I have more in common with people twenty years my senior than I do with people seven years my junior." On a mountain face in British Columbia, my own moment of clarity on all of this had arrived. It turned out

I vastly preferred the way things used to be. I longed for a pre-Internet reality. For a time that I could never bring back and increasingly could not even access within myself.

After summiting the peak, hearts hammering in our chests, my friends and I settled in for lunch. Seated atop the mountain, the teal ocean stretched below us and the looming mountain ranges across the valley evoked awe and wonder. We listened for the call of the peregrine falcon, for whom the Chief is a nesting habitat.

But we couldn't hear much over the din. The group next to us had someone on speaker phone and was engaged in a loud, animated conference call. Across the ridge, on an adjacent peak, another group was directing a drone. The floating device made a tremendous amount of noise, and they were all jumping up and down as they directed it around the mountain.

We had made the hour-long drive from Vancouver, battling traffic on the winding Sea-to-Sky Highway and navigating parking lots packed with tourists, with one purpose in mind: to get away. We wanted a break from the nonstop bombardment of information and noise, from the madness of modern life.

We wanted to sit atop this ancient mountain, breathe in the clear, heady air and feel, just for a few moments, blissfully present. At home in our bodies, our lives, the moment. Instead, we were met with an elaborate—and pointless—press conference. I could feel an instant spike in my cortisol, my blood flooding with stress hormones, my nerve endings suddenly raw and exposed.

Somehow, I managed to stop myself from scolding the

media-obsessed adventurers at the top. This turned out to be a good thing, because the way down required all the feel-good community bonding one could drum up.

The rocky gullies carved into the side of the mountain were formidably steep, and so packed with hikers that getting through was a dizzying, high-stakes game of Twister. People were, finally, forced to put down their phones.

We laughed and encouraged each other. We offered assistance. We assured the sweaty, scared hikers on the way up that the views were worth the effort.

A very slight, very brave eleven-year-old girl who'd gotten separated from her family was attempting the descent with a baby Chihuahua in hand. We relieved her of her tiny burden, cradling the trembling puppy as we made our way precariously down the mountain one foothold at a time, cheered on by hikers ahead.

When we reached the bottom of the cliffs—preparing for a good hour of stumbling through the forest down wooden stairs, dodging rocks and roots, legs shaking with fatigue—we stopped to revel in the hard-earned endorphin rush. We drank water, smiled at each other and petted Tucker the Chihuahua, who appeared more than a little relieved to be on solid ground.

On an unusually snowy day in Vancouver when I was in my mid-twenties, I went for coffee with a famous author whom I greatly admired. He was tall, and keenly intelligent, with kind eyes and a gentle smile. We sat in an empty coffee shop in South Granville with a mutual friend and talked about writing. Flurries swirled outside. Buses rolled slowly past on snow-packed streets. Hardly anyone was out.

I would have liked to tell this author, then, that the only time I felt at ease was when I was in airports. When I was about to fly somewhere, say New York or L.A., my restlessness evaporated. It felt like a window was opening to my future life. Something bright and colorful beckoned in the distance. As I rushed along airport corridors, dragging my suitcase, every step I took delivered me closer to this new reality.

I would have explained, if I could, that it was very much like the feeling I got when I was looking for a new place to live. Out viewing apartments, I would walk into a heritage walk-up with hardwood floors and sloped ceilings and glass doorknobs, windows looking out over towering trees, leaves fluttering in the breeze. Suddenly, I would feel at home. I could see my bookshelves there, filled with hardcover titles. I could envision my bed, piled with pillows. I could smell the Thai curry simmering on the stove, or a pot of strong espresso brewing. I would then know, with every fiber of my being, that this was a place I would soon inhabit.

It was the same when I was about to board a plane. A sort of boldness and an easy confidence would steal over me. I was headed somewhere. At my destination, I would find my place in the world, occupy the psychic space I so longed for.

The life I craved, the adventure, was coming. But it wasn't coming fast enough. I could not locate the door to cross over into that other life. I could not step across the threshold.

The author seemed to intuit all of this without me having to say anything at all. And so he offered me the answer to my riddle: the Internet.

You need for people outside of Vancouver to read what you are writing, he said. *You need to connect with people all over the world. You need a blog.*

So I left that day and started one. And then, miraculously, I got a grant from the Canada Council for the Arts to research global hip-hop. Sitting in Internet cafés in Tokyo and Bangkok, I could see from my blog's statistics that people were reading. They were reading in London, in Lisbon, in Lagos. The music journalists at big American publications began contacting me, and referencing my writing on their own blogs. Seemingly overnight, I was part of the young, ambitious, global set I'd yearned to belong to.

Soon I was having the kinds of conversations that I'd longed to have. On the phone, over email. In person in New York, in Midtown sports bars and in slick Meatpacking District lounges with DJs spinning old-school rap records, at four in the morning. In Tribeca faux-French bistros and Harlem bodegas, on park benches in Little Italy over fresh-baked cannoli. On a terrace at a grand Upper West Side apartment overlooking the Hudson, and on a Brooklyn rooftop with burgers on the grill, underground hip-hop beats blasting, the Manhattan skyline visible in the distance, sparkling with promise.

The stimulation was electrifying—a catchy, high-decibel chorus, with a constant, low-level bassline of satisfaction humming below. I wanted to sing that song always.

The author had handed me the key, unlocking the life I'd been craving. A vast new universe opened up with satisfying suddenness, yawning with possibility.

Several years later, I found myself in a fight with a rapper. By that time, I was writing my column for *XXL* from Canada, and living a good deal of my life on the Internet. So much so that friends often had to remind me that the people I was talking about all the time were people that I had, in fact, never met. It was easy to forget this.

It was the early, idealistic days of social media, before Facebook or Instagram or Snapchat. Even then, though, the tone of the online world was beginning to emerge. There was a nastiness to my daily life that had never existed before. Nobody had ever said the things to me that were now routinely being shouted in capital letters in the comments section of my blog.

I would post a long piece about, say, intergenerational poverty, and one of the regulars would reply, "SHOW US YOUR TITS." It was difficult to know what to do with this. Firing back was often read as overreaction. Doing nothing was interpreted as weakness. Laughing it off, meanwhile, felt inconceivable.

XXL was incredibly popular at that time. And as you might imagine, there was a strange sort of notoriety that came with the gig. I would be on the phone with an IT guy on a computer help line, and he would ask me if I was the Tara who wrote for *XXL*. Or, if I posted a critical review of a book by Jerry Heller, who once managed NWA, Jerry Heller himself would call me up to dispute it. Down visiting friends at the Brooklyn Hip-Hop Festival, strangers would stop me in the street.

On the one hand, this was rewarding, because it meant I had readers. I had a place to say the things I most wanted to say. (And, thanks to our exceptional editor-in-chief, the freedom to say it.) On the other hand, though, this level of exposure subjected me to a huge amount of online abuse, and it began to affect me.

In real life, away from screens, the men I'd met through my job—the rappers and the road managers, the record-label reps and publicists and promoters, the writers and editors—had gone to great lengths to look out for me. There were plenty of exceptions, of course. Men who tried to pull me onstage during booty-shake anthems, or made crass comments, or launched half-hearted, unsuccessful campaigns to coerce me into random hotel sex.

But overwhelmingly, the men I'd come into contact with had been respectful. As a journalist, I'd ventured into barrios and townships in developing countries, Manhattan recording studios in the middle of the night, clubs in New York boroughs where only a handful of women were present. I was forever riding around in cars with men I hardly knew. And nobody had ever taken advantage of that.

The misogyny online, however, was constant and vicious. And it wore on me. After a time, I began to confuse it with my day-to-day experience in the industry. I forgot all the care I'd been shown in person, and saw only the trolls. Felt only that ugliness.

All of this was brewing one day in 2006, a week or two after I'd moved to Toronto—months before I started at the women's magazine—when I was frantically searching the web for an idea for my column that day. I was under deadline pressure when I saw that a Toronto rapper I knew, Eternia, had written something.

She'd been performing at a show with the politically conscious rap duo Little Brother. Phonte, one of the rappers, had seen her backstage and called her "Titernia." She was appalled. "I have had dudes in the industry who were not interested in me beyond a piece of ASS treat me with more respect than that," she fumed on her MySpace page. "LB has lost a fan for life." Phonte replied: "Right now, you're looking like the 'crazy, emotional bitch female rapper' stereotype that your music does such a good job of debunking."

For me, this was a prime example of the sexism that I dealt with all the time online. In my column, I came out swinging, channeling an outrage that had little to do with the matter at hand. And making sweeping generalizations about men in the industry, as well as Phonte, whom I'd never had any contact with in real life.

It was a reckless move. And one I paid for. The hip-hop community exploded. Phonte was furious, and his fans were furious. He did an interview, also with *XXL*, calling me out and arguing that he was being asexualized, that women should expect that men in the industry wanted to sleep with them. They didn't want to talk hip-hop with us, he said, they just wanted to get laid.

This frustrated me to no end, since it often *did* feel like no men in the business ever wanted to talk to me. Men didn't care to hear my thoughts, no matter what countries I'd visited, or who I'd interviewed, or what magazine I wrote for.

More than a decade later, though, I can see that this was distorted thinking, and the distortion was coming from the Internet. The fact of the matter was I had a broad male readership, many of whom wanted very much to know what I thought, and logged on every day to find out.

But viewing my life through the hostile lens of the comments section had convinced me otherwise. And I'd wound up alienating the people I cared about most—the readers.

Thinking back on this, I can see, too, that I missed an opportunity. Eternia comments notwithstanding, in other contexts Phonte had struck me as a thoughtful guy. I'm pretty sure that if I had called him up instead of attacking him online, we could have had a conversation about all of this, and probably one that would have benefited everyone involved.

Instead, I remember walking the streets of Toronto in despair. Over the response my piece had gotten, how much animosity I'd attracted. Over the sexism forever in the background. But also over my own actions. I had allowed the speed of the Internet, the accelerated news cycle, the pressure, the temptation to be self-righteous and snide, to draw me into a conflict—and then actively make it worse. I had allowed myself to become flippant, casually malicious. I had become part of the problem.

Unable to settle, I called up a writer friend and asked her for advice. "Here's what I suggest," she said, after thinking a while. "Every time you sit down to write your column, meditate on love. Then write from that place."

So I did just that. I sat down and got quiet. I thought about how much I loved the music. The fans. All the artists I'd met over the years who'd shared their stories and their souls.

So many of the men I interviewed, I related to on a deep level. So many had told me about growing up in poverty, watching their single moms struggle. Many had felt enormous grief and anger, as I had, over absent fathers. Many had watched those they'd grown up around drift into the arms of trouble. Many had worried constantly about money, and felt ashamed of their dingy sneakers or where they lived or worked. Many had watched their dreams stymied by forces beyond their control.

I did not know these men, but I felt a fierce love for them. It was a love born of shared pain, but also of shared joy, at managing to make something beautiful from this mess. At putting this pain into words, and having those words mean something to somebody else. Ease others' pain, in however small a way.

These men, for all our outer differences, felt like family to me. And I didn't ever want to forget that.

So I wrote from that place for many months, and it wound up defining, for my whole career going forward, how I approach writing and interviewing.

At some point, I decided to put all this into words—to say it all directly—and I penned a piece about hip-hop and the Internet for *XXL*. I wrote about not having the stomach for the cutting, irreverent commentary that had become de rigueur on the web. About having to ask myself: *Why am I ripping to shreds the culture that I purport to love so much? Am I writing for my own amusement, or am I writing to contribute something?*

Once you'd sat across from someone and heard in detail about their lives, I wrote, it was hard to see them as anything but a human being. In his collection of essays *Never Drank the Kool-Aid*, music journalist Touré touches on this very point. After Tupac was shot the first time, Touré published a scathing essay in the *Village Voice* critiquing the exaggerated character he felt Tupac was presenting to the media. But Tupac was a man, not some mythic figure, and the rapper cried when he read the piece.

In other words, it wasn't cool to carelessly lob shots out into the abyss of the Internet. We needed to remember that more often than not these shots hit their target. And they hurt.

None of this was to say that music critics shouldn't go ahead and critique music. Nor that we, as women in the music industry, shouldn't call out the sexism inflicted on us. But we needed to be thoughtful about it if we ever wanted to end the cycle of suffering.

And so, going forward, I was profoundly wary of online culture. I knew the Internet was responsible for my career. I had gone from writing for a small independent weekly on the West Coast of Canada to being a columnist for a top New York outlet. The Internet had done this.

But I also knew its dark side, years before it was widely acknowledged. The mob mentality, the trolling, the callousness and cruelty. How it had the capacity to bring out the worst in us. In me.

Real life was big enough to hold numerous contradictions and contexts simultaneously. Real life could allow both myself and the men in hip-hop a complex humanity. But the Internet did not appear to be capable of this.

So, after I retired my column, I steered clear. I never did join Facebook, LinkedIn, Snapchat, WhatsApp or any number of other platforms. Twitter was my sole social media platform, and years later I watched the same dynamics I'd experienced play out there, turning it from a collegial place to share articles and ideas to a vehicle for outrage and discontent and, in the Trump era, political polarization.

My Luddite leanings have only increased over time. I now spend a sizable portion of my waking hours resisting Internet culture, with all its spidery tentacles. This, of course, is an utterly futile position to take, akin to trying to bail out a boat with a teacup. Is it even possible to unplug in a world that's always wired?

One of the biggest problems I have with the Internet is how it's changed the nature of consciousness. No big deal, right? Just radically reordered our minds and reshaped the very experience of being human.

As I write this, for instance, I can feel the pull of my smartphone. I want badly to check it. Despite the fact that on a deeper level, what I want more is to dive into this paragraph, these thoughts. There's a tug of war going on inside me. Even in this, this most exquisitely solitary hour of my day.

In addition to the digital addictions I battle and the impotent rage that sometimes engulfs me on Twitter, there is, too, an urge to broadcast my life that wasn't there when I was younger. When I briefly had an Instagram account, I began to feel so wedded to posting that it was as if experiences hadn't fully happened if they hadn't been captured online. Was there a point to that dinner, that trip, that stunning vista, if nobody else had seen it? Did it even count?

Given how little time I spend on the Internet—at least in comparison to the twenty-four hours a week the average North American spends online—I'm surprised at the impact it's had on both my writing and my sense of self.

In 2015, before leaving Toronto, I made a radio documentary about being thirty-nine and childless. It was difficult to make something so personal, something that cut so close to the bone. But I knew from my daily interactions that many women were experiencing this, in an age in which almost half the adult population was single and birth rates were plummeting. It was the most personal piece of journalism I'd ever done, and the riskiest emotionally. But it felt integral to my experience of being alive in this era, and I figured maybe some other women would feel the same way.

The public's response defied all expectation. The documentary had a huge audience and resulted in countless emails and texts and tweets from listeners. It even won a finalist certificate at the New York Festivals International Radio Program Awards.

I made the mistake, though, of reading the comments on the show's website, which were numerous, harsh and dismissive. Sitting down to write this chapter today, those comments still haunt me. Before I can stop myself, I wonder: Will anyone even care what I have to say?

In the wake of a breakup, the British writer Olivia Sudjic once fled to Brussels, on a writing residency, where she camped out in a grand apartment and found herself unable to go out, let alone write. She'd recently published her first novel, *Sympathy*, which had earned near-universal praise, but the new fan base effectively ended her feeling of anonymity. She had previously felt like she was writing into a void, and there was a freedom to this, especially for someone who suffered from anxiety. But now the awareness of a crowd lurking online amplified her anxiety to unbearable levels.

In order to write, Sudjic needed to be alone with her thoughts. But in the Internet era, we are never truly alone. None of the old classics about the writing life seemed to address this reality. So the twenty-nine-year-old wrote a new one.

Exposure is about being a writer, and a woman, and someone who deals with anxiety, in this strange, surreal, hyper-connected age. It was written in a burst of energy, and it perfectly captured the current moment—the bizarre hollowing-out of the self that occurs when bombarded with digital detritus. The mental exhaustion, the physical paralysis, the acute isolation amid extreme connectivity.

Sudjic received wave after wave of messages from readers, male and female, young and old, writers and not, all of whom related. "Sometimes it's the thing that you write in a matter of weeks—that you think probably only speaks to you, and doesn't contain any universal truths—and that's the thing that people end up really responding to," she told me, when I called her in London.

The digital world now felt utterly inescapable, she said, for all of us. "Even if you don't want to participate, all you are really doing is putting your head in the sand," she explained, "which can generate its own forms of anxiety and paranoia of what you don't know."

She wondered if it might be a bit easier for older generations, who hadn't grown up with the Internet in the same way. Perhaps for them, being wired didn't feel like second nature or unavoidable. Perhaps they felt like they could either opt in or opt out, or at least access a mental state pre-Internet. "Whereas I feel like it's absolutely an extension of my body," she told me.

"My consciousness has really been shaped by it," she added. "It's not that I have developed my writing voice, and then the Internet happened. My writing voice has been developed *by* the Internet. So choosing to avoid it will only feel like a kind of artificial hiding, rather than an authentic switching to a different psychic place within me."

There's a whole lot more at stake, too. The threat social media now poses to our society is profound. So much so that Internet gurus are now publicly acknowledging it.

Sean Parker, the first president of Facebook, recently admitted he and Mark Zuckerberg and Kevin Systrom of Instagram understood that the systems they were building exploited a vulnerability in human psychology—and went ahead and did it anyway.

"It literally changes your relationship with society, with each other," he has said. "It probably interferes with productivity in weird ways. God only knows what it's doing to our children's brains." Meanwhile, Chamath Palihapitiya, a former vice president of user growth at Facebook, has argued that social media's short-term, dopamine-driven feedback loops "are destroying how society works," leading to a lack of civil discourse, and misinformation and mistruth.

Jaron Lanier, a computer scientist and start-up pioneer, is now among Silicon Valley's chief critics. He draws attention to these admissions in *Ten Arguments for Deleting Your Social Media Accounts Right Now*, and paints a picture of social media as a large-scale behavior-modification apparatus that's highly manipulative. It's driven by social attention—the carrot of approval, of course, but more importantly the stick of criticism, which generates the most intensity, or "engagement."

"There is no evil genius seated in a cubicle in a social media company performing calculations and deciding that making people feel bad is more 'engaging' and therefore more profitable than making them feel good," he writes. "Or at least, I've never met or heard of such a person. The prime directive to be engaging reinforces itself, and no one even notices that negative emotions are being amplified more than positive ones."

This form of manipulation—"intermittent reinforcement" in psychology circles—has proven to be one of the most devastating dynamics in human relationships and is, in fact, a common theme in abusive relationships. It breeds addiction; the intensity of longing it engenders is unparalleled. The human brain is designed to want to crack the code, to figure things out, to somehow return circumstances to the honeymoon stage of pure approval. When the brain can't see the logic to something, it will return again and again, trying to locate a pattern, to somehow make sense of the senseless.

Homing in on the most potent and powerful emotional drivers, social media has also resurrected old conflicts to engage users with more and more fierceness. One need only look to the rise of white supremacy in the U.S. for an example of this.

In this dystopian realm, virality trumps morality, and our sole purpose as individuals is to "optimize" the social media machine—a mission that many of us now spend a huge portion of our waking hours carrying out.

According to Lanier, social media has turned people into lab rats, placing them under constant surveillance. Pointing to a growing body of research, he argues that it's making people angrier, more depressed, more isolated, less empathetic and less informed about the world. It even makes people less able to support themselves financially, since social media disrupts so many industries, from taxis to journalism.

All the while, network effects lock people into social media systems, making it more and more inconvenient—

and, in some cases, impossible—to step away, because of either strong social pressure or economic necessity.

If that all wasn't bad enough, Lanier says this finely tuned, highly manipulative behavior-modification apparatus is available for rent to anyone looking to influence the public. And it's often utilized by nefarious entities we know little about. As, I would point out, was the case with Russian interference in the 2016 U.S. election.

The constant stream of data, and the algorithms that tweak subsequent efforts to sway us, are not just used to sell soap, of course, but also to influence politics. And as we learned in the American election, the Silicon Valley giants sometimes don't even know who their customers are.

In Lanier's opinion, the only reasonable response is to deprive these companies of our data, and force them to come up with a better business model. It is, in fact, "the most finely targeted way to resist the insanity of our times."

Quitting Twitter was, perhaps, a place to start. I resented all the hours devoured by constant checking—of social media, of apps, of texts, of emails. I hated the way that my awareness of time would evaporate once I logged on. I hated how even on the days I managed to avoid Twitter and all forms of messaging, I *still* spent the whole day looking things up online on my laptop as I wrote. How my whole world essentially revolved around the Internet, whether I liked it or not.

To understand what else might be done to reclaim my life and my mind from the daily digital onslaught, then,

I needed to find someone courageous enough to give it all up. Sadly, it wasn't going to be me.

I flirted with the idea of surrendering my smartphone, sure. But I was dependent on it to be in touch with family and friends. I needed to communicate easily with my editors. I couldn't even drive without it, since I used it for car sharing.

I couldn't, on my own, conceive of any acceptable tech-free model for my life. So I started looking for someone who'd already undergone an extreme digital detox. And could tell me what it felt like.

Paradoxically, this journey led me back online, where I found a man by the name of Mark Boyle. Boyle, a thirty-something Irishman, had lived for three years without money, writing several books, a column in *The Guardian*, delivering a TED Talk and earning the nickname "the Moneyless Man." When he stopped using money, he began to depend on other people in a way that he had never had to before. Like many we've met in these pages, he traded consumerism for community.

Boyle now lived and worked on a property in rural Ireland without electricity, fossil fuels, running water or technology. He had, in essence, retreated entirely from civilization. This is something few would be willing or able to do. But we could all benefit from what he'd learned about humanity by giving up texting, emailing, surfing the web and streaming TV shows.

"The consequences of this ever-intensifying industrialism," he wrote in a 2018 *Guardian* piece, "are clear: widespread surveillance in our pockets; the standardization of everything; the colonization of wilderness, indigenous lands and our mindscape; cultural imperialism; the mass extinction of species; the fracturing of community; mass urbanization; the toxification of everything necessary for a healthy life; resource wars and land grabs; 200 million climate refugees by 2050; the automation of millions of jobs, and the inevitable inequality, unemployment and purposelessness that will follow and provide fertile ground for demagogues to take control."

With 7.7 billion active phone connections now on Earth, he pointed out, his personal protest was unlikely to make much of a difference. As people told me all the time: you simply can't resist technology. It's a done deal.

Still, while Boyle was under no illusions that he could stem the tide, he'd chosen to focus on preserving the old ways of life that were most valuable to him.

"There remains a timeless simplicity about this way of life," he noted. "I've found that when you peel off the plastic that industrial society vacuum-packs around you, what is left could not be simpler. There's no extravagance, no clutter, no unnecessary complications. Nothing to buy, nothing to be. No frills, no bills. Only the raw ingredients of life, to be dealt with immediately and directly, with no middlemen to complicate and confuse the matter. Simple. But complex."

He added: "When you're connected to wifi you're disconnected from life. It's a choice between the machine world and the living, breathing world, and I feel physically and mentally healthier for choosing the latter."

This was a useful way of looking at technology, a

continuum I could locate myself on, even if I was not planning to live off-grid in Ireland.

I wasn't going to disconnect from Wi-Fi permanently, but I could, quite happily, try to connect more to life. I could tip the balance in favor of the old ways I loved too. I could do small things to reject the machine world—leave my phone at home sometimes, keep it out of my bedroom at night, call people on my landline instead of texting them. Look up, talk to people in the street and in the coffee shop. Unplug with silent meditation retreats, increase my tech-free activities like hikes and yoga classes. Try an Internet Sabbath here and there.

Connecting more to life, though, invariably meant connecting more to people. And I quickly discovered there were other barriers that didn't involve me having too little time or consuming too much tech.

I wish I could tell you when the loneliness started. I wish I could pinpoint the day, or the month, or even the year, when I started to feel so profoundly disconnected from other people. But it crept up on me slowly. Sometime during my stretch at the women's magazine, I woke up on a holiday Monday in my spotless condo, made coffee and washed the windows, and then wandered my neighborhood alone, listless. I thought: *I don't like this. I don't like this at all. This is not how I want to live.*

Over the decade that I grappled with this loneliness, I discovered that almost every person I knew was silently struggling with the same thing. Scrolling and swiping away, haunted, hungry, sad. Craving something we could no longer really fathom. Afraid to reach out in real, human ways. Losing the skills of small talk, phone calls, casual connection. Needing something as much as we needed air, but unable to grasp it.

I spent much of my thirties in that vortex. With a million friends and plenty of dates and loads of fun places to go in the week—but nevertheless roaming my neighborhood on the weekend, utterly, completely alone.

Waking up alone. Eating breakfast alone. Coming home alone, to an empty apartment, the details of the day banging around in my head, echoing off the walls of my psyche. Texts pinging constantly, doing nothing to alleviate the ache.

CHAPTER SIX

The Void

Where all of this left me was on my couch. Which, actually, was not a bad place to be. Many months had now passed since I'd left the newsroom in Vancouver. I was still getting chest pains, but the meditation and the yoga and the healthy food and all that time in the wilderness had begun to energize me. I had started freelancing, had paid off my student loans, and was now gloriously debt-free for the first time in my adult life. I could feel the weight of that old albatross lifting from my neck. I could breathe again. And I could dream.

In keeping with all I had learned, I unplugged, regularly leaving my phone at home. I lived a minimalist life. If I needed to go somewhere, I walked or biked or took the bus. I cooked. I hiked, had friends over, listened to podcasts for entertainment and did travel writing, which allowed me to head off on local adventures. I reviewed books, so I got those for free. I went to a beauty school for deeply discounted haircuts. I rarely bought anything, but if I really needed something, I got it on Craigslist.

What surprised me most was how little it took to make me happy. I had come from a world where you only wore cocktail dresses once, for fear of being photographed in the same outfit twice. But that sparkling realm hadn't made me even remotely happy. Those years, thrilling as they were, had been among the loneliest of my life.

What gave me joy, it turned out, was pretty simple. Waking up every day without an alarm. Reading all the books on my nightstand. Eating when I was hungry, resting when I was tired, staying at home when I was under the weather. Moving my body every day. Being outside. Cooking for people I cared about.

The key to contentment, I realized, was time. And the more time I had, the less money I needed. I didn't need treats to boost my spirits during a rough week, because my week was never particularly rough. I didn't need lavish vacations because, as *Your Money or Your Life* put it, my daily life was not something I needed to vacate. When my true needs were met, I did not need to compensate with stuff.

And practically speaking, since I didn't go to an office every day, it didn't really matter what I wore. Putting on lipstick made me feel sufficiently spruced up.

The wide-open expanse of my life—and, consequently, my mind—was infinitely better than presenting a polished image to the world. So much so, I almost couldn't believe it.

One of the best parts of my moratorium on spending was, as the Toronto Tool Library folks had predicted, not having to maintain, clean and repair new possessions. For the first time in my adult life, I reached the end of my to-do list. There were no loose ends. No tasks I'd procrastinated on. No sweaters to hand-wash, or gadgets to fix, or shoes to return. Nothing pressing to do with myself or my time.

Strangely, though, my anxiety did not lift. It was as if nobody had bothered to inform my body how relaxed my life had become; it still seemed to think I was in the newsroom. I had chest pains all the time: walking around my neighborhood, reading in bed, visiting friends.

So I did the only thing there was to do: I curled up on the couch and stared into the void. The gaping, blank, oppressive emptiness. I knew something was coming—whatever it was I'd been running from all those years. Whatever the never-ending lists, the relentless pace, the achievement had kept at bay.

In my early thirties, I had once gotten caught in a tropical thunderstorm in Bangkok. I was leaving a salon, where I'd chatted with a group of Thai women as they washed and blow-dried my hair. The air was thick, humid, heavy as I stepped out onto the street.

Then the sky opened up and crashed down, hurling rain onto the cracked pavement. Tuk-tuks and motorcycles pulled over to the side of the road as the streets flooded ankle-deep with water. I huddled under a noodle vendor's umbrella. Everything came to a complete standstill. The storm demanded total surrender. There were no individual agendas. There was just the deluge.

Something about those cold, quiet months in Vancouver reminded me of this. There was no avoiding the storm. All I could do was take shelter and let it run its course.

During the spring of 2014, the British journalist Johann Hari found himself in Hanoi, doing research. He was walking down a side street, hungry, when he spotted an apple at a stall. "It was freakishly large and red and inviting," he writes in *Lost Connections*, his game-changing book on depression and anxiety. He bought the piece of fruit, took it back to his hotel room and, despite a bitter, chemical taste, ate half of it before going to bed.

Within hours, he was struck with violent food poisoning: stomach pains, a spinning room, a blur of sickness. Having experienced this before, he wasn't particularly alarmed. He drank a lot of water and figured it would pass.

But after a few days of agony, he writes in the book, he began to fret about wasting his time in Vietnam. He called his translator and insisted they drive into the countryside to conduct interviews. Which is how he found himself in the hut of an eighty-seven-year-old woman, talking about the bombing of her village and then projectile vomiting.

At the woman's insistence, the translator delivered Hari to a rural hospital, which had likely never treated a foreigner. Roiling in agony, he begged the doctor to give him something for his extreme nausea.

"The doctor says you need your nausea," his translator informed him. "It is a message, and we must listen to the message. It will tell us what is wrong with you."

Reading that, I realized, as Hari had, that I needed my distress. My anxiety was telling me something was wrong. To move forward, I suddenly understood, I would have to return to the past.

———

In her *New Yorker* profile of the late American novelist Madeleine L'Engle, poet Cynthia Zarin recalls a friend once telling her in college, "There are really two kinds of girls. Those who read Madeleine L'Engle when they were small, and those who didn't."

I was among those who did. And like so many others, I absorbed the world she created on the page. It was a realm of lyrical prose, magical child-heroes, mystical spirituality, ancient archetypes and myths, and reverence for nature, science, art and literature. A world of epic battles between good and evil, where nothing less than the future of humanity hung in the balance.

When I was a child, all I wanted was for my life to be like a Madeleine L'Engle novel. I related to the heroines in her books, girls who longed for adventure and felt perpetually out of place. They were sensitive and awkward and in search of something. For these girls, wondrous things happened. They met brooding boys who fell in love with them; they formed friendships with wise priests who explained the meaning of life; they cooked enormous pots of spaghetti, which they ate on terraces overlooking the sea with their loud, affectionate families. They glimpsed the Great Reality.

My life was, in comparison, if not dull, at least a little bleak. My parents were bright people who talked about books and exposed me to art and culture. But our family was small and, after my parents' divorce, decidedly lonely. The low-income housing complex in Vancouver where my mother, my brother and I lived was neither gracious nor welcoming. We did not travel, nor did we associate with many people—certainly not the Manhattan concert pianists and Episcopalian priests who peopled the novels I adored.

But there is something to the power of imagination. If you can envision it, sometimes you can create it. L'Engle radically expanded my vision for my life. In her books, I discovered a world of deep connection—to others, to nature, to the magic of the universe. I yearned for the world contained there. And then one day I found it.

I started reading *A Ring of Endless Light* when I was thirteen. The novel follows Vicky Austin, an ill-at-ease teen spending the summer on an island off the New England coast, as she comes to terms with her grandfather's terminal leukemia.

Gathered together to nurse him, her family reads Henry Vaughan poetry ("I saw Eternity the other night, / Like a great ring of pure and endless light"), listens to Brahms and Bach, debates theology and contemplates the cosmos over dinner. Meanwhile, Vicky is courted by three young men: Leo, a childhood friend from the island; a dashing, rich city kid named Zachary, who has followed her there; and Adam, a university student researching the local dolphin population. In quiet moments, Adam shows Vicky how dolphins communicate—telepathically, it turns out—and Vicky learns to call them.

Out in the ocean, the dolphins swim with her, their bodies pressed against her side, silently letting her know that she is cared for, that she will survive the loss of her grandfather and the confusion of youth. That she is going to be all right.

Near the end of the novel, with Zachary at the hospital where her grandfather has finally been admitted, an epileptic child dies in Vicky's arms. Zachary abandons her, unable to cope. Vicky is alone, flooded with despair, and enters a state of shock. In her moment of crisis, she calls out telepathically to Adam. He hears her, somehow, and arrives to deliver her back to the sea. There, the dolphins surround her, affirming all that is good in the world. Hope and faith are restored. The despair is banished.

The moment offers a mystical way of thinking through the grief of being human. Vicky must accept that she lives in a world where children sometimes die in emergency rooms. She must accept that her grandfather will die. She must accept, too, the anguish that threatens to pull her under. As in all of L'Engle's books, though, she does not have to do any of this alone. She has the friendship of the universe—in this case, the dolphins—to give her comfort and courage.

At the time I read this, I happened to be in the midst of my own crisis, as my father walked away from our family, shattering my sense of trust.

My mother, meanwhile, was forced to fill both roles, juggling parenting with low-wage work, eventually going back to school.

By the time I entered high school, I was desperate for someone to pay attention to me. The first meeting I attended of the Environmental Youth Alliance was held at the second-floor office of Oxfam Canada and chaired by a bearded twentysomething named Doug. I was fourteen. I have no idea why I went. But sitting around that conference table, my opinion suddenly counted for something. So I went back again the next week, and the week after that.

Soon I was writing articles for our newsletter, organizing rallies, speaking at conferences and being interviewed on the radio. Being a leader of the environmental movement brought me closer to L'Engle's vision of a spiritual universe, a creative life, awe-inspiring wilderness—and the satisfying symbiosis between those things. Plus, who knew where it would lead? I might find myself visiting remote jungles, meeting famous scientists, dining with anthropologists who forged links to ancient cultures.

As it turns out, all of this came to pass. And more.

Six months later, weeks before my fifteenth birthday, several dozen of us stood at the arrivals gate at the Vancouver airport, holding handmade signs with phrases in the Penan language, as news cameras looked on.

We were there to welcome tribesmen from the Malaysian state of Sarawak, on the island of Borneo, two of whom belonged to the Penan, one of the last nomadic hunter-gatherer tribes on the planet. The men were on the Voices for the Borneo Rainforest world tour, protesting the twenty-four-hour-a-day logging of their ancestral lands.

When I first met him, Mutang Tu'o was in his early twenties. He walked into the cold airport terminal in a loincloth and traditional headgear, carrying a single flower.

From the start, he and I shared a feeling of close kinship.

Over the weeks that I visited with him, he taught me to play the nose flute and made me carved bamboo bracelets. He played the guitar and sang and told me stories. I promised to visit him one day in Borneo.

Mutang made me feel seen, heard, appreciated. Things I was not feeling in my family at the time.

I was drawn to his bright mind, his sense of fun, the stillness that he carried within him, the reverence with which he talked of his homeland. The way he spoke had a familiar poetry to it; it reminded me of L'Engle. "Whatever happens next, I am only putting my confidence in those who are out there in the world, because we are in their hands," he said in a statement during the tour. "Let us be married in spirit, loving each other so that our friendship be strong and eternal. Let the indigenous people and the people of the world be together like the moon and the stars that shine in the darkness."

He believed in the power of human connection. He trusted in our interconnectedness, and the sense of purpose that came with it.

Around that time, we both joined a delegation of young environmentalists on a trip to Galiano Island, led by famed environmentalist Thom Henley (no relation). During the retreat, we played games in the forest, greeted the wind, water, air and earth in song, and ate elaborate meals cooked over campfires. We combed the shoreline, taking photos of the sandstone formations, marveling at the purple starfish, the eagles overhead, the silence.

Early on, we were each encouraged to find a "spirit spot," a quiet place where we could sit and contemplate life. For these daily meditations, I would hike off to mine—a rugged, mossy bluff—and sit staring out at the ocean. Out on the bluffs, I felt a sense of connection to the universe around me and, in the fullness of that connection, a gentle reprieve from my pain. From my own complicated humanity.

Toward the end of the retreat, each of us went on a "vision quest" intended to help us find inner courage. Supplied with food and fire (a potato and a match), we were sent off in the afternoon, sleeping bags in hand, not to return until morning. I hiked along the rocky shoreline, up steep cliffs and then down into dark, foreboding bays. Eventually, I found a friendly-feeling bluff, near a lighthouse, and settled in. I could not start my fire and had to eat my potato raw.

After several long hours, dusk fell and I became afraid. I listened to the forest behind me, aware of each crinkling leaf, every snapping branch. Were there animals out there? Humans? Was I safe? I sat up, stricken, most of the night.

But at some point before dawn, a peace settled over me. In that moment, the world no longer seemed like a hostile place. I understood that I was looked after. There was something, some presence, with me. It communicated to me through the stars and the rustle of the trees and the fullness of the moon hanging over the glittering ocean. This quiet harmony reached back—to the past, to my childhood, to the world I'd connected to in L'Engle's books. And it reached far into the future, to a life I did not yet live and an understanding of the world I did not yet grasp.

After the retreat ended, Mutang returned home. Sometimes when you say goodbye to someone, you know you will miss them for the rest of your life. This was the case with Mutang.

After he went back to Borneo, I placed a photo of us on a side table in my room, with a bracelet he had made for me. I looked at this strange little altar every day, and at my lowest points, as our family chaos spiraled out of control, I would say a sort of prayer, reaching out to him across the ocean, across time zones and continents and cultures, envisioning him sitting in the longhouse. I would imagine that he answered me.

That year, I had a dream. I was in Borneo, with a friend, in a longboat on the river, paddling toward Long Iman, Mutang's village. The green jungle canopy hung low and lush overhead. Cicadas buzzed. Mists rose off the water. The air was thick with humidity. I was being drawn, pulled by some powerful force. I woke up and wrote down the details of my dream. I still have that crumpled piece of paper.

A decade later, at twenty-four years old, my life felt, in many ways, like the L'Engle novels I had so wanted to emulate. I had followed my love of books into grad school, and planned to become a professor. I still read and reread her books. Still sought the world of connection, and purpose, and justice outlined in their pages.

The beginning of grad school was exhilarating. That August, I moved into an attic suite in a heritage house, in a neighborhood filled with writers. I made new friends. Had fascinating conversations over strong coffee. Bought new books. Started to sketch out one of my own. But I had been having bowel trouble for months, and finally, after I began bleeding, a specialist ordered tests.

In early September, I went for the first of many colonoscopies. Lying on a hospital table in a pastel gown, I felt the drugs enter my bloodstream, a jarring sensation. Alertness, followed by long stretches of absence.

The nurses were my age; this put me on edge. One of them told me she was going to a bachelorette party after work. They'd ordered a cake shaped like a penis, she said with a laugh.

In my drugged state, I watched the screen as a scope probed my colon. And then I heard the doctor say, "Oh my God." Panic seeped in. What was going on? Then, there was pain—deep, aching pain. The room filled with a tense excitement, slightly euphoric. The doctor held something up to the light. It looked like a large, bleeding raspberry. I wanted to touch it. I reached out. He fumbled and dropped it in my lap.

I woke up in the recovery room. A blond woman across from me was muttering incoherently, lipstick smeared across her cheek. I had the vague sense that something important had happened. When my friend arrived to help me dress, I told her they'd found a tumor, realizing it as I said it.

Sitting in an abandoned waiting room afterwards, the doctor made a drawing of where the polyp had been located and how he'd removed it. I laughed, in shock. I would have to wait several business days to find out if it was cancer, he said.

That week, driving around in a car with friends, I felt raw, fragile, like precious glass. Like a thump on the back would shatter me. I felt detached from everything and everybody. It seemed bizarre to me that life could be continuing on as usual for everyone else. I envied my friends, their triviality—their social faux pas, their new shoes, their consuming crushes. I wanted that oblivion back.

Over dinner one night, I forced my friends to look at the photo of the growth. They were disgusted, but I didn't care. I could not shoulder that image alone. That giant, swollen yellow orb with its slippery sheen. I wanted others to help carry it, break it up, distribute it. Somehow minimize its horror. I wanted sympathy, maybe. Or protection.

I knew something was wrong, and I was afraid. The fear was liquid; nothing could contain it. It spilled out into every minute, infecting every second with blackness. I called my mother at night. "I don't want to die," I sobbed into the phone.

But the next morning, I went for a walk. The September air was fresh and cool. I walked past brightly painted houses, trees resplendent with jewel-toned leaves, gallivanting dogs, overflowing flowerbeds—signs of life. I thought: *Maybe this is how you choose life. Maybe this is how you choose the light over that consuming darkness. Maybe it is as simple as heading outdoors, feeling grateful for this moment of sunshine, this crisp autumn air, this reprieve.*

I went home and scrubbed the kitchen floor, reorganized the cupboards, cleaned the bathtub. I lit some candles and had a bath. Finally, sitting in the steaming water, I felt like it was going to be all right.

I had the energy to survive whatever was coming. I would not give in to this raging fear. I would make it through this.

I knew when I heard the message from my doctor's receptionist, asking me to come straight in, that it wasn't going to be good. I picked up the message on campus and drove to the west side of the city in a daze. Double-parked in the lane behind the office. I was shown to a treatment room right away. There, my GP opened a file, stared evenly at its contents and told me the tumor was cancerous. "This is not a death sentence," he said gruffly. "We caught it early."

He released me into the bright afternoon. I drove to my mother's apartment building and sat on the steps in the hot sun in a leather jacket, unable to remove it, waiting for her to come home.

Finally, responding to messages I had left on their pagers, my two closest friends came and found me. Later, my mother arrived, shaking. We made tea and cried, all of us together on the couch. The closeness was both touching and excruciating. Simultaneously satisfying and devastating.

My mother and I went to Topanga, where my brother was working in the kitchen, and sat on the patio until he finished his shift. When we told him the news, he cried too.

The two of them—my constants, my solace in life,

then and now—slept in my room that night, in my attic apartment. I had to get up at four in the morning to sit in an armchair in my study, too afraid to sleep. Reality had taken on a surreal quality. Lights were too bright. Sounds were too loud. Everything felt unreal.

How had my life changed this fast? One moment I was worried about a bad haircut, and the next I was worried about my life.

In the following days, friends and family flooded my tiny apartment, arriving with bags of food. Roasted chickens, whole lasagnas, homemade cookies and muffins, salads and soups. The threat of death, it seemed, made people hungry.

But during the weeks that I waited for my surgery, I could not eat. I could not sleep. All I could do most days was stay in bed and read Margaret Atwood novels.

I was afraid of many things: the surgery itself, the anesthetic, the possible complications. Mostly, I was afraid of losing control, of lying unconscious on that metal table, naked and exposed.

As the days progressed, there were fewer and fewer people I could talk to. My fears were too real; they startled people into silence. My need was a dark, gaping, ugly hole. It was bottomless, and it frightened people away. So I stopped talking, stopped telling anyone anything.

At one o'clock one morning, overcome, I prayed for a sign that I was going to survive. I broke down and called a friend. As she answered, I saw a dark outline beside my bed. The rational part of my mind could see that it was a shadow, perhaps cast by light shining behind the tree outside my window. But it didn't feel like a shadow; it felt like a presence. I opened up to my friend, finally releasing all of my fears, like dozens of frantic mice. I named each one of those creatures, every single terror that had been gnawing on my courage, devouring my hope from within.

She decided to read my tarot cards. The outline was still visible over my bed, and it comforted me. I felt light-headed and calm.

The first card she read was for the past. It marked not respecting one's bodily limitations. The second card was for the present. It signified being surrounded by true love—the kind of love that sees you for who you truly are. And then came the card for the future. "You are battling a dragon, and you will triumph," my friend read. "If you are a student, you will gain success. If you are a writer, you will publish."

I fell into a deep, serene sleep.

I was extremely lucky. That same September, I underwent a successful colon resection and discovered the cancer had not spread.

After the surgery, it took a week to be able to walk down the stairs from my attic apartment and another week to reach the end of the block. Longer still to regain my equilibrium.

The pain in my abdomen was like an appendage, like a new limb. It did not go away.

The visits stopped in early October. My friends and

family returned to their lives. My fridge emptied out. Those long, lonely weeks proved the hardest. I was suddenly, staggeringly, alone. I had no energy. I could not get groceries, or make food for myself, or clean my house. I could not work, or study, or cash my student loans, since it wasn't clear I'd be able to stay in school. I could not pay my rent.

I felt disappointed by everything and everybody. I could not contain my grief. It leaked out of me, perpetually spilling over. I did not trust. Not in my body, not in those around me, not in the universe. My connection to all was shattered.

In between crying, I felt numb. The sorrow was so immense, so vast, that I had to sip it slowly; if I'd allowed myself a big gulp, I would have drowned.

I wondered: *How can I be this filled with darkness when I've essentially been saved from death? How do I dig myself out of this pit of rage and despair? How do I get my life back? My relationships? How do I forgive those who've failed me, who've been unable to show up? How will I ever feel normal again?*

I made the mistake of going back to class. The effort it took to get to campus, to walk down the hall to the classroom, to speak to my peers, was incomprehensible. Sitting there, shaky and vulnerable, I thought, *I need to be a million miles away. I need to be in Mexico or Italy or Thailand. Anywhere but here.*

When I returned home, I happened upon some words from Frank Church, a courageous politician who'd sponsored the Wilderness Act and had been among the first U.S. senators to oppose the Vietnam War. Who'd himself survived cancer. "I had previously tended to be more cautious," he was quoted as saying, "but having so close a brush with death at twenty-three, I felt afterwards that life itself is such a chancy proposition that the only way to live life is by taking great chances."

Reading that, I realized that life was never going to be ordinary again. Much as I wished it, I could not go back in time. I could not go back to those first few optimistic weeks of grad school, when I stopped for a cinnamon bun and a coffee in the mornings on the way to campus. I could not go back to a time when I never thought about life or death.

And if I could not go backward, I would have to find a way to go forward.

A plan slowly formed. I would take the following semester off school and go traveling. When I was sick, I'd regretted that I hadn't seen more of the world. I could remedy that. I could walk out into the arms of adventure, the wider world L'Engle had so lovingly portrayed, and see what I found there.

The decision instantly energized me; it made me feel alive again. I found the courage to ask for help—for home-cooked dinners and grocery runs and company and more—and the help began to come. My grad school allowed me to do the semester from home. I was able to get my student loans, and thus pay my rent. I began to sell off my possessions, saving up money for a plane ticket.

Around that time, I read a Margaret Atwood story, "Scarlet Ibis," in which a tourist family takes a bird-watching boat trip on a river. The story describes rising mists, and reading it, I flashed on my dream of Sarawak from all those years ago. On my promise to visit Mutang. I suddenly wanted to be on a boat, too, making my way down a river, heading off into the mists. Into the mystery.

I wasn't sure I was brave enough to go to Borneo. The jungles of Sarawak seemed remote, impossibly dangerous, filled with lethal insects and parasites and, moreover, dangerous loggers and corrupt government officials. But I could head in that general direction, couldn't I? I could go to Southeast Asia. I could hope the courage materialized to carry me further. I couldn't fathom going alone—as in L'Engle's narratives, a quest is rarely taken solo—but I had a close friend, Ian, who offered to come with me.

A few months later, we found ourselves walking through the airport in Bangkok with two other friends, hit by a wall of heat and humidity, and a pungent scent, difficult to place—some combination of rotting garbage and jasmine blooms.

Back at our hotel, we all slept the drugged sleep of international travel, and awoke to sit by the pool and drink instant coffee. And then walk the city streets, entranced.

The Saturday market was a teeming maze of crates and stalls and sweating human bodies. There were vats of sweet-smelling soup, shelves of silk scarves and carved wooden chopsticks, cages of iguanas, insects and puppies, vendors serving pancakes dripping with sweetened condensed milk.

The city was like a sauna. I drank bottle after bottle of cold water, pouring it over my head and hands. I was covered in a thick film of sweat. My skirt stuck to my body; my normally straight hair was an explosion of wispy curls. I struggled to take it all in. To adjust to the dirt, the grime, the gentle filth of the city. The ever-present drone of motorcycles; the toilets that were just holes in the ground; the heavy air; the lazy, languid heat.

In the backpacking district, Khao San Road, everything was neon bright and loud and frantic. In every direction, there were people our age. Sitting at plastic tables on the street, drinking Singha beer and eating plates of white rice and spicy beef. Spilling out of tattoo parlors and bars. Lugging huge backpacks and laughing, Britney Spears blasting from giant speakers.

We walked down twisting back alleys, past massage parlors, where bored-looking prostitutes sat outside on porches in fancy dress and full makeup, waiting to be selected. Past fragrant soup carts manned by young rural girls with wide smiles. We drank musty sweet tea and ate plates of pad thai, sitting on plastic chairs at stands under bridges, motorcycles speeding past.

My eyes burned from the chili smoke. My nostrils filled with the scent of flowers, overripe fruit, temple incense. We settled into our hostel, run by a Thai family. Every morning, the mother would go to market and return with breakfast: lychee jam for our toast, sweet sticky rice, coconut dumplings, rose apples, dragon fruit, mango, durian.

Then, at a beach just outside Bangkok, my thinking and thinking and thinking about Borneo solidified into a single word: *go*.

So Ian and I booked an overnight train south to Krabi,

to the environmentalist Thom Henley's eco resort. The sea there was jade green, surrounded by towering limestone cliffs and dotted with brightly colored longboats.

The morning after we arrived, we ate a breakfast of deep-fried banana and sweet sticky rice and coconut cakes in a gazebo surrounded by fuchsia flowers. That night, we sat on the beach as a thunderstorm erupted, watching the lightning illuminate the bay in quick bursts of electric blue. Transparent crabs scuttled across the sand, geckos lurched for cover, bats screeched by. The air was pregnant with possibility. We stood in silence, terrified and exhilarated, watching the rain pound the sand. Drenched, we returned to our thatched hut, cocooned ourselves in mosquito nets and awoke in the night to more thunder.

I thought, again and again, of the lush jungles of Sarawak that awaited us, of my friend Mutang. I was afraid of leeches. I was afraid of ticks. I was afraid of malaria. I was afraid of the Malaysian government. I was afraid of all the things about the jungle that I didn't yet know enough to be afraid of.

But Thom gave me a book he'd written about the Penan, and reading it on Valentine's Day in a Starbucks in Kuala Lumpur after a long bus ride down south, I found a quote from Franklin Roosevelt's 1933 inauguration speech: "The only thing we have to fear is fear itself."

That gave me the final push I needed. We booked flights to Miri, an oil town in Sarawak, on the island of Borneo. I called my mother from the airport, waking her in the middle of the night, needing to hear her voice before we boarded the plane. Needing to hear her tell me I was doing the right thing.

Illness makes you question everything. It forces you to go deep within, to face your greatest fears. To ask yourself the most important question in life: *Will I give in to the darkness or will I choose the light?*

I had chosen the light. And that choice had opened me up—not only to myself and to the world around me, but to those I loved. At home and here, many miles away, bound for one of the world's most remote jungles.

During those grueling days of travel to Borneo, I thought a lot about my life. I thought about Mutang and how his quest to save Borneo's ancient rainforests symbolized all that was good and true in the world. About how much I wanted to be a part of that—the struggle, essentially, for the future of humanity. About how much I wanted to live.

I began to understand, too, that there was a kind of energy that was somehow linked to being unwell. A sort of franticness, a pushing of things too far. A Western mindset of *more, more, more*. Of packing too much into too little time. Of doing instead of being. Of rushing around all the time. I began to understand that this really must be avoided. Going forward, I knew I must find a way to dwell in the calm of the overnight train ride south from Bangkok, gazing at the moon from the caboose as families around me stirred in their sleep. Or the silence in the courtyard of a Buddhist temple as monks filed inside and a pink sun slipped behind an arched roof.

I suddenly knew, too, that there had been a lot of things in my life that I had needed to say but had been unable to. And that I was going to need to find a way to say these things. I was going to need to find my voice.

In Miri, our packs filled with oatmeal, coffee, canned beans and peanut butter, Ian and I boarded another flight, this time a twenty-seat propeller plane bound for Mulu National Park, located near Mutang's village. Flying over the jungle, I stared out the tiny windows at the lush forest below, at the mist rising off the tree line, as I'd always known it would.

We landed at noon and hired a boat to take us upriver. As we made our way, the jungle canopy dripping low above us, I felt a shock of recognition. The lush forest overhead. The buzz of the cicadas. The heat and humidity. The swirling mists. The feeling of the moment—it all was identical to my dream from a decade before. "We are all strangers in a strange land, longing for home, but not knowing quite what or where home is," L'Engle once wrote. "We glimpse it sometimes in our dreams, or as we turn a corner, and suddenly there is a strange, sweet familiarity that vanishes almost as soon as it comes."

I don't know how that boat trip in Borneo felt like a homecoming. But it did.

Once we docked in Mutang's village, we were shown to the home of the boat driver's father, a longhouse in the center of the village. Someone left to run to the rice fields, where Mutang was apparently farming. Suddenly, he was there, standing in front of me. He was the same: open face, mischievous smile, kind eyes. "Tara!" he exclaimed. It was clear, immediately, that our friendship had been as important to him as it had been to me. That I had been right to come.

Mutang welcomed us into his immaculately clean longhouse, where we slept on the floor at night on woven mats. The walls were decorated with advertisements from magazines, old greeting cards, hand-drawn pictures, official documents from his travels, letters he'd received from abroad.

Rain often rumbled overhead, bombarding the roof. During downpours, we sat in the longhouse, talking, remembering. Mutang pulled out photos of us from all those years before. He played the nose flute as an audience of rapt children crept into the room. He shared his handwritten Penan/English dictionary with me and encouraged me to copy it out. *Akeu*, I. *Bakêh*, friend. At night, we dined in his small kitchen building, adjacent to the longhouse. A chicken was killed, greens harvested from the jungle. I sat on the floor with Mutang's sister, laughing, chopping vegetables.

It was hot and my anti-malarial medication left me susceptible to the tropical sun; my face burned and blistered. Mutang climbed a tree and pulled down a coconut, advising me that its water was healing for sun sickness. We trekked deep into the jungle, and he told us about the plants and their many medicinal uses, for everything from virility and fertility to the common cold. He showed us how to make umbrellas and spoons from hardy leaves. He took the boat downriver and returned with mosquito coils, toilet paper, candles for me to write by.

His kindness humbled me. The whole tribe's kindness humbled me. Here were people who were losing everything— their forest, and with it their home, their food supply, their security, their medicine and their spirituality. But they had not lost each other. They had not lost the capacity to love. They gave so much, and with so much tenderness.

I felt enormous grief that the world tour had not worked, that these ancient rainforests could not be saved, that I could think of no way to help Mutang and the Penan. That the only thing I could do was show up and be a witness. That the only thing I had to offer was my friendship.

The night before we left, I sat with Mutang in his long-house, drinking tea and talking. He told me he'd had a dream that I was coming two weeks before. Right around the time I'd boarded the plane to Bangkok, in fact. Working in the rice fields, he'd told his friends. When they went to get him to tell him we had arrived, they exclaimed, "Mutang, your dream was true. The woman is here!" The village had been expecting me.

I had been waiting my whole life for those few days in the rainforest, for the deep feeling of connection that I experienced there, and the sense of purpose that flowed from it.

The Penan gave the great gift of mattering, and in the most essential way possible. Of seeing how love can cross cultures and continents and countries, even whole eras of human history.

As we said a heartbreaking goodbye once again, Mutang asked me to tell his story—the story of his people, of their mattering. And, over the years, I told it again and again.

The story became my north star, setting the course of my life toward connection. To the natural world, to belonging, to love. I had lost this, though, to the insanity of modern life. And during those long months on the couch, I knew I had to find a way to get it back.

An image kept returning to me as I lay in my living room in Vancouver, trying to find a way forward. The morning Ian and I left Borneo, Mutang had walked us down to the dock and watched as we climbed into the boat that would deliver us back to Mulu National Park and its tiny airport. Sitting in the water just off the riverbank, I glanced up to see the entire tribe gathered on the cliffs to say goodbye. Young and old, all were there, standing together, smiling and waving.

I began to cry, and when I looked to the back of the boat, I could see that Ian was crying too. There was something so moving about seeing the tribe gathered in this way, standing together, demonstrating their care.

In the Penan's ancient tribal culture, though, this gesture that we found so touching, so generous, was commonplace. In fact, nothing about the surrounding set of circumstances—so extraordinary to me—seemed unusual to them at all.

It was not strange or eccentric that, faced with death, I had traveled across the world to reconnect with someone I cared about, and meet his people. It was a natural human reaction, this outpouring of love, this desire to translate emotion into action, this need to show others that I cared about them. It was utterly, completely normal to want to be close with people in this way.

It was normal, too, for them to embrace me in the way they had. To see me immediately as one of their own. To feed me (though they had little food) and shelter me, cook with me and sleep near me and include me in their children's lives. To joke with me, and tease me, and begin to teach me their language. To tell me their stories and their problems, and sing songs and celebrate with me too. To draw me into the fold in a way that made me feel essential. That made me matter.

This was what was missing from my life. What had always been missing from my life.

The thing about us humans is that we need each other. And not in an "I'll shoot you a text" or "Maybe let's grab coffee next week if schedules permit" kind of way. We need to be woven into the fabric of each other's daily lives. We need close, intimate, unbreakable bonds. We need to rely on each other as if our very survival depends upon it. Because it does.

As the former war correspondent Sebastian Junger writes in *Tribe: On Homecoming and Belonging*, throughout history we have needed each other to hunt and gather, to defend against attacks from animals and other humans, and to brave extreme weather conditions. But now, as we buy prepackaged meals at supermarkets and live alone in secure, climate-controlled condos, that need is no less powerful. We are still hardwired for connection, for interdependence. And when we don't have it, we sink into despair.

Without a tribe, we are lost. Group unity is the force that buffers against the horrors of the human condition. When we lose that, we lose everything.

I think this is why my grandmother spoke so nostalgically about the Blitz. During the eight months of those punishing air raids, as Junger points out in his book, Londoners came together in remarkable ways. Bombarded night after night by bombs, people slept shoulder to shoulder in shelters, protected each other, shared food and water, and lifted each other's spirits. Strangers became friends. Family, even. A feeling of common cause, purpose, brotherhood pervaded society. Nobody was in it alone.

Psychiatrists at the time were amazed to see that many patients' symptoms improved. Indeed, admissions to psychiatric hospitals went down.

The lesson observers took from this, as Junger notes, was that modern society disrupts the bonds that define humanity—whereas catastrophes like the Blitz throw everyone back into a more ancient way of relating. One in which class, sex, income and race dissolve, and people are judged solely by what they are willing to sacrifice for the group, the greater good. One in which people feel profoundly close to one another.

My anxiety, I could now see, was a reasonable response, both to my past and to the society I was now living in.

Of course I felt anxious in a society where a homeless man could stand outside a gourmet grocery store, largely ignored, selling community newspapers to make enough money for a sandwich, while mega-mansions a few blocks away sat empty and unused. Where teachers could not afford to rent studio apartments, but multimillionaires flooded the streets to protest minuscule property tax increases. Where tensions between white and Chinese, millennial and baby boomer, male and female, right and left, capitalist and environmentalist, employer and employee, cyclist and driver, spiraled out of control, making everyone miserable.

Where single people had nobody to call when they were sick with the flu, and parents had not a single moment to see friends, and the elderly had no visitors for weeks at a time. Where everyone everywhere reported unprecedented levels of loneliness.

This was what I was suffering from—this was the void. It was not an individual problem; it was a collective problem. And I was going to need to find some collective solutions.

CHAPTER SEVEN

The Tribe

Building community from scratch is a daunting exercise. The enormity of the task really cannot be overstated. Exactly how does one create the kind of ancient structures of relating that took thousands of years to evolve—and have been systematically demolished by contemporary life? How does one stem the tide of modernity, resist the alienation entrenched all around us? Especially when reaching out to others in any significant way is now often read as inappropriate, intrusive even. Especially when people are so incredibly overwhelmed, either by their stressful, busy lives or their personal pain and suffering, that they cannot commit to coffee, let alone community. Especially when you yourself are doing the reaching out under duress.

This sort of effort inevitably involved, for me, sending out a bunch of texts or emails to friends and acquaintances, and getting back a bunch of responses reading, *Maybe . . . play it by ear?* or *That might work* or *Work is nuts right now— touch base next month?*

Still, looking back at the illness in my twenties, I understood that my grief had resulted from a failure of the tribe—and that my healing had come from a restoration of the tribe. What was now broken in my life, I knew, could only be repaired in relation to other people. I needed to seek out community, however elusive that proved to be at this particular juncture in history.

For all these reasons, I had to start at the easiest place possible. I had to start at the coffee shop.

The café that I wrote in every day was a hub for my neighborhood, a rare space in which neighbors actually spoke to one another spontaneously. There were toddlers racing around, and dogs tied up outside. People had business meetings, and nervous first dates. They shared muffins with church pastors, and sat down for advice from graduate thesis supervisors. They had carefully worded conflicts with friends, and boisterous chats with family. New moms came in for conversation, and freelancers for company. Clerks from the bank across the street came in for breaks. My horticulture-therapist neighbor (and former executive director of the Environmental Youth Alliance) stopped by. As did a folk singer friend from Ireland who lived blocks away, and the young City Beet farmers who transformed local lawns into veggie plots.

The artistic director of the Vancouver Writers Festival met with authors at corner tables. A retiree watched shows on his iPad in the afternoons. A bus driver biked over on his days off to read the books he bought in bulk at a local thrift store. A construction worker in a safety vest pored over the *New York Times*.

It was the kind of place people returned to at the same time every day, so much so that you could set your clocks by it. In this way, we all became part of each other's routines. We gathered deliberately, again and again, seeking some small slice of town square.

The staff, of course, played a big role in this, gently coaxing the rest of us out of our stubborn isolation. *See that person over there?* they might say. *She's a writer too.*

Battling self-consciousness, I pushed myself to open up. In doing so, I learned that the staff were all voracious readers. I was by then a freelance book reviewer, and since I regularly got sent stacks of books and read them quickly, I started taking in bags to the team. It was an easy way to express my gratitude for giving me such a welcoming place to go. The unexpected bonus was that I got to learn all about their reading habits and, as a result, their lives.

One was studying library science; she had a knack for zeroing in on the books that would become bestsellers or go on to win big literary prizes. Another had a sister who was transgender and was interested in emerging voices in Canadian literature. Another, a charming Brit, loved nonfiction books and was fascinated by learning about the world. Another was an illustrator who made the most exquisite drawings.

Pretty soon, I knew all sorts of other things about them, too. I knew when one had tooth pain and had to go to the emergency room, or another extended his work visa. I knew about partners and pets, roommates, trips to Mexico, New York, Portland.

The turning point came in the summer of 2018. I was feeling especially low and was spending more time than usual in the coffee shop, embarrassed to be always hanging around. The manager approached me one day when I was putting cream in my coffee, and told me that it always made her happy when I came in, that my warmth and good energy were a gift to her. To the whole staff. I promptly burst into tears.

After that, I stopped doubting this impulse to know and be known. I gave myself over to it, understanding that it was an answer—not just for me, but for us all.

People have all kinds of ideas about anxiety, given how prevalent it is these days. And as I attempted to cope, and build a life that made sense, I found myself inundated with suggestions.

People told me to meditate. Or else check out TED Talks, podcasts, self-help titles. They told me to exercise and cut out caffeine. But some went even further. Some told me that my unhappiness stemmed from what I was focusing on. Everyone is unhappy sometimes, they said. Our happiness cannot be dependent on a partner or kids, on whether friends are free this weekend. We must find happiness within. Collective wisdom held that whatever you lacked in life, it wasn't about your circumstances—it was about your thinking.

All of this was well-intentioned, and made sense in the speaking. Sure, okay, happiness is an inside job, and shouldn't be contingent on outside factors. Life is uncertain, and if you place your happiness in other people's hands, you'll always be unhappy.

To be fair, much of this advice came from friends with husbands and children and hectic, jam-packed schedules. They had the opposite problem to me; they desperately

craved alone time. They found it hard to see just how cor-
rosive too much of it could be.

Ultimately, though, the main problem with this "it's
a matter of perspective" approach was that it didn't work.
I had tried listening to podcasts and reading self-help
books. I had tried thinking relentlessly positive thoughts.
I had tried taking action and letting go of results. I had
tried counting my blessings. I had tried to stop trying.

The fact remained that I was still spending the bulk of
my time by myself. And no matter how many times I
reframed this for myself (and others), I simply didn't like it.

It was British journalist Johann Hari's *Lost Connections* that finally helped me see that my longing for more
closeness—and despair over not having found it—was
a perfectly normal human response to modern society.
I was not broken, his work insisted; I was a human being
with unmet needs.

Driving this point home in the book, Hari cites a study
from the late neuroscience researcher John Cacioppo, who
charted the body's response to loneliness. Through saliva
tests, Cacioppo discovered that when people are feeling
disconnected, their cortisol levels skyrocket, as much as if
they'd been physically attacked. Being deeply lonely, Hari
notes, seems to "cause as much stress as being punched by
a stranger."

Other studies cited in *Lost Connections* demonstrate that
loneliness reduces immunity, and that isolated people are
two to three times more likely to die. Indeed, Hari writes,
"Almost everything became more fatal when you were
alone: cancer, heart disease, respiratory problems." In all,

being lonely has as much of an impact on your health as being obese. Just as striking, research shows loneliness is not just a factor in depression, but in fact *leads* to it.

According to Cacioppo, this massive impact on our physical and mental health has to do with our evolution as a species. Humanity originated on African savannas, where we existed in small hunter-gatherer tribes. Our survival depended on cooperation. And being separated from our group spelled grave danger. "You were vulnerable to predators, if you got sick nobody would be there to nurse you, and the rest of the tribe was more vulnerable without you too," Hari writes. "You would be right to feel terrible. It was an urgent signal from your body and brain to get back to the group, any damn way you could.

"So every human instinct is honed not for life on your own, but life like this, in a tribe," he adds. "Humans need tribes as much as bees need a hive."

Interestingly, there's a scientifically proven snowball effect to loneliness, as Hari goes on to point out. Brain scans show that lonely people become increasingly suspicious of social contact, perpetually scanning for threats. On a subconscious level, Hari explains, they know nobody is looking out for them, and so they become hyper-vigilant. Which, in turn, makes them difficult to be around.

This dynamic may be where the self-help change-your-attitude approach originates. But in reality, people who are suffering need extra reassurance, love and support to heal, not pull-up-your-bootstraps judgment and criticism. So the self-help bromide winds up being a classic case of the cure being worse than the disease, with such sentiments serving only to accelerate the spiral of isolation.

To truly end loneliness, Hari concludes, what people need is to experience reciprocal protection and aid.

Think about that: what we need, more than anything, is security. We need to know that our tribe will feed us, shelter us and defend us. We need to know that we can count on people in tangible ways. And we need to offer the same to others.

This, of course, calls not for individual solutions, but deeply communal ones.

Hari's research convinced me that I'd hit the limits of self-help's usefulness. The data on anxiety and depression is extensive. It points not to a need for attitude adjustment, but to a need for stronger social connections.

Understanding that my distress was normal was a huge relief. The self-help solution had proven horribly elusive. How exactly does one surrender? How does one shift one's own thinking? How does one find peace within? Recognizing that I needed to spend more time around other people, on the other hand, was wonderfully straightforward. Depending on some mystical set of principles left me paralyzed; aiming to get closer to other people gave me a simple game plan.

As an aside, it's also worth noting that surrender is not necessarily healthy, anyway. I recently spoke with a yoga critic, Matthew Remski, author of *Practice and All Is Coming: Abuse, Cult Dynamics, and Healing in Yoga and Beyond*, who stressed that sometimes surrender can actually be a fatal form of passivity. If the evolutionary response to a threat is fight, flight or fold, we maybe shouldn't be championing the fold option, he pointed out. We might want to remember that folding is something you do when you die.

Anyway, in modern culture, we keep telling people to find the answers within, disregarding thousands of years of culture and psychology and biology. "This is a denial of human history, and a denial of human nature," Hari stresses in his book. "It leads us to misunderstand our most basic instincts. And this approach to life makes us feel terrible."

We're not meant to take care of ourselves. We're meant to take care of each other.

Luckily, around this time a friend invited me to her company's three-day workshop on non-directive coaching—a crash course on how to be a tribe.

My friend, Carollyne Conlinn, worked for a food-service management company for thirty years, eventually becoming a vice president. In the mid-nineties, when she was in her early fifties, she started to find the constant travel taxing. She had two preteens at home, and found it exhausting to always be on the road, away from her family. After much deliberation, in 1996, she took early retirement.

Significantly, this decision grew out of an unorthodox living arrangement. She and her husband and kids had just moved into a cohousing complex in a Vancouver suburb, an arrangement in which each family had their own living quarters but shared common areas, tasks and community.

"I felt like my children were cared for more than just by me, and that there was a strengthening of our family unit because we were living in community," she told me over tea at her new apartment, in another cohousing project, this time in North Vancouver. "I found the courage, actually, to unleash myself from the corporate stronghold. Because living in a single-family home in the middle of suburbia, I felt like it was all up to just us—my husband and me. But somehow in this community, I started to think of other ways to earn a living. It just really opened my eyes."

Around that time, Conlinn stumbled upon a free workshop on one-on-one coaching, and there, she realized what a difference that kind of support would have made to her while she was in her corporate job. Though she'd initially been skeptical, she found herself feeling quite inspired. She'd never experienced anything like this, and she decided to enter the coaching world, to offer it to others.

Conlinn felt it was essential to free people up to interact as human beings with the people they worked with. The principles she was learning introduced humanity, empathy, meaning and purpose into the workplace. She could see what a difference this made to how people worked with one another, allowing them to have richer, more satisfying, less depleting work lives, with more energy left for family and friends and life outside of work. "I could just see so much potential for people who were—like I had been not that long before—in a way dying on [the] job," she said. "Getting it done, but part of me was . . . sacrificing my family, my lifeblood."

Two decades later, the company she'd co-founded, Essential Impact, had trained thousands in non-directive coaching, in public, nonprofit and corporate settings. The coach's sole aim, as they saw it, was to be present, listen and ask insightful questions, allowing the person the space to speak freely and arrive at her own solutions.

Giving someone a non-judgmental space to talk through their lives, Essential Impact maintained, had become so rare in our society that it could be life-changing.

Truth be told, I doubted this, as I tend to doubt most things. Particularly in group settings, and particularly if there's any hint of New Age spiritualism in the mix. (Show me a "sharing circle" and I'll show you the exit sign.)

But I'd also become aware that my instinct in groups was to be critical, to tap into my reporter mind and poke holes in proceedings, or else withdraw entirely—and this was obviously not ideal for tribe-building.

So, in the spirit of getting closer to others, I put these critical impulses on hold. And I began to notice that the workshop was, in fact, incredibly pragmatic. As coaches worked with participants on real-life work issues in front of the group, modeling techniques like active listening, presence, non-judgment and "holding people capable"— i.e., believing that participants knew best what solutions would work for them—it became clear how powerful these simple skills could be. As Conlinn explains, the work was intensely practical—"not woo-woo," she said with a smile— and really just focused on giving people better tools for relating to one another.

Add to that, my fellow participants were marvelous

human beings. Many worked for faith-based charities, on the front lines of poverty and addiction in our city. They were on Vancouver's ravaged Downtown Eastside offering food, shelter and friendship to those who needed it most. Listening to locals, and trying to act on what they heard. These were remarkable people, people whose moral strength moved me. People who had, in many cases, overcome tremendous obstacles in their own lives. And were determined to make things better for others.

Hour by hour, as we learned how to be a group together, I could see how each individual played a pivotal role in the whole. How one person's logical mind encouraged us to think about the best processes for achieving fairness for all, and another's altruism soothed those who were distressed. Another's action-oriented nature, meanwhile, helped us accomplish our goals. Group well-being depended on all of these energies. All these people.

As I appreciated these qualities in other people, I could appreciate them in myself. I could see that my analytical mind served an important purpose, as did my empathy.

During the last day of the workshop, we were paired up and instructed to tell our partners what we most wanted to be validated for in our lives. Then our partners would do just this, commenting on what they'd observed about us over the three intense days that we'd spent together. We switched partners again and again, until we had performed this ritual with many in the group.

This was, it must be said, harder for me than just about anything I'd ever done. Asking people to give me what I needed emotionally—to be seen, heard, appreciated—felt so unnatural, a root canal would have been preferable. I did like to see, though, how this exercise affected others.

Almost always, the things people yearned to be recognized for were the very things that I'd already noticed and admired about them. They simply wanted validation for what was already true. I was surprised to discover how much we had all picked up about the character of every person in the room, even those who spoke very little. The strengths we each possessed, our fundamental goodness as individuals, was immediately clear when we took a few minutes to focus on it. With just a little attention, we could easily identify and articulate each other's unique gifts, and express real gratitude for them.

The workshop concluded with, you guessed it, a sharing circle, in which a designated participant who'd been secretly observing you for the entire workshop told you, in front of the group, what they most admired about you. Nearly everyone was crying.

There was a strange sort of magic to this—some other force operating, on some sort of mystical level. On the first day of the workshop, when we'd drawn names from a hat, I'd gotten a woman in her early thirties who worked for the Union Gospel Mission on the Downtown Eastside. As I watched her day after day, in exercises, at lunch, in coaching sessions, I was struck by many things about her. She had a kind of throwback 1950s glamour to her, with her red lipstick and polka-dot dresses, and it brought a lightness and levity to everything. She was also extremely witty, though her jokes never came at others' expense.

But the thing that stood out most was her intelligence. She was so smart. The kind of smart that takes highly complex ideas and distills them into plain language that anybody could understand. The kind of smart that's infused with kindness for others, with empathy.

I told her so, in front of the group, as she cried. When it was her turn to speak, she told us she was crying because she was, at that time, struggling with confidence. She had just begun graduate school, undertaking a master's in community development, and was unsure she was up to the task. She was the first person in her immediate family to even graduate from high school, she said. For someone to tell her, publicly, how smart she was meant a lot.

When my turn came, a quiet man stood across from me. On the surface, we had nothing in common. He was of another generation, a salesman, a married father, Christian, Chinese. Despite our differences, I trusted him. His quiet, gentle presence served as a sort of anchor for the group. In the circle, he told me that I was amazing to him, and all the reasons why, as tears streamed down my face. In fact, he told me the things I'd most wanted to hear for my entire life.

I could see, in that moment, that something had broken in me in my turbulent childhood when my father left, and then again during those weeks alone after the cancer, triggering a profound mistrust of groups—indeed of other people. But that day, in the chapel of an old church in East Vancouver, that thing was mended, at least a little, by the kind words of a stranger. I felt seen, heard, appreciated. Valued for simply being who I was.

It was a practical application of Hari's research. And to say that it was life-changing would actually be an understatement.

In the days and months afterwards, taking this newfound confidence—and understanding of how to better serve others—out into the world, I began thinking a lot about groups and how I could access one. I did not, of course, want to spend my weekends sitting on my couch, waiting for the bad days to pass. I wanted to have fun. And for me, fun was getting out on my bike first thing in the morning and pedaling around the city, through forests and beaches and winding mountain roads. Stopping somewhere for a sandwich and a hot cup of coffee and a lively conversation.

Back when I had been reacquainting myself with the woods, I had joined an online hiking club to head off on local adventures. But it hadn't worked especially well. A lot of the hikes were too strenuous—way beyond my fitness level—and there's nothing worse than summiting a peak and realizing you don't have the energy to scramble back down again.

At some point, it occurred to me that if I didn't like how grueling these outings were, I could propose something gentler. I could myself become an organizer. This decision changed everything.

I started posting cycling trips on the group email list. I posted rides around the University of British Columbia, and to Stanley Park. To Steveston along breathtaking dykes, and across the Lions Gate Bridge to Ambleside

Park. Through East Van on lazy Sundays, stopping for espresso and pastries on colorful Commercial Drive. With some three thousand members on the list, there was always someone around to bike with.

Quite quickly, I met a wide circle of friends, many of whom lived close by. These people were highly accomplished—doctors and architects, creative directors and project coordinators for local developers. They were from all over the city, and all over the world. They all wanted to get out every weekend, and were reliable about doing so. And every last one of them adored food.

I had set out to meet activity buddies, but I hadn't expected to, within months, form close, genuine friendships. And I hadn't expected that my efforts to evade loneliness would bring joy to other people's lives.

I was soon seeing these friends all the time, celebrating their birthdays and meeting their broader social networks. We went to farmer's markets to buy foraged mushrooms and homemade ginger beer, and took weekend trips to cycle the Galloping Goose Trail on Vancouver Island, pedaling through sheets of rain, singing loudly as we crisscrossed through bear country, the damp autumn leaves an explosion of color.

When Thanksgiving came around, we held a big potluck at my place. And when Christmastime arrived, we baked cookies together and visited seasonal markets, went caroling and listened to choral CDs, drinking lemon ginger tea by the fire. We looked after each other in the wake of medical procedures, too, and helped each other wait for results.

We went to dim sum for Chinese New Year, and debated traditional Chinese medicine, and shared theories on the housing crisis. We cycled to suburban malls to eat noodles in Hong Kong–style food courts and buy fresh, sweet tofu in syrup. We frequented Chinese bakeries, sampling coconut tarts.

By now, I was no longer just sending out texts about the weekend; I was getting a whole bunch myself. Invitations to dinners and rides, yoga classes, brunches, pub quiz nights. More often than not, now, I had places to go, with people I very much liked going with.

I could now text these friends if I found myself with a free evening that I wasn't sure how to pass. Rather than sitting alone on my couch, I could pop by their homes for tea or takeout.

In the postscript to *Tribe*, Sebastian Junger mentions a book called *Moral Origins*, by Christopher Boehm. In it, the famed anthropologist references Eleanor Leacock, who studied the Cree in Northern Canada. She'd once gone on a hunting trip with a Cree man named Thomas, and out in the wilderness they'd come across two strangers who'd run out of food and were very hungry. Thomas gave them his flour and lard and, as a result, had to end his trip early. When Leacock pushed him to explain why he'd done this, he became exasperated. "Suppose, now, not to give them flour, lard," he said. "Just dead inside." In other words: not sharing what we have makes us feel dead inside.

I thought about this story all the time, walking around

Vancouver. I thought about it every morning when I passed the young man lying in a sleeping bag in front of Starbucks or, later on, diligently sweeping the street in front of a sign detailing his homelessness and mental illness, and requesting help. I thought about it every afternoon when I passed the steadfastly polite man who sold newspapers in front of the grocery store.

Ignoring these neighbors, as Thomas predicted, felt unhealthy. And so I stopped turning away and started engaging. In doing so, I learned that the man who sold the *Megaphone* was named Bob, and that he was one of the original vendors for the newspaper, which was produced and sold by people experiencing homelessness and poverty. I also learned that he took his coffee decaffeinated and black, that he was sixty-six years old, that he enjoyed the work very much but that as he'd aged he needed to work shorter hours. I learned, too, standing on the street with him, that he was a favorite of many in the area, a steady stream of friendly faces who stopped to buy the paper and chat.

One day Bob told me he had an article in *Megaphone* (which I later discovered he sits on the board of directors of). The essay was about his youth in Winnipeg, and also about working various jobs for twenty-five years before selling newspapers. Of all the jobs he'd held, he liked this one the best. He loved our neighborhood, had experienced a lot of kindness here and made lasting friendships. As a result, he wrote, he may never retire.

Standing on the street offering conversation—highlighting the vital role of community with his very presence—Bob showed me the way forward. It was a move to step outside of myself, toward others. A move to acknowledge our inter-connectedness. And it had an outsized impact on my despair.

Our brains are wired for collaboration, cooperation. Serving others gives us a rush of oxytocin, and the sense of belonging so many of us are lacking these days. It goes back, again, to tribal life, and how much we've always depended on each other for survival. And it's why experts often suggest volunteering to people who are suffering.

These days, though, volunteer work has gone the way of other work, becoming intensely bureaucratic, competi-tive and all-consuming. I knew that I needed to get more involved in my community. I needed to be useful, to be connected, to hear other people's stories—and to find a way to step into them in a meaningful way. But applying to become a volunteer was, I soon discovered, exactly like applying for a job.

I filled out lengthy forms, wrote essays, submitted résumés, sat through interviews and sent off for criminal-record checks. I campaigned to contribute—sold myself, my worth, my value, to each and every organization. For a good long while, nobody was buying. This was all so exhausting and, frankly, dispiriting that I almost gave up.

But one organization stood out, for the warmth I was greeted with. I had applied for a paid communications job at Take a Hike, a local alternative high school for vulnerable youth that offered kids classroom instruction, outdoor education, community service opportunities and ongoing therapy. I did not get the job, but the executive director's email informing me of that fact was so friendly and personal—commenting on an interview I'd recently done with author David Sedaris and generally acknowledging me as a human being—that it made me want to get involved anyway. I met with the volunteer coordinator and liked her enormously too. When the next school year started, I began visiting one of the classrooms, a twenty-minute bike ride from my apartment.

The school's approach made sense to me, and fit with all that I'd researched to this point. I had just been reading Dr. Nadine Burke Harris's brilliant book, *The Deepest Well*. Harris is the Vancouver-born founder and CEO of the Center for Youth Wellness in San Francisco (and now the Surgeon General of California). Her work examines how adversity impacts the physical health of her patients; in effect, the science behind what Scottish rapper Loki introduces in his own book.

In *The Deepest Well*, Burke Harris outlines how the study findings are applied at her center. Its strategies are designed to heal the dysregulated stress response in kids. Sleep, therapy, exercise, meditation, yoga and nutrition were all key, but just as important was having healthy adults in their lives who were trustworthy and nurturing. Just as important was the tribe.

At Take a Hike, this model came to living, breathing life. The kids were offered exercise, meditation, therapy, nutrition and education. They went on bike rides and hikes, and on weeklong kayaking excursions. They learned how to snowboard. They took mindfulness breaks. They cooked food together in the classroom kitchen, which was always stocked with groceries. They had counseling sessions. Most significantly, their needs for community were taken seriously. Take a Hike provided students with a supportive place to return to every day, and a circle of caring adults committed to addressing the conditions of their lives. Take a Hike understood that for an individual to thrive, they needed a tribe to take them in.

It was a wondrous, heartening thing to watch, to take part in. And also felt like the most natural thing in the world. Like: of course. Of course they need others. Of course we need others. Of course *I* need others.

It reminded me of a story in *Lost Connections* about the work of South African psychiatrist Derek Summerfield, who had traveled to Cambodia to study the impact of land mines on mental health. Hari went there to interview Dr. Summerfield, and he said villagers had shared a telling story with him.

They said a local man had stepped on a land mine, which blew off his left leg. He was fitted for an artificial leg and continued his work in the rice paddies, becoming more and more distressed. In response, the townspeople came together with the man and his doctors, and talked about his life. They learned that working in rice fields with an artificial leg was incredibly painful and had caused the man to become stressed, dreading his future and losing hope.

The villagers realized that dairy farming would be much less physically taxing, and also wouldn't expose him to painful memories of the accident in the rice fields, and so they all pitched in and bought him a cow. He took to the new profession, and in the ensuing months his despair lifted. To these Cambodians, the solution to depression was, as Hari puts it, "the community, together, empowering the depressed person to change his life."

This was the approach to healing that I was witnessing every day at Take a Hike, and it filled me with energy and optimism.

My first assignment was to interview the teens about their lives for an English essay. We'd talk on tape, transcribe the interviews and then edit them down to a page or two. It was a narrative of where they'd been in life, what had changed, how they felt now.

The kids were, I soon discovered, eager to tell their stories. In spite of formidable challenges, they sat in front of me, hopeful, bright-eyed, determined. Some told me what a difference the wilderness trips had made—how simple things were out there in the wild, how in-the-moment they felt, how much they learned about life from setting up tents and cooking food. Others talked about what it meant to suddenly have a circle of close, supportive peers and adults. For some, this was the first time in their lives that they'd experienced this.

We do everything together, one seventeen-year-old told me. We eat together and go on trips together. It's like a family, he said. I can have a horrible day at home, and then I come here and it changes my mood. By the end of the day, I feel okay again.

As I sat typing away in the corner, transcribing interviews—moved by the kids' tenacity, their humor, their unique aptitudes for storytelling or writing or interviewing, their *specialness*—I watched as they all reassured and comforted one another. They were incredibly tactile, forever hugging each other. They were still teenagers, of course, burping loudly, making jokes and wrestling around, knocking over chairs. But there was a total absence of scorn among them. It was as if there was an unspoken agreement that they'd experienced enough of that already.

At this school, these kids felt seen, heard, appreciated. And they thrived in this atmosphere of love and respect, in spite of ongoing and very real stresses. (Take a Hike had a graduation average of 88 percent, higher than the provincial average of 84 percent—and way higher than the alternative-school average of 34 percent.)

Talking to teachers, following students' progress, recording their stories, applauding their triumphs, filled me with joy. In affirming their mattering, I felt like I mattered too.

Profound healing is possible. Probable, even, under the right conditions. But in order to foster these conditions, we have to stop telling the story of healing as one of individual triumph, and start acknowledging the role of the tribe.

We have to focus on what we must do for each other, instead of what we must do for ourselves.

I was reminded of this when I went to see the attorney, author, TV host and former presidential advisor Van Jones speak at a forum on the future of work, hosted by Simon Fraser University, my alma mater. Jones was appearing with Anne-Marie Slaughter of the New America think tank (and the viral *Atlantic* article "Why Women Still Can't Have It All"). The conversation was fascinating, touching on everything from the pressures of automation to the need for a more diverse workforce.

Jones argued, and rightly so, that we were wasting so much talent, allowing so much human potential to go untapped. To illustrate his point, he referred to a man called Shaka Senghor at MIT's Media Lab. Senghor, he told us, frequently posed challenges to MIT students such as making a tattoo gun or a hot plate from random materials like batteries and dental floss. When the students—some of the so-called brightest minds in America—failed to solve these challenges, Senghor pointed out that such engineering feats were accomplished every day by prisoners. The idea was to highlight how many brilliant people are wasting away in prison. But also: how different skills are viewed in different contexts. What's seen as trouble-making in prison is viewed as genius at MIT.

In talking about all this, Jones touched briefly on Senghor's biography. Senghor, he said, was convicted of murder as a teenager in Detroit and sent to prison for almost two decades, seven years of which he'd spent in solitary confinement. Spending even fourteen days in the hole can cause mental health breakdowns, Jones reminded us. But during those long, painful years, Senghor had experienced an awakening instead. "Somehow, in those circumstances, he reached inside himself and he transformed himself in a way that was so remarkable that by the time I met him he was out of prison and was a fellow at MIT," Jones explained.

How had his healing taken place? What had made his radical transformation possible? I wanted to know. So I decided to find Senghor and ask him.

As I worked to track him down, I read his *New York Times*–bestselling autobiography (remarkable), watched his TED Talk (1.5 million views and counting), streamed his Oprah interview (he cried, she cried, I cried). Clicking on clips from his recent appearance at President Obama's My Brother's Keeper Rising! event, I marveled at this man's journey. What a leap to make in one lifetime, from the block and the prison to the presidential podium.

When word came that he would sit down with me, I booked a ticket to Los Angeles, where Senghor now lives and writes and works in criminal justice reform. Until weeks before, he had served as the executive director of the Anti-Recidivism Coalition.

Landing at LAX, my shuttle drove through South Central, surrounded by the pastel hues of crumbling corner stores, walls adorned with colorful murals, palm trees set against a hazy sky. Homes with barred windows, empty front porches and yards.

An elderly woman in a Dodgers T-shirt sat in the front of the van chatting amiably with our driver, who delivered her to the front door of her impeccably kept house, gallantly helping her out. Ten minutes earlier, he'd announced to the rest of us, "We're in South Central, home of . . ." His words hung in the air. "Hip-hop," he finally finished, grinning proudly. "I was wondering where you were going with that," the old woman had said, laughing.

I checked into the Ace Hotel downtown, which housed the ornate 1927 Spanish Gothic United Artists Theatre, with its vaulted ceilings and mirrored dome and mythic murals of stars. The building was situated on a strip of Broadway famous for its dilapidated Old Hollywood theaters, seemingly all in the process of being restored. It was a neighborhood, now, too, of hipsters whizzing past on motorized scooters, and shiny mid-century modern furniture boutiques coexisting with jewelry shops advertising "hip-hop gold" and crammed snack shacks and hustlers calling out.

After a late lunch, as I walked back to my hotel from a taqueria, a shirtless, shoeless young black man with open sores on his face paced the corner, looking feverish, petrified, out of his mind. As I passed, he was barked at by some sort of city official. "Get out of here," the man shouted, his voice thick with cruelty, with scorn. "Move on, get. Go!" The look on this young man's face was one of pure terror as he scurried away, but then it morphed into a kind of agony. "I'm not *doing* anything," he howled in pain, hurling his agitated body about, as if to literally shake off the indignity.

Back at my hotel, I numbed the sadness I felt with a peach cobbler and an Ali Wong Netflix special. The day's light finally fading, I gazed out at the glittering towers of downtown L.A. and wondered what the hell we were all going to do.

———

The next afternoon, I found myself in Koreatown, in the lobby of an upscale building, buzzed up to a high-level floor, where I navigated a tranquil hallway to Senghor's front door. He opened it, smiling, and ushered me into his apartment, which was airy and bright, with high ceilings and floor-to-ceiling windows that looked out over the city. In his living room were framed album covers: Jay-Z, Nas, Slick Rick, Kanye. On his sleek kitchen counter, near where we settled across from each other on stools, was a stack of books and a collection of photos with family, and one with Oprah. His home felt peaceful, relaxing. Senghor himself exuded calm, kindness.

He'd grown up on the east side of Detroit, he began, in a middle-class neighborhood, in a home that looked, from the outside, like a good one. His father worked for the state and was in the Air Force Reserve; his mother was a homemaker. They were the first black family on the block. He had lovely neighbors, he said, including an Italian family who cultivated peach trees and always shared their food, and an Irish woman who was famous for her pear preserves. As a young boy, Senghor was an honor roll student with dreams of becoming a doctor.

At some point, though, white flight took hold. Factories closed. New neighbors moved in, old bonds dissolved. Crack arrived on the streets. And Senghor's parents' marriage ended.

The physical abuse he'd long experienced at the hands of his mother escalated, and she eventually told him he'd have to go live with his father. "I interpreted that as there was something wrong with me," Senghor told me. The violent beatings were one thing, but the things she said to him were something else—cruel, dehumanizing. He craved the acceptance of his mother, he said, craved her love.

He struggled with this, and then at thirteen he decided to run away, soon finding himself homeless. "I thought that one of my friends' parents would say, 'Oh, there's this smart kid, he deserves to have a safe, healthy space to live,'" Senghor said. "And that just wasn't the reality. Sadly, it is not the reality for a lot of kids who end up in these spaces.

"I internalized that rejection as well," he added. "Like, *Something must be wrong with me. Nobody wants me.*" It took a long time, he said, to undo that psychological damage.

Eventually, local drug dealers took him in, offering food, shelter, clothing and safety in exchange for manning the local crack spot. He went from being a naïve child to being deeply immersed in drug culture, eventually experiencing all of the horrors that come with that life. His childhood friend was murdered; he himself was beaten close to death. He became addicted to crack for a stretch.

And then, at seventeen, he got shot. "It completely changed me," Senghor said. He became anxious, afraid, alert to every sudden movement, every approach of every car. Forever aware of his mortality. And still just a young kid.

"I think that's one of the things that oftentimes gets left out of the conversation when it comes to inner-city gun violence," he reflected. "These are very young kids who are experiencing these high levels of gun violence. And there is no space—even going through the hospital—where anyone thinks about it through the lens of trauma."

In other words, as he points out in his talks, nobody hugs you, comforts you or counsels you. Nobody lets you know that you are going to be okay. The hospitals just patch you up and send you back to the same streets you just came from.

Senghor often wonders what would have happened if someone had intervened at that point. Offered him someone to talk to, a place to work through his feelings.

Instead, back in his community, terrified, he began carrying a gun. And fourteen months later, in a drug-related exchange, he fired it, ending a life.

Senghor found himself in county jail a month before his nineteenth birthday, now exposed to even more extreme levels of violence. Facing a long sentence—at an age where most kids can't think past the next week—he rebelled, getting into trouble, running schemes and raging against authority. Experiencing racial antagonism from guards. He spent a lot of time in solitary confinement, seven years in total.

As we talked quietly, in the background we could hear sirens, helicopters. Reminders of the streets below, away from this oasis of calm in the clouds.

Senghor was fortunate in that some of the older guys in prison saw something in him that was redeemable, he said. He began reading a lot, trying to expand his mind, but he was still caught up in prison culture, still navigating its daily violence. "You become numb to it," he told me. "Every day when the cell door opens up, you don't know if there's going to be a conflict or not, but you've got to be prepared for it."

The mentality in prison valorized this violence, validating a man's worst instincts instead of his best. It was hard to find a way to step outside of this.

One turning point came in the hole, in the form of a letter from his eleven-year-old son. The young boy had just found out what landed his father in prison. He reminded his father that Jesus teaches us not to kill, and asked him to pray. Senghor was floored; he had never considered that his son would see him as a murderer.

"There was just something about hearing that from my son, and realizing that not only had I robbed him of a father—by being taken away before he was even born, out of the womb—but I also had created this idea in his mind," Senghor said. "I knew he would see me as a monster if I didn't do anything about it.

"I didn't want to go through the rest of my life being shaped by that moment in time, and having that be the only representation of myself that he had access to."

And so Senghor dove into autobiographies, looking to see how other people had overcome adversity, how other people had healed. "I really want to learn how people have arrived at the spaces they've arrived at," he told me. "What were the practices? What were the things they learned on the journey? What were their fears? What were their failures? What were their accomplishments? What were the moments when they've had to discover courage that they didn't know they had? What were the moments where they had to be more resilient than they were willing to give themselves credit for? Those things are really intriguing to me. I've always loved reading other people's autobiographies and memoirs, and putting myself in other people's shoes."

Eventually, he began to write, pouring it all—his life, his joy, his pain—out onto the page.

Another letter had arrived, too, this one from the god-mother of the man he had killed, telling Senghor this man's story, this family's pain. But also forgiving him, telling him that she loved him, no matter the circumstances, and launching a correspondence that continued for years. "You may think your life is a mess," she wrote in one letter, "but you are special. And God is able to pick you up and help you go on. He can clean up your messes, no matter what they are." She believed in transformation, and she believed it was possible for Senghor.

He was finally able to fully comprehend what he had done. Senghor eventually wrote the man he'd killed a letter, expressing how sorry he was for taking his life, for taking him away from his family. And vowing that his life would not be in vain, that Senghor would find a way for this man's story—their story, their shared pain—to help other people.

After that, Senghor was able to start forgiving himself. And forgiving all those who had hurt him, understanding that they too had been hurt.

Reestablishing love in his life, he began to let love in. There had, in fact, been a lot of people who supported him—his father, older prisoners, even some staff—people who saw who he was, heard him, appreciated him. Encouraged his natural leadership skills.

One man, Tom, stood out. He was a recreation supervisor Senghor had worked for in the prison—"one of the most incredible human beings I've ever met."

Tom extended all kinds of kindnesses to him. When it was hot in the prison, he would request Senghor, getting him out of the cell for a few hours, whether there was work to do or not. During the holiday season, he'd bring pizza in for the prisoners. His wife baked the inmates cookies. And when Senghor wrote a piece for the prison newspaper, Tom praised his storytelling and took the piece home to his wife, who worked in publishing, reporting back that she said Senghor had raw talent and should keep writing.

"Those early moments of being affirmed as a human being for something positive, that meant a lot to me," he told me. "It took years for me to really understand how much it meant. When I wrote my first book, the first person I thought about was Tom, saying, 'I believe that you can become a serious writer.'"

After Senghor was transferred to another prison, he lost contact with Tom for fourteen years, since staff were not allowed to befriend prisoners. But when Senghor got out, and began mentoring youth, he wanted to express his gratitude. "I just wanted to let him know that he impacted me in a way that my life is now impacting other people," he said.

He called up Tom, who promptly invited Senghor up for a college football game. Tom welcomed him into his circle of correction officer friends, who were tailgating and drinking beer. He later invited him up to his lake house for the weekend and visited Senghor at his apartment.

Fellow prisoners, too, played a big role in Senghor's transformation. He used to run a class, Houses of Healing, for other inmates, he told me. "It was really interesting— when I proposed the class, the administrators were like, 'Nobody is going to show up for that, men don't talk about how they feel,'" he said. But they were wrong. The men did come, and they did open up. Senghor wrote discussion questions. *When was the first time that you were physically hit?* "You would see these grown men just break down, and talk about the first time they were struck, and then the depth of the abuse they experienced," he said.

"Through that process, I realized that most of the men that I encountered while I was in prison were just broken little boys," he continued. "And that they had come through these very tough circumstances, high levels of abuse. Gun violence, drug violence, sexual abuse. And they were trying to find the language to articulate what that was." Because of low literacy rates, that language was often violence—"but you could really sense that there was this deep, deep desire to turn things around, and to stop the suffering."

Senghor believes in the power of storytelling, which fosters, he said, deeper human connection, compassion, empathy. He sees it as powerful not just on a personal level, but on a systemic level, too. A lot of the things that separate us, whether racism or sexism, are rooted in individual fears, he said. When you create space for people to acknowledge these fears openly, it can be life-changing.

"That's what I think the role of the storyteller is," Senghor said. "To create a space for honest conversations. Once you get to that space, that's where transformation becomes possible."

And he sees these kinds of transformations all the time, he said. In other prisoners, in the youth he works with, in the men who line up to talk to him after events. There's always this awkward dance, he said, where they ask if they can have a hug. Men crave this, he said, this ability to express love in a healthy way.

"The story of love is one that has been told to men, at least in America, in a way that's completely unhealthy," Senghor said. "We've been told that it's weak, that it's weak to be vulnerable. But in reality, love is empowering."

If solitary taught him anything, he said, it was how much we all need life-affirming contact. When he was in the hole, there were long stretches where the only physical contact he experienced was officers handcuffing him or patting him down. To survive this, he said, you had to detach from your body. And so healing required a reestablishment of physical affection, of open, healthy expressions of love.

Love, he thought, was ultimately about acceptance. About being accepted for our differences, and also for our similarities.

Back at home in Vancouver, I walked the streets, playing the audio from the interview in my headphones, listening, absorbing. Sitting in the park near my apartment, Senghor's voice in my ears, I was struck by how much we had in common.

There were the obvious things, of course. We both loved hip-hop, had both started our publishing careers writing album reviews for local newspapers. We were both voracious readers, particularly of nonfiction, of memoir; both fascinated by other people's lives. We both adored food, and associated a lot of our happiest childhood memories with it.

But there were deeper commonalities, too. We had both, at around the age of thirteen, experienced the rejection of a parent, a rejection that had had practical and emotional consequences that had shaped much of our lives. We both held within us that child who'd wondered, *Why can't you see me?*

We'd both, as young people, been forced to confront our mortality in pretty dramatic ways, too. And, at critical moments, had had to face our fears alone. He'd been shot and I'd had cancer, extremely different circumstances, but the result was the same—we'd both been stripped of the feeling of safety, of faith in the world. To restore it, we'd had to go on a journey of learning and growth. And of seeking out deeper human connection. In the process, we'd been shown tremendous kindness. And had gotten to experience the wider world in miraculous ways.

Ultimately, we had both sought out story as a way of transforming ourselves, and then worked to offer this tool to the world, to other people in need of transformation.

Senghor's healing was an expression of all this—of the

power of human connection, of love. As all healings are. As mine was. And is.

One drizzly Friday morning, I found myself in a trendy café in Gastown, on the edges of Vancouver's Downtown Eastside, talking with Kari Bergrud, the master's student from the coaching workshop.

Thinking back to the validation exercise that was so powerful for both of us, Bergrud marveled at what ordinary people were able to do for each other. "It's not like it's this skilled, professional group of people that know how to read into and observe others," she said. "It was an arbitrary group that just facilitated a space that gave you the time to do it. It made me think maybe this is more natural than we give it credit for. We've made so many of these things professional—if you are a counselor or an inspirational speaker, you can see this. But no, literally everyone can. This is a human skill, not a professional skill."

We needed to do this regularly in our workplaces, she thought, and in our families and friendships. Validation is a form of connection, of noticing. It's a way of saying: *I see you, I hear you, I appreciate you.*

And in this context, extraordinary things happened. Bergrud pointed to our exchange in the last sharing circle, and others like it that day. In those moments, she felt herself connecting to others on an almost spiritual level. There was no way that people should know exactly what we needed to hear, when we most needed to hear it—and yet, somehow, they did. "There are things outside of ourselves that connect us to one another, that we can't see and don't understand," she reflected. "That science has yet to explain to us. But that are very prevalent and very real. We are much more intertwined than we give ourselves freedom to express, or experience."

Bergrud said she'd learned a lot about the power of community from working on the Downtown Eastside, where people regularly took back public space, parking their lawn chairs out on the street, and continually watched out for each other, sharing food, offering up compliments freely.

She'd learned a lot from her church, too, from showing up every week somewhere and seeing the same people, and doing the same thing together. This kind of close community doesn't have to be religious, she said. There are knitting groups, and Meetups for everyone from wiener-dog owners to vintage-BMW enthusiasts. There are so many ways to find people that you have things in common with.

But also, she said, there is something really lovely about finding people you have nothing in common with. "At church," she said, "I have a fleet of two-year-olds that I know, even though I am a single woman with no children. That's magic. And I also have a little granny who prays for me all the time. That's also magic. And I have nothing in common with either of these two groups, except for the fact that we're in the same space together.

"I think that's something I appreciate about the Downtown Eastside," she continued. "There's a lot of people that we have nothing in common with each other, in one sense. And then in another sense, we actually have a lot of things in common with each other. They're just hidden."

CHAPTER EIGHT

The Home

Things were shifting. But I was, after all that, still crying every day. It was monsoon season in Vancouver, dark and gloomy and wet. People were hibernating. Meanwhile, freelancing had slowed down, my rent had just been raised for the third time, and my savings were gone. I had too much time to fill, and no idea how to fill it. I trudged down the street every day in the rain, tracing a loop from couch to coffee shop, drenched, solitary, listless.

Still, my thinking about what was required to heal had radically changed, and I wanted to test this new theory out. Would my anxiety and despair fall away if I was part of a close, loving community? One where I felt useful and necessary?

I wanted to see how I would feel in the middle of a busy household, in a close-knit family with lots of kids and a number of relatives, in a deeply communal society. What would it feel like to transport myself into a ready-made tribe?

My brother, in one of our daily phone calls, offered me exactly that (plus a plane ticket). He lived in Dublin with his Irish wife and their two small children, among an extended family of roughly one hundred, most of whom were within ten minutes' driving distance of one another. Eight months prior, his wife had lost her father to cancer, so the four of them had moved back in with her mother. I joined this intergenerational household, which also included one of my sister-in-law's nephews, aged twenty, who was back and forth from Donegal for school. My sister-in-law's sister lived down the road with her husband and a large brood of boys. There were always people coming and going, always a kettle on. At no point in the day was I ever alone.

I immediately found myself part of a complex web of meals and chores and routines. In the morning, my sweet niece and nephew would wake me, either by singing quietly in the next room or else by shouting that it was time for everyone to get up. Some mornings, after we got them off to school, my brother, sister-in-law and I would drive to a local farm restaurant for breakfast. Other mornings, I would eat porridge with the children and then take the tram into the city center to work. After writing for a few hours at a packed café (which, my brother pointed out, had a strict "no laptops" policy on weekends to encourage community), I would head back in time to eat a late lunch with the kids. I'd pass the rest of the afternoon and evening drinking tea, coloring, eating the beautiful vegan meals my sister-in-law prepared, baking cookies, reading *Anne of Green Gables* to my niece, talking books with my sister-in-law's mother and attending the yoga classes that my sister-in-law taught. Even then, in Shavasana—the most meditative, and therefore the most private of poses—I was never alone, as my sister-in-law would pad over in the darkness to rub essential oils into my temples.

I visited my niece's school with my sister-in-law's

mother, and felt my heart swell at my niece's delight. Seated on my lap during show-and-tell, she beamed proudly as I told her class the story of how her Irish mother and Canadian father had met, years ago, in Australia. Fridays, her school day kicked off with a dance party in the gymnasium. Her mother, her father and I stood at the back, laughing and awkwardly following the steps on a giant screen as children from Pakistan and Poland, Malaysia and China, all jumped up and down together to the theme song for *Ghostbusters*.

On the weekends, I went to the kids' gymnastics classes, and we made pancakes to serve to their parents. Or else we'd all drive to the fishing village of Howth to walk the rugged cliffs at dawn, gazing out at the Irish Sea, surrounded by teams of cyclists. I cooked my brother's favorites, lasagna and shepherd's pie. Drank coffee and talked with him. Strolled the cobbled streets of Temple Bar with my sister-in-law and her mother and my niece, stopping for tea and treats. My nephew, meanwhile, took to calling me into the bathroom, gleefully bestowing the honor of wiping his bottom.

It was, needless to say, a level of interdependence that I hadn't experienced in decades. My whole being relaxed. I slept deeply, contentedly, despite the fact that many nights my three-year-old nephew shouted for his soother, waking the entire household. Other nights, my six-year-old niece would sleep with me, sprawled out across the double bed or else nuzzled into my side, her arms around my neck, her tiny hands pressed against my face. I was surrounded by people, by family, by love.

My despair evaporated the day I arrived. The rumination, the anxious thoughts, the loneliness—it was all gone.
This, even though I was facing extreme financial pressure,
not even sure how I would pay the next month's rent. In
the embrace of the Irish tribe, the stress dissipated as a
mist clears when the sun rises in the sky.

Had it even been foggy out? I could hardly remember.

The concept of home is a tricky one in the twenty-first
century. For those of us born with Western passports, there
are now endless options for how and where to live. But this
mobility is a gift and a curse. Rising rents, stagnant salaries
and precarious work often make such relocations compul-
sory, scattering people across the globe, forever chasing the
multinationals, on the hunt for a decent standard of living.
As globalization spreads, we of fortunate birth fan out, following the jobs from one country to the next, losing each
other as we go.

Many of my peers were constantly on the move.
Singapore. London. Seoul. Hong Kong. Dubai. Moving
apartments, moving jobs, moving cities. Moving from relationship to relationship. Moving friend groups. There was
little stability for any of us. Nothing we could hold to, or
build on. Nothing we could call our own.

Over tea, my mother-in-law told me about a very different way of life. She'd been born in the tenements of
Dublin, where families as large as thirteen all crowded
into a single room, living without heat or running water.
Her father, a religious man, corresponded with Mother

Teresa. When the government built council housing in the suburbs, her extended clan migrated to the outskirts of Dublin, where they've remained, eventually buying houses in adjoining estates. Now, grieving her husband, she was surrounded by an army of siblings, cousins, nieces and nephews, in-laws, children and grandchildren—a huge solace, she said. She'd been with her husband fifty years when he passed away; they'd lived out their entire lives in this twenty-mile radius.

In contrast, since I'd moved out at seventeen, I had probably lived at twenty different addresses, in three different cities. More if you counted brief stays in New York and Bangkok. I longed to settle down, put down roots, and had tried to do so in Vancouver. But the economy was not cooperating.

During the weeks I spent in Dublin writing, I contemplated my next move. Would I return to Vancouver and continue pushing the boulder up the hill? Watching my rent steadily tick up and my freelance rates fall, waiting for the point (swiftly approaching) when I'd be forced to leave the city? Would I return to Toronto? What about the land of my mother's birth, London, England—or would Brexit preclude this? Perhaps I should join my brother and his family in Ireland, somehow scraping together the sky-high rent for a studio apartment in Dublin?

Any way I thought about it, the puzzle pieces refused to fit together. There were too many moving parts, and always a major structural issue to contend with, delaying decisions indefinitely. And so I felt homeless. As in: I had no feeling of home. It was hard to envision any kind of future.

I began to wonder about this. There must be others grappling with this phenomenon. How did the nomads of the twenty-first century address this desire for a more solid, rooted life? How did they stop living in the weightless present, stop swiping left, stop hopping planes, forever dwelling in the liminal space between contracts, sublets, time zones? Trading permanence for one shimmering mirage after another, always slightly out of reach. How did they find their way back home?

This is how my sister-in-law and I came to be standing at an iron gate at the end of a narrow dirt road, far out in the Irish countryside. We were looking for Mark Boyle, the *Guardian* columnist famous for swearing off money and technology, who was now living on a small acreage near the town of Loughrea, outside Galway. When we came upon the fence, we'd been driving for several hours through miles of picturesque rolling hills, complete with grazing sheep. Now the satnav was out of ideas. The road had come to an abrupt end, and the car was surrounded by ankle-deep mud.

"Should we get out and walk?" I asked my sister-in-law.

She pointed to her white sneakers. "I'm wearing my Guccis," she said with a laugh. Ideal footwear to meet the Moneyless Man, we agreed. I got out and walked a few minutes. There were no houses in the distance. Since Boyle didn't text or email, or even have a landline, there had been no way to let him know we were coming. And, now that we were here, there was no way to tell him we were lost.

I had checked one of Boyle's books out of the library

some five years before, when I was living in Toronto and working in radio. *The Moneyless Man* was about the period that he'd given up money, and it was chock-full of the kind of practical considerations that readers were bound to wonder about. Before retiring the use of cash at the age of twenty-nine, Boyle had sold his houseboat and used his life savings to launch a barter website that had taken off, making the "freeconomy" trendy. The site was founded on the principle of paying things forward. People did favors, or gifted items, without any expectation of something in return. Money is to giving and receiving what prostitution is to sex, Boyle was fond of saying, in his book, in interviews, in a TED Talk.

He began to locate his sense of security in his social circle as opposed to his bank account, and it felt good. As he watched the freeconomy movement take off, Boyle decided to take the experiment to its logical conclusion and refrain from using cash altogether. To celebrate, he hosted a giant party, completely gratis, serving food that had been foraged or sourced from dumpsters.

He then found a free twelve-by-six-foot caravan on the Internet and arranged to volunteer on a farm near Bristol, England, in exchange for land to park it on. He grew his own food, cycled everywhere, installed solar panels to power his laptop and built a compostable toilet. He bartered for anything he couldn't buy. Or else made it himself, as was the case with a pair of flip-flops he'd fashioned from an old abandoned tire.

I'd been fascinated by his story back in Toronto, in part because he'd been a pretty ordinary guy before all of this. He'd grown up on a working-class estate on the edge of the Atlantic, in the coastal outpost of Ballyshannon, the oldest town in Ireland. He lived on a street of eighty houses (with one phone among them), in the house his father was born in. After doing an economics degree at university in Galway, he moved to England and wound up working in the organic food industry, in the process becoming acquainted with our looming planetary disaster. Ten years later, he was a vegan environmentalist and had concluded that the best way to resist the madness of modern life was to stop using paper currency. As with all the counterculture folks I was learning about, I was struck by the extraordinary lengths such a regular guy would go to to resist twenty-first-century corporate capitalism.

I was also struck by how much his example appealed to others. Anyone that I mentioned the Moneyless Man to was instantly intrigued. And his efforts were now rippling out, sparking similar movements in far-flung places. Like Vancouver, for instance, where a new barter Meetup group had just formed.

I was struck, too, by how much it appealed to me, living as I did back then in a shiny Toronto condo, donning cocktail dresses and dining at trendy restaurants. Boyle's life, I think, represented a simpler way, a mode of living that could, maybe, connect me more. To nature, to food, to place and to others.

Now in his late thirties, Boyle was apparently using money again, in small doses. (And had stopped being a vegan, to eat a hyper-local Irish diet that included fish.) Ironically, he later told me, his book about giving up money had sold well, and he'd used that capital to set up a project in rural Ireland. The cost of land is one of the main obstacles to people experimenting with this kind of life, he said, and so he wanted to remove that obstacle. He bought three acres and a farmhouse, built an off-grid tiny house for himself and his partner, and constructed a cob-and-cordwood hostel, the Happy Pig, where people could gather rent-free and live off the land.

He'd now lived there for almost six years, the past two without any technology. His smallholding had no electricity, gas, running water, cars or Wi-Fi.

The problem, of course, was finding it. It was starting to look like Boyle didn't particularly want to be found. As we circled the area, I was forced to ask myself a pressing question: What would I have done before smartphones?

Talk to people, I realized with a laugh. So we drove until we found a stone cottage that was being renovated by builders. Did they know the Moneyless Man, perchance? They did not. But, these men said, they had friends who might. One of the builders called someone, and then he got in his car and led us to the spot his friend directed him to. The same fence, unfortunately. But at least we knew we were on the right track. And now we'd met some friendly builders, too.

Eventually I went door-knocking, which led to some lovely chats with elderly neighbors, in doorways and out kitchen windows—ten years ago, we'd have been invited in for tea, my sister-in-law noted, before the rash of rural break-ins—and one finally sent us to the right place. I rapped on a farmhouse door, and miracle of miracles,

Boyle stood before me, bearded, barefoot, a bit puzzled by my presence. But game to talk.

It turned out he was just putting finishing touches on some work for his new book, *The Way Home*, a philosophical treatise on living without technology. He showed us to the cottage he'd built himself, a whimsical hobbit house with a woodstove, where we waited for him. After he finished seeing to his business, he joined us. He'd just baked bread, and offered us some.

We sat on a wooden bench, gazing around at shelves packed with books on camping and woodcraft and Irish fishing, survival, self-sufficiency and gardening. There were framed quotes from Thoreau lying about, and an axe, and a bowl of salad greens he'd harvested. Plus a copy of Kevin Kelly's *What Technology Wants*. To the side of the cabin, there was a vegetable garden, brimming with stalks even in the chill of early January. I asked for a bathroom, and Boyle said I was very welcome to pee under a tree, or use the composting toilet in the hostel. I opted for the tree.

That summer, he told us, he'd parted ways with his partner Kirsty—a classic Sagittarian, he said fondly—who was intent on travel and adventure. She was gone now, along with everyone in the hostel. He was feeling frustrated by how transient the community had become. You had to keep starting over, rebuilding time and time again, he said. Nobody wanted to commit to anything.

He was staring down forty, and wanted something more stable for this next stage of life.

People would come and stay awhile in the hostel, he

told us, and then they'd move on. I pictured these people—
including "a yogi, two sailors, an anarchist, a circus per-
former and a musician," I later read in Boyle's book—sleeping
in the hand-built bunks, drinking Boyle's homemade cider
at the free bar, leafing through books by Naomi Klein and
Paul Hawken from communal bookshelves, perhaps offering to help out with the wormery, or the compost heap, or
the firewood. Or a thousand other invisible farm tasks I
couldn't fathom. Then, I imagined these same people packing it in, discouraged by the hardships of this life, craving
hot showers, flush toilets, Instagram. Lured away by the
sparkling realm of the Internet, the promise of endless
excitement, romance, novelty, distraction.

Even here, in rural Ireland, Boyle could not escape the
same tides of change that I myself was struggling with.
Even in the middle of nowhere, at an address that didn't
seem to register on Google Maps, bulldozers were ever-
present. Pubs were closing, and post offices. Locals were
becoming less and less connected.

"I need a tribe," Boyle said, shaking his head.

Even so, living without technology had proven so rich and
rewarding, he never wanted to go back. It had forced him
to be present in his immediate life, Boyle explained, without interruption or interference. His engagement with the
natural world had grown exponentially. He never wanted
to own another phone.

His main motivation in the beginning was ecological, he
said. He knew from studying economics that industrialism

destroyed the environment. He pointed to a recent report from the World Wildlife Fund; in the past forty years, 60 percent of wildlife had disappeared. "If I'm campaigning about not wiping out life on planet Earth, then I need to construct a life for myself that isn't based on the fruits of that system," Boyle said. "Nothing else makes any sense to me. I can't be arguing for or against industrialism, and still have all the products and still want to use them all." He knew his one-man ban was unlikely to make much of a difference, but for him it was a question of dignity. I couldn't help but respect this.

He had other powerful cultural and personal reasons for withdrawing, too. These gadgets were a massive social experiment, he believed, the consequences of which we could not yet know. He saw their impact in rising rates of anxiety and depression, and children growing up with no connection to the natural world. A recent book he'd read from British author Robert Macfarlane, *Landmarks*, tracked the changes to the *Oxford Junior Dictionary*. Words like *bluebell* and *acorn* were being replaced by techno-terms like *cut-and-paste*. It horrified him to think of children growing up not knowing what a conker was. (A horse chestnut, as far as I can tell.)

I don't think Boyle had read *The Age of Surveillance Capitalism* by Shoshana Zuboff then, because it wasn't yet out, but his thinking anticipated so many later conversations I had about it, in Vancouver and New York and Toronto. That following summer, it was as if everyone I knew, and casually met, and interviewed, had suddenly arrived at Boyle's conclusion simultaneously.

Now that he'd given up tech, he told me, his interactions with people were a lot more meaningful. He visited friends and family face-to-face, wrote letters. He'd slowed down a lot, and relished this new way of being. "It's not the fast-paced, got-to-be-productive thing that it used to be," he said. "My time is now spent going down to collect spring water, growing some food, cycling to the post office sometimes, going fishing for the afternoon, reading in the evening."

And writing, of course, in pencil, and often by candle-light. When I returned to Canada and his publicist emailed me his book, I was struck by how timeless the prose felt. The elements felt like a living, breathing reality, characters in themselves. The natural world came alive on the page, with its sea buckthorn berries and burdock root, its icy Siberian winds and deluges of rain, its orchestra of swallows. Boyle skinned a deer he found dead on the road, cycled to the local pub to meet a fellow writer for a standing weekly date, built a rocket stove so he could make tea, washed his dishes in wood ash and water. Thought deeply about the world, and his place in it.

The book had been written by hand, but the time eventually came when it had to be submitted to the publisher. So Boyle had been forced to break his tech ban, sitting in front of the computer twelve hours a day, typing up the manuscript. He would stagger away from his desk every night, feeling drugged, dissociated. Afterward, it took days for the landscape to return to him.

Not long after that, Boyle told us, he'd had a visit from a friend who was working on rewilding projects, allowing land to return to wilderness. This friend knew the BBC presenter Bruce Parry, who had a show called *Tribe* that Boyle thought I should check out. (Back within Googling range, I discovered that Parry had just made a film about the Penan.)

Parry was apparently thinking of starting his own tribe, in Wales. People could come and live off the land for free, Boyle said, but you had to make a serious commitment. You had to agree to stay for the rest of your life. "He's realized that the tribe is the only way forward, ecologically speaking and socially speaking," Boyle said. "A lot of people are really interested, but none of them want to commit for life."

Many of our attempts at tribal life these days are unnatural, Boyle went on. We are lacking familial bonds, shared history and a sense of belonging, even the kind of deep closeness that emerges over years. Boyle had lived in a number of intentional communities, and funnily enough, he said, it was the religious ones that seemed to last. There had to be a strong common purpose for communities to sustain, he'd concluded.

With all this talk of tribes, my sister-in-law pointed out that I'd traveled to visit a tribe myself. And so, sitting in this cabin in rural Ireland, I told Boyle the story of Borneo, of my friendship with Mutang, of getting sick and regretting not having been to visit him, about all the flights and buses and trains and propeller planes and boats upriver, about finally finding myself at Mutang's Penan village. Finding that he had dreamt I was coming.

"That's a beautiful story," Boyle said. "The more I learn about the non-human world, and the human world too, those stories aren't surprising anymore. There's so many different levels on which the world operates that we can't tap into anymore." But some people were keeping those understandings of the world alive, he said with a smile.

He often wondered how much he'd lost, living in this culture. How many of the old ways we were forgetting. It was affecting our mental health, and our sense of place. "We don't feel at home in the world anymore," he said.

East London, the following day, felt like a universe away. Transported from the subdued green hues of the Irish countryside, with its mud and muck and birdsong, I walked the paved streets of the East End. It was raining, the sky gray and gloomy, the streets Technicolor. I walked past women in printed hijabs, vendors hawking cheap dresses and plastic children's toys, butcher racks of brightly plumed pheasants, not yet plucked. I walked past Colombian coffee shops with names like Hermanos. And social venture boutiques, where you were encouraged to WhatsApp the Kenyan artisans who'd handwoven the baskets on display. There were yoga studios offering full sensory immersion, with ultra-magnetic light and sound and aromatherapy designed to support circadian rhythms, where people took time out of the busy workday to meet on the mat. And juice windows where you could share the intimate details of your biology and receive carefully crafted remedies for a cold, the flu, jet lag.

Everywhere I went, people wanted to talk. At the Beehive, a not-for-profit café located in the Bethnal Green Mission Church, the barista, a tried-and-true East Londoner named Rich, told me how they planned to offer training to vulnerable youth in the area, schooling them in the art of coffee culture. Rich sent me to a local pizzeria, Sodo, located down a winding graffiti alley. There, over a Margherita pie with sourdough crust, the young Italian server told me about another local gathering place, the Love Shack, described online as "a plastic-free patch of vegan paradise in the heart of Hackney"—part plant-based eatery, part event space. The mission there was simple: "to stop wasting time lining the pockets of people that don't give a fuck and . . . make the world a little less shit by simply making a really nice place where people can come and hang out for a bit."

Alone in my hotel room that night, I listened to the sirens and watched the latest Brexit developments on a giant TV, and thought about Britain's minister for loneliness, appointed in 2018 by Theresa May to curb the epidemic of social isolation, a state which is apparently worse for your health than smoking fifteen cigarettes a day. I remembered George Monbiot's famed essay in *The Guardian* proclaiming our era the age of loneliness. "We are shaped, to a greater extent than almost any other species, by contact with others," he wrote. "The age we are entering, in which we exist apart, is unlike any that has gone before."

I wondered if the social venture efforts I'd observed that day in East London—reassuringly visible without even scratching the surface of the city—chipped away at any of this. I wondered if they helped people feel more at home in their neighborhood, their country, their lives.

—

Two Tube rides and a double-decker bus later, I was seated in another café, this time in the suburb of North London, waiting for *Lost Connections* author Johann Hari, who'd coincidentally just undergone his own digital detox, unplugging for several months.

I wanted to talk with Hari about self-help, an ideology I had realized I'd been steeped in without ever having consciously chosen to subscribe to it. I may have scoffed at talk of "manifesting" and rolled my eyes at sharing circles, but when it came down to it, I'd been convinced that solving my despair was my job. And mine alone.

People had quite literally told me so.

The Vancouver self-help scene had presented a complex formula for healing that involved meditation, prayer and a Jedi-like attitude adjustment—a sort of Eckhart Tolle–inspired imperative to let go of "human world" concerns and stay in the present moment. Plus a good dose of positive thinking, visualization as per *The Secret* and a hodgepodge of therapy-like "inner work." (Not to be confused with actual therapy, which I found profoundly helpful.)

All of which I'd been slogging away at for years. But the only real relief I'd experienced was in Ireland, surrounded by loved ones, spending the bulk of my time and energy simply enjoying those around me. Doing no emotional heavy lifting whatsoever.

I wanted to interrogate these ideas I'd unwittingly absorbed in my childhood, and in progressive circles in Lotus Land. And Hari seemed like the ideal person to do this with.

While working on *Lost Connections*, he had traveled the world for three years, interviewing leading experts and examining data-driven research. The book's conclusion? Those of us suffering from anxiety and depression were not broken. We simply had psychological needs that were not being met. Because modern society was terrible at meeting them.

"The concept of self-help is part of the problem," Hari confirmed, after greeting me with a hug and settling down in front of a bowl of porridge. "The idea that the solution is to help yourself is part of the problem."

Hari pointed to research from Dr. Brett Ford, at the University of Toronto. Dr. Ford had wanted to investigate what would happen if someone consciously dedicated more time to making themselves happy. Would they actually become happier? The team conducted research in the United States, Russia, Taiwan and Japan. But the findings were perplexing. In the U.S., if you tried to make yourself happier, you wouldn't become happier. But in other countries, you would.

What they eventually discovered was that in the U.S., if you wanted to become happier, you did something for yourself. "You buy something, you show off on Instagram, you work harder—things that I used to do all the time when I started feeling bad," Hari explained. Whereas in these other, more communal countries, if you wanted to make yourself happier, you did something for someone else: friends, family, community. "We have an implicitly individualistic idea of what it means to be happy," Hari said. "And they have an instinctively collective idea of what it means to be happy."

But we are a tribal, social species, Hari reminded me, one that originated on the savannas of Africa. If we had been a species whose goal was to help ourselves as individuals, we never would have survived. Many of the ideas that we now take for granted—the Facebook platitude, for example, that "the only person who can help you is you"—are very recent, and quite ideological.

Also: totally untrue, Hari added with a laugh. Every single person on the planet has been helped by someone else; we wouldn't be here if we hadn't been. It's a sign of how awry our culture has gone, he said, that even our most banal clichés are wrong.

We have absorbed neoliberalism in mainstream culture, he continued. Viewing each person as an isolated, rational, self-interested individual whose sole purpose is to maximize the economy is an "extraordinary simplistic, thin, hollow way of thinking about what it is to live."

Our ways of working are now failing us, sucking up all of our time and energy and leaving us depleted and exhausted, he said. Our increasingly disconnected communities are failing us. Our very values, in fact, are failing us.

We're all now living in a machine that is constantly telling us to work more, then buy more and show it off on Instagram—"junk values," Hari went on. "We're living in a hurricane of messages telling us to do that. And when you are trying to extricate yourself from that, as clearly you are, you are still in the middle of the hurricane.

"So," Hari concluded, "we have to try and dismantle the machine."

It's a bit like dieting, he said. There is a certain amount you can do with individual self-control. But the two most effective things you can do to help yourself are actually collective: you can join a group like Weight Watchers, where you get peer support, or you can change your environment.

"We have a food supply where it's extremely hard to eat well," Hari pointed out. "And we have cities where it's very hard to walk around and bike around. It's not that people in Copenhagen are somehow less greedy, or more morally impressive. It's that in that city it's really easy to get on a bike, and walk around, and their food supply is fresh and nutritious and cheap. People in Kansas City don't have any of those things, and as a result, they put on a lot more weight."

We've been trained, he explained, when we're confronted with a problem, to ask: *What is the individual solution? What do I do, as an isolated individual?*

And so when Hari tells people, "Yes, there are things you can do as an individual, but the truth is we're much more powerful as citizens, banded together, doing things collectively, making things easier for ourselves and everyone else"—to many, it sounds pie-in-the-sky.

But in fact, the prevailing self-help groupthink—the stance that life will always be uncertain, and so we'll have to find our peace within—desperately needs to be put into historical context.

"You could have said to women a hundred years ago, 'I know you feel bad because you're not allowed to have a job and you're not allowed to have a bank account, and you're essentially the property of your father or your husband—that's never going to change,'" Hari said. "'But let's think about *your thought processes*, and how you can reconcile yourself to this dreadful reality.' Your life would be absolutely terrible now if women had thought that way. Fortunately, they did not.

"While there are some things we can't change," he added, "there are loads of things that we can change."

CHAPTER NINE

The Commons

Back in my hometown after London, it felt like all roads led to the Downtown Eastside. This handful of blocks had haunted the city's imagination for as long as I could remember. Here, as a society, we were at our worst and our best. Against an Instagram-worthy backdrop of mountains and ocean, the neighborhood's crowded, urine-drenched alleyways contained the height of human suffering, a reminder of all those we had abused, abandoned, failed. But in the neighborhood's residents, health care workers and addiction activists, we saw, too, the height of human tenderness, kindness, unconditional love.

So I wasn't too surprised when I found myself back down there again, seated in the lobby of what was once the Vancouver Police Department headquarters, for many years home to our jails. It was now reborn as an enormous co-working space, with polished concrete floors, sandy wood beams, an airy atrium, clusters of quiet conference rooms and a young, smiling concierge in a checkered shirt. There was something so symbolic about this trans-formation. Once a site of so much human misery, it was now a place for creativity, idealism, optimism.

On cue, in walked Charles Montgomery, author of *Happy City* and founder of a consultancy firm of the same name, located in the building. As my focus had shifted from individual to communal solutions, I had moved from back-to-the-land radicalism to data-driven urbanism, which just so happened to be his specialty.

I had begun this journey thinking about the modern city, and here, now, I returned to it.

Montgomery and I walked down East Cordova Street, past shuffling addicts gazing into the middle distance. Past Harbour Light Detox, where tattooed men gathered out front, laughing, smoking cigarettes, talking recovery. Then, through the doors of the hipster haunt The Birds & the Beets, where more tattooed men served up miso barley bowls.

Just over a decade ago, when he was a journalist in his late thirties, Montgomery told me, he'd had a kind of awakening. "I used to feel angry and anxious a lot," he began. He'd grown up in the Cowichan Valley on Vancouver Island, a gay guy in a small town, and had been drawn to city life early on. But moving to Vancouver, Hong Kong, Mexico City—all wonderful cities, he stressed—he noticed that he often felt trapped and frustrated.

"We live in an age where people say the solution is self-help," he said. "You know, *You need to improve yourself.*

"I certainly do need to work on myself, and I've gone to therapy," he continued with a laugh. "But it dawned on me that these systems that I was living in were nurturing or corroding my everyday happiness. Why didn't I get to see my friends when I wanted to? Why didn't I get to see my family when I wanted to? Why did I have a sore back? Why did I arrive at work frustrated, anxious and uptight? The answer was always that I was stuck within a system—usually stuck within a car—in cities that just weren't performing so well."

He lived with this frustration for some time. Then, in the late aughts, he met the man who would change his life: Enrique Peñalosa, the current (and former) mayor of Bogotá, Colombia. At the United Nations' World Urban Forum in Vancouver back in 2006, he had heard a talk given by Peñalosa, who claimed to have, during his first tenure as mayor, redesigned his city with human happiness in mind. Being a reporter, Montgomery was skeptical. But a few years after the Forum he traveled to South America to investigate, and witnessed a city that had been in deep crisis—"one of the worst places in the world to live at the end of the last century," Montgomery said—now radically transformed.

At the turn of the century, within a few short years, Peñalosa had reprioritized public space. As he detailed in a later TED Talk, he had given much of Bogotá's roads over to buses, and built 350 kilometers of protected bikeways. He had added a new network of parks, plazas and greenways for seniors to walk in and children to play in. (In his talk, he noted that ten thousand kids were killed every year worldwide by cars.) He built new libraries, schools and daycare centers. He reduced rush hour traffic by 40 percent, and planted a hundred thousand trees.

He had, in fact, reimagined the city, with democracy as a guiding principle. "The first article of every constitution states that all citizens are equal before the law," the mayor explained in his talk. "That is not just poetry. It's a very powerful principle." If that was true, he went on, a bus with eighty passengers had the right to eighty times more road space than a single driver. We'd become so accustomed to inequality, he said, we sometimes didn't see when it was right in front of us.

Protected bikeways, he added, were also a powerful symbol of democracy, because they showed "that a citizen on a $30 bicycle is equally important to one in a $30,000 car." (It's worth noting that as he redistributed space to the poor, the young and the elderly—insisting that everyone now had the right to mobility and safety—he was almost impeached.)

Montgomery recalls biking with Peñalosa to pick up his son from school during the annual car-free day in the Colombian capital, a well-loved tradition that the mayor had implemented. The streets filled with children, businessmen, young women, vendors selling arepas; the air was clear. On a day when kids all over the Western hemisphere were being killed as they traveled to school and back, Montgomery told me, and parents everywhere were getting stuck in traffic, and getting angry, and polluting the atmosphere—here was an alternative.

"That's when I set out to find out if he was right," Montgomery told me. "If it was true that the city itself could be a device for nurturing—or breaking—our happiness."

Inspired, he traveled the world, researching, and all he learned made him hyper-conscious of urban design's effect on well-being. After returning home, he made numerous adjustments to his own life, including starting to commute by bicycle. "The science says that I arrive at work more refreshed, happier, friendlier towards my colleagues and more hopeful than those who drove, or even who took public transit," he said. "That's what the science says, and I absolutely know it to be true in my own life.

"As long as I follow safe, separated bike routes," he emphasized. "If I bike in traffic, I arrive as angry as anybody else."

In the absence of bike lanes, in fact, barely anybody was willing to risk it. "The American self-help approach to well-being and mobility would have it that we all toughen up, get on our bikes, get out into traffic and not be scared of cars. That's the American approach: be a hero." We'd been designing cities using that approach for ninety years, he said, and the result was that bike commuters were predominantly young and middle-aged men. Not women. Not children. Not seniors.

By using the traditional self-help approach, he pointed out, we'd excluded most people from the means of mobility that's most associated with human happiness.

"This is why when we are giving advice to cities now, we tell them, if you want to build a mobility system that's healthy—but also *equitable*—then you need to build safe, separated bike infrastructure," he explained. "Not just pieces of it. You need the entire network. So that all of us feel safe moving in that way. And when that happens, we see massive spikes in bike ridership."

For Montgomery, then, a series of strategic choices accompanied his decision to get around on two wheels. Instead of buying a house in the distant suburbs, he shares a place in the city with three other adults (which, by the way, is a sixteen-minute ride from his office, which a study has determined is the optimal commute time).

He pays more for housing, sure, and has less personal space, but he knows he's happier. Every single day.

The question of whether perilous, pricey, emissions-heavy vehicles had the right to hog public space—crowding out, endangering and limiting the movements of the poor, the elderly, the disabled and the young—had actually never occurred to me before.

But when I thought about it, it was the assumption on which my hometown had been built. Vancouver was a car city; as a result, inequality was embedded in our very design. We had effectively elevated the interests of car owners over the greater good, right down to the level of the grid. (This has begun to change in recent years, with a big push for bike lanes, the creation of which allowed me to take up cycling.)

As a lifelong transit rider, it was pretty stunning that this assumption that had underpinned so much of my existence was only now becoming clear to me. In Toronto, Montgomery pointed out, where I'd experienced so much stress on the subway, a large chunk of 2019's infrastructure budget was going toward repairing the Gardiner Expressway. Far less than what was being spent on the embattled Toronto Transit Commission, on which millions relied every week. (When I looked it up, I discovered that the TTC is the least subsidized transit system in North America. And on average, it accommodates a staggering 1.7 million passenger trips per weekday.)

There were other invisible assumptions shaping cities,

too, which Montgomery highlighted as we ate our lunch.

"Social science has demonstrated that individuals and organizations and societies and civic leaders—we get happiness wrong all the time," he said. "We make a series of predictable errors in calculating how current actions will lead to future happiness. Vancouver is a great example of this."

In our own city, he said, we'd focused on creating the "greenest," healthiest, most picturesque place, prioritizing the visceral over the systemic. "We think the beauty of the city will make us happy," he said, "forgetting that actually it's our relationships that keep us happy and strong."

And so, "while we were busy building the most livable city in the world," he explained, "we allowed global capital to play a massive influence in our housing market. So now we have a beautiful, livable city where most people who were born or who do regular jobs here can't live."

Shortly after our interview, in fact, new numbers on the housing market came out from the Canada Mortgage and Housing Corporation. Analysts reviewed the data and found that foreign owners had captured $75 billion of the Metro Vancouver real estate market. Eleven percent of condos were owned, at least in part, by people living outside Canada. And, according to the *Vancouver Sun*, this was before authorities delved into the vast network of corporations and shell companies that owned property in Vancouver, some of which likely had directors or owners based overseas.

So, a super livable city, but a super unaffordable one. This insight made so much sense to me. On the surface, my lifestyle in Vancouver was pretty wonderful. Unlike in Toronto, I enjoyed the benefits of clean air, (relatively) easy mobility, gorgeous scenery, plentiful park space, trees galore. The only problem? I couldn't actually afford to live here. And neither could many people I knew.

"So, how is Vancouver doing on happiness?" Montgomery said. "Terrible. We've blown it. Because we were blind, like many cities were, to the rapid influence of global capital."

Recent developments—like six hundred new units of temporary modular housing built over the previous year—had made him feel more optimistic, though. "I think we can be hopeful that Vancouver, and other cities across Canada, are starting to figure out that if the city is not for everyone, then it is failing everyone."

If we truly want to address anxiety, Montgomery said, we must address this question of inclusion. How much is everyone invited to benefit from the riches of the city?

There are many causes of stress in our lives, he added, but the single greatest cause of stress is social isolation. It's absolutely brutal; it pumps stress hormones into our systems every single day.

And yet, we've been designing cities that deepen social isolation—for marginalized people, of course, but also for the rich.

Studies of big American cities have shown that people who live in auto-dependent neighborhoods on the far edges of a city report lower levels of trust in neighbors. They are less likely to know these neighbors, or to have them over for dinner; they are less likely to volunteer, or play team sports. They are even less likely to vote. They simply don't have the time, Montgomery said.

A Swedish study, too, showed that couples who had a forty-minute commute one way were 45 percent more likely to get divorced after ten years than couples who enjoyed a short walk to work. "These distances that we have built into our cities are stealing the good life from us," he said. "They are ripping apart our relationships."

Not for nothing, driving in traffic can have a greater effect on stress levels than being a riot cop in a protest, according to one study.

"We've invested in a system that makes people sick, fat and isolated," he said. And angry, and stressed. And broke—as gas prices skyrocket.

In North America, he added, we are now suburbanizing poverty. Wealthy people have figured out that we feel much better walking to work and shops, and have been buying up all the city land, pushing out everyone else. Relegating them to a life lived on the road.

"I want to talk about home," Montgomery said, as he spooned up the last bite of miso-drenched barley from his bowl. The individualist ethos that we'd been talking about didn't just play out in our self-help culture, our distribution of public space, our dispersal of cities and our blindness to the impact of global capital on the greater good.

It also shaped what kind of dwellings we built. In Vancouver, Montgomery said, we'd been doubling down on studio and one-bedroom apartments for twenty years. But there was almost no social infrastructure in these buildings, he pointed out, and no room in these tiny condos to entertain.

Montgomery himself had learned this the hard way. He'd gone through a difficult breakup a few years before, and had gotten an apartment and lived on his own. "I found myself not just sad, but anxious," he told me. "That anxiety was: *Am I going to see anybody this weekend? Or am I going to be all alone?*"

He knew he was not the only one; many people these days felt a lot of social anxiety. He wondered: What if we lived in a system that removed the need for that anxiety?

And so, in his darkest hour, at the height of Vancouver's affordability crisis, Montgomery joined a group of twenty-five other households who were in the process of building a cohousing complex together, not far from where I lived. He expected to move in within a few years.

Cohousing, of course, was radically more social. Individuals had their own small apartments, but the whole community shared amenities like kitchens and entertaining spaces and gardens. Friends of Montgomery's who lived in cohousing had told him that all they had to do was leave their front door and head to the common room, and something was always going on. And, remarkably, Montgomery said studies showed that people who live in cohousing report paying $1,500 less a month in childcare, solving a huge problem for cash-strapped young families. At his cohousing meetings, Montgomery saw this dynamic in action as parents handed off babies for hours at a time to the others, who were more than happy to get a good cuddle in.

"We evolved for tens of thousands of years in village environments and nomadic societies, where we were constantly surrounded by a small group of people," he said.

Here it was again: we evolved for the tribe. And for shared public space, shared living, shared resources, shared land. For the commons.

All this made me think, again, of Peñalosa. Though his legacy was eroded in the years when he was out of office, in the immediate wake of the mayor's policies, as Montgomery reported in his book, twice as many people cycled to work, saving the average minimum-wage worker the equivalent of a month and a half's salary every year. Citizens who lived near the new parks exercised more, especially seniors. The buses worked so well that traffic moved faster for everybody, and commute times fell by a fifth. Air quality improved. Traffic fatalities decreased, as did accidents and even, amazingly, murders. People reported feeling more optimistic.

"What are our needs for happiness?" the mayor is quoted as saying in *Happy City*. "We need to walk, just as birds need to fly. We need to be around other people. We need beauty. We need contact with nature. And most of all, we need not to be excluded. We need to feel some sort of equality."

I had, it must be said, not expected to arrive at this conclusion. I had assumed my journey to find a saner life would involve some combination of "life hacks" like meditation, sleep, healthy eating and digital detoxes, and would likely culminate in building an off-grid tiny house on some sliver of land in rural B.C., where I'd work twenty hours a week writing freelance articles (with what Wi-Fi connection, I'm not sure), and spend the rest of my time growing food, reading, hosting potlucks and walking a chocolate Lab.

Not so much, it turned out. For one, I wasn't too interested in living without running water or electricity. I'd proven pretty resistant to even giving up lipstick. For two, as an extrovert with unmet social needs and a huge appetite for intellectual stimulation, I was hardly the ideal candidate for living alone in the woods. Finally, freelance writing in this day and age was unlikely to support the Lab, let alone me. And who had the cash to build a cabin, or buy land in an astronomically expensive region?

No, connecting the dots on the epidemic of overwork and anxiety had not led me to unplug from society, leaving a trail of helpful tips for readers in my wake. It had instead led me here, to the most pressing issue of our time: economic inequality.

Underlying every single issue that I'd explored— from food culture to transportation—was the reality that we live in a massively unequal society.

As I finished writing this book, Bernie Sanders penned an op-ed for the *Wall Street Journal*, arguing that the three richest men in America—Bill Gates, Jeff Bezos and Warren Buffett—now owned more wealth than the bottom half of the American population. That's 160 million people. And worldwide, according to a 2017 Oxfam report, eight billionaires now owned more wealth than the bottom half of humanity. Oxfam also reported that 82 percent of the global wealth generated in 2017 had gone directly to the one percent.

In Canada, things were pretty bad too. Between 1982 and 2010, the incomes of the bottom 90 percent of Canadians increased only 2 percent, while the top one percent of the country enjoyed income increases of 160 percent.

And yet as recently as February of 2016, editors of *Income Inequality: The Canadian Story*, a volume published by the Institute for Research on Public Policy, found themselves having to make the case that this issue was even worthy of public consideration. "What we have is a lack of consensus in Canada as to whether inequality is really a problem, and whether it needs to be addressed," editor France St-Hilaire, Vice President, Research, at IRPP, and co-editor of *Income Inequality: The Canadian Story*, told the podcast *Policy Options*.

There seemed to be a huge disconnect in our culture, a wide-scale cognitive dissonance. Few seemed to be drawing the link between people's hectic, harried lives and income inequality. Between the suffering of the many and the concentration of wealth in the hands of the few.

Thinking back to the doctor I'd interviewed in Toronto—who'd told me, remember, that in unequal societies everyone gets sicker—I began digging into the data. And what I discovered was astonishing.

One of the world's preeminent researchers on the subject, Richard Wilkinson, professor emeritus of social epidemiology at the University of Nottingham, has demonstrated that unequal societies perform worse on numerous indexes that assess the health of a society. Life expectancy, literacy, infant mortality, imprisonment, murder rates, obesity, teen birthrates, mental illness (including addiction), social mobility and, crucially, trust—all get worse as the gap between the rich and the poor increases.

The Nordic countries, some of the world's most economically equal societies, perform among the best on such metrics, while the U.S., one of the most unequal, performs among the worst. "It's an extraordinarily close correlation," Wilkinson stressed in a TED Talk.

And this was, just as the Toronto doctor had said, true for *everybody* in a society, rich or poor. While income equality made the biggest difference to those at the bottom of the scale, it also predictably delivered small benefits to those at the top of the hierarchy.

Worried that people might think they were manufacturing evidence to suit their argument, Wilkinson and his team also published a paper in the *British Medical Journal*, this time using the UNICEF index of child well-being as its basis. The index included forty different components, ranging from immunization rates and bullying to levels of communication between parent and child and the availability of books in the home. It showed the exact same outcome, with kids faring far worse in economically unequal societies.

"What we're looking at is general social dysfunction related to inequality," he said. "It's not just one or two things that go wrong—it's most things."

What was at work here? What exactly was it that was so destructive, across so many different areas of society?

"I think I'm looking [at] and talking about the psycho-social effects of inequality," Wilkinson explained. Feelings of superiority and inferiority. Of being respected and disrespected. Status competition, which he believes is also driving the consumerism in our society. And which leads to widespread feelings of insecurity, even violence.

To explain, he pointed to recent studies in the field of social psychology. Researchers reviewed 208 studies in which volunteers in psychological labs had had their stress hormones measured. The review was looking to pinpoint what kind of stressful tasks most reliably spiked cortisol levels. The answer? Tasks that included "social-evaluative threats." Threats to self-esteem or social status.

"The average well-being of our societies is not dependent any longer on national income and economic growth," Wilkinson said. "That's very important in poorer countries, but not in the rich developed world. But the differences between us, and where we are in relation to each other, now matter very much."

My early question—How does one measure the soul of a city?—was actually quite easily answered.

As was the mystery of my fragile health. "The big change in our understanding of drivers of chronic health [problems] in the rich developed world is how important chronic stress from social sources is in affecting the immune system, the cardiovascular system," Wilkinson noted.

Significantly, the question of what, if any, interventions could bridge the gap between the rich and the poor was also easily handled. There were a range of solutions on offer, all already tested in rich, developed market democracies. Sweden narrowed the gap between the haves and the have-nots through taxation and a generous welfare state. Japan, meanwhile, had lower taxes and a smaller welfare state, but less extreme differences in income. No matter how governments achieve greater economic equality, it results in healthier societies.

The most talked-about intervention these days, though, is probably universal basic income, which has been written about extensively by Rutger Bregman, a Dutch historian and writer for *The Correspondent* who rose to prominence with his book *Utopia for Realists*.

Launched in Manitoba in the 1970s, the pioneering universal basic income experiment resurfaced in 2009, when professor Evelyn Forget at the University of Manitoba rescued some two thousand boxes of data that had been languishing in an attic of the national archives in Winnipeg for decades.

The experiment had run thirty-five years earlier in the small Manitoban town of Dauphin, with a population of roughly 13,000. Providing a guaranteed base income, it raised about 30 percent of the town, or one thousand families, above the poverty line. As Bregman documents in his book, a legion of researchers was on hand to observe the impact of this subsidy on work, family life, society and physical and mental health. Truckloads of data were generated.

But after four years, the Liberal government was ousted by the Conservatives and the funding stopped, ending the "Mincome" experiment. The research was boxed up, not to be seen again until Forget discovered it many years later.

When she and her team finally ran the data, there were some startling discoveries. There had, of course, been concerns at the time that people would stop working if they were handed free money. But the opposite had been true. The only exceptions were students (mainly young men who would otherwise have quit school at sixteen to farm), who used the money to finish school, and new mothers, who took slightly longer maternity leaves.

But, as Bregman reports, the most stunning piece of data to emerge from this experiment was that hospitalizations decreased by 8.5 percent, carrying huge implications for healthcare spending.

A few years into the experiment, domestic violence was down, too, as were mental health complaints. "Mincome had made the whole town healthier," Bregman writes. "Forget could even trace the impacts of receiving a basic income through to the next generation, both in earnings and in health."

If we know what the problem is, and we have a range of different ways to solve it, what's stopping us from doing so?

In 2015, the former *New York Times* columnist and correspondent Anand Giridharadas stood at a podium at the Aspen Institute's Action Forum, preparing to blow up his life. "I was asked to speak to you today about forgiveness," he told an audience of friends, colleagues and fellow

Aspen Global Leadership Network fellows. "As I considered what I wanted to say to this community that [my wife] Priya and I so cherish, the topic grew and meandered. But in one sense, it has stayed true. After I have spoken, I will need your forgiveness."

He proceeded to lay out a devastating critique of the worldview belonging to the elite he was speaking to—the bankers and CEOs, philanthropists and tech moguls. The private-jet class. The multimillionaires and billionaires. The one percent.

It was a critique that helped me to understand everything I had been writing about, in a way that I hadn't grasped until now.

In his speech and subsequent book, *Winners Take All*, Giridharadas unpacks an ideology that has impacted my life in countless ways.

He calls this ideology MarketWorld and defines it in the book as a rising, powerful elite operating on contradictory impulses—to both do well and do good, "to change the world while also profiting from the status quo." This new class is made up of "enlightened businesspeople and their collaborators in the worlds of charity, academia, media, government, and think tanks." It has "its own thinkers, whom it calls thought leaders, its own language, and even its own territory—including a constantly shifting archipelago of conferences at which its values are reinforced and disseminated and translated into action." MarketWorld is both a professional network and a community, but it is also a culture, a state of mind. And one that fervently believes that "social change should be

pursued principally through the free market and volun-
tary action, not public life and the law and the reform of
the systems that people share in common; that it should
be supervised by the winners of capitalism and their
allies, and not be antagonistic to their needs; and that the
biggest beneficiaries of the status quo should play a leading role in the status quo's reform."

This worldview, according to Giridharadas, had been
fomenting for forty years. Contributing to it were decades
of Republican attacks on the very idea of government,
and also major Democratic leaders like Bill Clinton, who
moved from championing governance to championing
market solutions. (Think of the famous line in Clinton's
1996 State of the Union address, "The era of big government is over," and, in fact, the entire premise of the
Clinton Global Initiative, which brought together business leaders to solve the world's most complex problems.)
This is how we got the irony of post–White House Obama,
who, in considering how he could help make democracy
more vital, turned to management consultants McKinsey
& Company to help.

In fact, companies like Goldman Sachs and McKinsey,
Giridharadas went on, played a pivotal role in creating
MarketWorld. They did a brilliant job of selling this ethos
to the younger generation in order to recruit the so-called
best and brightest to its firms. The line they sold to this
next generation was this: in order to be effective change-
makers, one needed to apprentice in the business world
first and learn the tools of change. This, Giridharadas has
argued in interviews, effectively took the most idealistic

young people, those historically best positioned to make change, and defanged them. Whether this was a deliberate move to coopt idealism or simply a power play to hoard talent is unclear.

Regardless, what this young cohort learned in the corporate world slowly infiltrated all the institutions they then went on to lead, from academia to the nonprofit sector.

The toolkit they absorbed, and then deployed all over the world, involves a kind of step-by-step, linear thinking that often compartmentalizes problem-solving and discourages looking at the wider context. And, more often than not, this McKinsey-esque brand of analysis results in bite-sized, easily actionable takeaways. All presented with the polished, breezy optimism born of profound privilege.

So often, as Giridharadas pointed out, this sort of upbeat, "win-win" thinking fails to take into account the losses experienced by people on the other side of the equation. And those losses are very real. The "productivity revolution," embraced by corporations everywhere, taught businesses to optimize everything—as Jia Tolentino so beautifully articulates in her essay on optimization—trimming supply chains and decreasing the volatility of income statements. "This optimization, of course, made companies less hospitable to workers, who faced such things as layoffs, offshoring, dynamic scheduling, and automation as the downside of corporate progress," Giridharadas writes in his book. This was "part of why their wages stagnated while companies' profits and productivity rose."

Productivity, in fact, has risen more than 70 percent since the 1970s. And we're all feeling the crunch.

If the work world feels like a mad scramble, that's because for many of us, it is.

The final piece of the puzzle that Giridharadas deconstructs has proven the most insidious, and the hardest for me to write about, since so many of those involved are clearly well-meaning and sincere.

In pouring so much time, energy and money into philanthropy and social ventures, MarketWorld effectively took over the business of social change, steering it away from historic ways of transforming society—street protests, grassroots community organizing, wide-scale government interventions—and instead toward private, market-based efforts.

In the process, it directed our very thinking about social change away from broad, communal solutions that benefit all, to individual solutions that benefit a handful.

To improve education, then, Giridharadas argues, we moved away from the notion of funding schools by raising taxes for the wealthy (or even making them pay what they already owe under current tax law)—and instead watched the rich donate to charter schools that helped a handful of kids in Harlem get into Harvard.

From standard, boring civic responsibility to flashy acts of individual generosity. But generosity, as Giridharadas points out, is not the same thing as justice.

This is how it's possible to have an elite that is at once incredibly concerned with saving the world and incredibly concerned with amassing wealth. The same elite that gives back also fights for policies that concentrate wealth, resisting taxes on financial transactions and inheritances, pushing for carried interest to be taxed at lower rates than income, and "insisting on a sacred right to conceal money in trusts and shell companies and really weird islands," as Giridharadas said in Aspen.

"This hoarding does not merely correlate with the have-nots' struggles," he continued in that speech. "It is, in a certain sense, a cause." Because, he stressed, this money was *the money*. It was the money that would have been spent improving the lives of the many, through vocational training and schools and infrastructure and financial aid and social insurance.

"We talk a lot here about giving more," Giridharadas said. "We don't talk about taking less."

One of MarketWorld's most powerful products, he argues in his book, is the ideas factory that obscures this truth. Its ideas are packaged in digestible soundbites, focusing on individual solutions to complex collective problems, conforming to an uplifting, inspirational story arc and offering simple, actionable takeaways.

This was obviously the TED model, it pained me to realize, and in Giridharadas's view it was no surprise the TED conference was exclusive, expensive to attend and carefully curated.

The problem is not that this model exists, but that it is now the chief mode of disseminating new ideas, and hands down the most effective (as evidenced by the fact that almost every single person I interviewed for this book had given a TED Talk).

One has to wonder: Who isn't being heard as a result? What isn't being said?

The whole conversation—the very *way* that we speak about social change—is dictated by the group that has the most to gain from society not changing in any significant way. This, at the exact moment in history when we most need change.

Thus, we arrive at Sheryl Sandberg. You had to know that was coming, right?

In an interesting coincidence, just as I finished this book, Giridharadas was making the talk show rounds, pointing to her as an example of MarketWorld's limitations.

Women's equality is one of the most pressing problems of our time, his argument ran; Sheryl Sandberg's solution, though, was not to advocate for policies that other countries have already effectively implemented to empower women—policies like maternity leave. These solutions work, but are expensive and invariably result in higher taxes. So instead we got her milquetoast imperative for women to speak up more, to "lean in."

Parental policy, I discovered, is not even an issue that Facebook is prepared to explore in-house. The company provides a four-month leave, which is better than the nothing that most American women get. But when women within Facebook pushed for more parent-friendly policies,

Sandberg and Mark Zuckerberg declined to move ahead.

This recently came to light when a Facebook data scientist and new mother was forced to choose between her job and her family.

She'd just given birth to her third child, and was overwhelmed by a long daily commute and juggling a high-pressure job with an infant and two young sons. So Eliza Khuner proposed to HR that she work part-time, or work from home, or take extra unpaid leave. She was refused all.

Khuner responded by resigning and posting on a Facebook employee page, calling on the company to do better by families. Around 5,500 employees responded and hundreds commented, letting her know she was not alone. "Mothers shared how they struggled to perform at work and be there for their kids, and how sad they were to miss the special moments," she wrote in an op-ed for *Wired*. "Fathers said they felt the strain of not being with their children."

Khuner went on to say, "Facebook has solved harder problems than this. . . . Companies like Facebook have the imagination and the resources to implement better leave and flexibility in working hours so parents don't have to choose between their children and careers. It may come at a cost initially, but the return on investment will be more women staying in the workplace, higher employee satisfaction, and the knowledge that we are doing right by our people and our children."

———

Sandberg's upbeat philosophy, then, disregards the crush-ing realities of the current labor market for women. "I believe telling mothers to raise their hands and try harder in the open sea of hostility we face in the workplace is like handing a rubber ducky to someone hit by a tsunami," Katherine Goldstein, a *Lean In* devotee-turned-critic, wrote in an essay for *Vox*. "I think it also inadvertently encour-ages us to internalize our own discrimination, leading us to blame ourselves for getting passed over for raises, eased out of jobs, not getting called for job interviews, and being denied promotions.

"I now believe the greatest lie of *Lean In*," she went on, "is its underlying message that most companies and bosses are ultimately benevolent, that hard work is rewarded, that if women shed the straitjacket of self-doubt, a meritocratic world awaits us. My own life, and my research and reporting, along with interacting with hundreds of mothers in the past two years, has convinced me this is untrue."

Instead of real change, then, we got Sheryl Sandberg fretting about the "ambition gap." Haranguing women to work harder—to work, in fact, up to the very moment they give birth. And, if Sandberg's own example means anything, to resume emailing from hospital beds immedi-ately afterward. What kind of life is that?

To harken back to Johann Hari's words in London, this is an incredibly thin way of looking at what it means to be alive. To be human.

If we're honest about it, if we look at the actual num-bers, overwork is essentially taking all of our precious life energy—all the hours we could be spending with family, laughing with friends, learning new hobbies, getting out into nature, exercising our bodies, eating home-cooked meals, sleeping, participating in our communities and creating real social change—and converting all of that time and energy and attention into profit. Profit, in fact, for a very small group of people.

This analysis—a bummer if ever there was one—explains so much of what has happened in my own life. And it certainly explains why I was so angry at the "lean in" phenomenon that I wrote an entire book in opposition to it.

Build a business, save the world. Somehow that already-quite-flawed idea has morphed into another, equally flawed idea: Work as if you're saving the world. No matter what you're working at.

This is how many in my generation, and the generations that follow, now approach our jobs. Even when we're doing no more than writing Meghan Markle listicles (fun as they may be).

We work as if we are changing the world. But leave the *actual* work of changing the world largely untouched.

Reading Giridharadas's book made me see that the "lean in" ethos that defined my generation—and, in fact, my life—originated with the one percent. It spread, through consultants, to various sectors (including the media), along the way picking up moral authority from idealistic philanthropists and social venture capitalists, and a utopian vision from Silicon Valley. In its travels around the thought leadership circuit, it was cemented into an ideology. One that is now sacrosanct.

At heart, though, it remains an ideology created by the few, promoted on behalf of the few and benefiting only the few.

Looking through this lens at the online culture of rise-and-grind, overtime-is-bliss, #ThankGodItsMonday, revealed it for the nonsense it was. This was not a recipe for meaning and purpose; it was a recipe for horrible physical and mental health, ruined lives, broken families, fragmented communities and shattered democracies. It was a recipe for societal disaster.

I knew this already, of course, because I had lived it.

And I was not the only one. All around me, people were waking up to the fact that the emperor had no clothes.

Around this time, Basecamp founders Jason Fried and David Heinemeier Hansson published a book, *It Doesn't Have to Be Crazy at Work*, calling bullshit on this whole phenomenon. Silicon Valley is not really that important, they argued. Tech could drop the grandiosity, scale back ambitions and build a calm office culture. One in which people's right to a stress-free life trumps stretch revenue targets and ridiculous messianic rhetoric.

Meanwhile, the *New York Times* published a think piece on what it called "performative workaholism," asking, "Why are young people pretending to love work?" And deploying perhaps the wittiest line in the debate thus far: "I saw the greatest minds of my generation log eighteen-hour days—and then boast about #hustle on Instagram."

"Welcome to hustle culture," tech correspondent Erin Griffith writes in this widely shared piece. "It is obsessed with striving, relentlessly positive, devoid of humor, and—once you notice it—impossible to escape."

The article goes on to unpack this never-ending "work rapture," in which everything from exercise to concerts is merely "inspiration that leads back to the desk."

This cultish culture is, as we've seen time and time again, far from beneficial for its adherents. So it shouldn't be surprising that most of the people "beating the drums" for overwork are, as Basecamp's David Heinemeier Hansson says in the piece, not the ones doing the work—but the ones profiting from it.

Griffith points in the article to a tweet from Elon Musk. "Nobody ever changed the world on forty hours a week," the Tesla founder claimed, ignoring all historical evidence to the contrary. (As one woman pointed out on Twitter, the scientist Alexander Fleming changed the world simply by going on vacation and leaving a petri dish out. Hello, penicillin.)

And what, pray tell, was the number of hours we should aspire to work instead? Musk figured eighty a week, sometimes a hundred. If you loved what you did, it shouldn't feel like work.

This was an echo of another absurd comment I'd written about five years before, a comment that sowed the seeds of the book that's now in your hands.

In an interview, "lean in" icon Marissa Mayer, then the CEO of Yahoo!, claimed to have worked 130 hours a week building Google. It was, she said, possible "if you're strategic about when you sleep, when you shower and how often you go to the bathroom."

So, here it was. Here was the logical conclusion of the worship of business in general, and entrepreneurs in particular, that MarketWorld had kick-started so many years ago. Here was what "lean in" actually meant.

A life that was totally, completely about work. A world, in fact, about this and this alone.

I will leave you to mull over a utopian future in which we all work 130 hours a week, declining to sleep, bathe or use the toilet. But I will leave you with one final thought first.

If I had to sum up all I learned during my three years of leaning out, all the books I read and the people I interviewed, all I experienced on my travels, all the suffering I saw and also all the wonderment, I could do it in one simple statement.

And that would be this:

We are all in this together. And if we want to save our society, we're going to have to start acting like it.

The Adventure

Iknew I was better when hip-hop returned to me. One day I was on the couch, feeling lethargic, and the next I was in my kitchen, dancing to Cam'ron's "Hey Ma." Jay-Z shouting over Otis Redding on the next track, "I guess I got my swagger back!" I couldn't turn it up loud enough.

The despair lifted, replaced by a white-hot determination, burning through apathy and disillusionment, obliterating all with its fiery vitality. Empowering, expansive, clarifying. I danced in my kitchen for a long while, feeling my energy return. Feeling myself return.

Meanwhile, Rutger Bregman was on every talk show, in the wake of his now-famous speech in Davos. "I hear people talking the language of participation, and justice, and equality, and transparency," he had told those gathered at the World Economic Forum. "But then, I mean, almost no one raises the real issue, of tax avoidance, right? And of the rich just not paying their fair share.

"It feels like I'm at a firefighters' conference and no one is allowed to speak about water," he went on. "This is not rocket science. We can talk for a very long time about all these stupid philanthropy schemes, we can invite Bono once more, but come on, we've got to be talking about taxes. That's it—taxes, taxes, taxes. All the rest is bullshit in my opinion."

Alexandria Ocasio-Cortez was all over the Internet, too, talking about the Green New Deal and proposing 70-percent marginal tax rates for the super-rich to pay for it. And, when Republicans dismissed her environmentalism as elitist, delivering a scorching speech.

"One year ago, I was waitressing in a taco shop in downtown Manhattan," the young congresswoman said. "I just got health insurance for the first time a month ago. This is not an elitist issue. This is a quality of life issue. You want to tell people that their concern and their desire for clean air and clean water is elitist? Tell that to the kids in the South Bronx, who are suffering from the highest rates of childhood asthma in the country. Tell that to the families in Flint whose kids, their blood is ascending in lead levels, their brains are damaged for the rest of their lives. Call them elitist. You're telling them that those kids are trying to get on a plane to Davos? People are dying!"

London's National Portrait Gallery was turning down a million-pound donation from the billionaire Sackler family, who owed much of their fortune to OxyContin and whose aggressive sales of the drug had been implicated in the opioid epidemic. (More than fifteen hundred entities filed federal lawsuits against the Sacklers' company, Purdue Pharma, over its role in the crisis.) Transparency International Canada was releasing a new report revealing the extent of money laundering in Toronto real estate. And that was all just in one news cycle.

There was a new dynamism gathering—a standing up, a speaking out. A collective cry on behalf of the tribe, the commons. A flooding of the town square.

It was spring in Vancouver. The sun was shining; crocuses were pushing their way up through the earth, cherry blossoms exploding into bloom. People were suddenly on the streets, in the coffee shops, in the parks, shedding heavy parkas, lacing up sneakers, greedy for fresh air, for sunshine, for each other. I was biking more, walking more, doing more vigorous yoga. As I stretched out my body, I felt strong. Drake and Lil Wayne in my headphones, constant companions once again.

Day in and day out I wrote, the words tumbling out of me, landing with precision on the page.

Notorious B.I.G.'s "Hypnotize" in the speakers, taking me back to the euphoria of my youth, driving around Manhattan in SUVs in the middle of the night, snow falling in fat flakes, the bass reverberating in my chest. In Tokyo before sunrise, sitting on a club's covered patio, gazing out over the rooftops of Shibuya with my friend and her boyfriend, a Japanese beatboxer. In a Brooklyn attic apartment on a dark, chilly fall evening, Eminem's epic anthem "Lose Yourself" on the stereo. In Victoria, B.C., at a Souls of Mischief show with my cousin, the crowd erupting as the first notes of "93 'til Infinity" dropped. Walking the streets of Johannesburg, Kanye's "Diamonds from Sierra Leone" blasting out windows as cars sped past. Dusk in Military Park in Newark, New Jersey, the air thick with humidity, Slick Rick on stage, a crowd of aging hippies in dashikis, young professionals in business attire and teen boys in oversized white T-shirts, fireflies flickering above. In the mountains outside Caracas before dawn, dancing with hundreds to Daddy Yankee's "Gasolina" at an impromptu block party, all of us moving as one, a single heartbeat pulsing in the darkness. Later that week, a bright fuchsia sun slipping over palm trees in a plaza downtown, M-1 from dead prez on stage, the crowd chanting the chorus: "It's bigger than hip-hop . . ." The rapper in a hotel restaurant, after a global hip-hop summit on healthcare, freedom, food, giving me a message for the rest of the world: "Wake up. We need you. Wake up."

Then, just as fast, Beyoncé's "711" transporting me to the Toronto newsroom the autumn it dropped, when we were all playing it all the time. The feeling it gave me of being at the very center of our city, our time. On the phones, out talking to taxi drivers, hairdressers, teachers, standing on street corners with microphones. *Tell us your story, tell us your story, tell the city your story.* Us, woven into the fabric of this place, living and breathing our shared destiny. Our common fate.

The feeling of agency, when it came rushing back, was a tremendous relief. I startled awake, as if from a dream. Well-rested, alert, ready.

I arrived in New York City in May, booking into a room at the Ace Hotel with a desk and a view of the Empire State Building. As I waited for interviews, I traced the footpaths of years gone by. I walked past the old blue awning of the Skylight Diner on 34th Street, where in my twenties I'd once eaten cheeseburgers at two in the morning with a rapper's entourage. Past an impressive tower on Avenue of the Americas where I'd met with my first literary agent, and then a shabby office block in Midtown where I'd met my first magazine editor. I walked past a Korean restaurant where I'd once eaten lunch with a DJ, delighted by all the tiny, delicious dishes that arrived at our table. Seaweed, kimchee, pickled vegetables.

I walked past Zabar's on the Upper West Side, where I used to buy bagels and lox, blocks from the room I rented from a retired professor in a sprawling, rent-controlled apartment on Riverside Drive with a wraparound deck and breathtaking views of the Hudson River. I thought of this professor again as I walked through the farmer's market at Union Square, where she'd once taken me to shop for salad greens, which she kept in bags stowed away in the fridge, safe from skittish cockroaches. I thought, too, of Madeleine L'Engle, who'd also lived on the Upper West Side for decades. Felt anew my grief at never having had the chance to meet her.

I walked past Jefferson Market Garden in the Village, its verdant greenery the backdrop of photos my cousin and I took the weekend before her wedding, five years before, when we were still in our thirties. I ate creamy frozen custard in Madison Square Park at twilight, as we'd done then too, surrounded by crowds of laughing strangers and the cacophony of the nearby playground, strings of lights twinkling against a dusk sky.

First thing in the morning, I walked down to the Hudson, jarred by the construction, the cranes overheard, the assault of jackhammers. The air smelled of smoke and asphalt and alienation. A haze of smog hung low. A woman crossing the street shouted at a truck that turned too slowly. I felt as if I was out walking in a mad, capitalism-fueled dystopia, where work never ceased and everyone, everywhere was miserable.

But then I slipped onto the High Line greenway, that renovated railway track above the streets, and in an instant I was in gardens where you could breathe again and people seemed to have the time to smile. There were wildflowers growing through the cracked pavement, and public art (notably, a massive clock with a banner that read "Time to organize"), and dogs and grinning toddlers. There was life. And there was hope.

I wandered down to the gleaming lobby of the Gansevoort Hotel, where I met the journalist, author and filmmaker Sebastian Junger for ginger beers as men played pool nearby and the mournful, melodic Rihanna chorus of Drake's "Take Care" filled the room.

Junger told me that he'd been thinking about community for much of his life, in part because the affluent Boston suburb that he'd grown up in had had zero community. "Teenagers notice things in a very poignant way—their hearts are wide open," he said. "And if you grow up in an affluent community, the thing that I think young people long for—which is human connection—they actually can't find around them. I grew up very, very aware of that for some reason.

"I look back on my twenties, and I was living by myself, making very little money waiting tables, struggling to be a writer," he said. "With no meaningful contribution to the world, no community to be a part of. I was an example of what I wrote about in my book *Tribe*, this sort of unaffiliated, unattached person."

In college, navigating an existential crisis, he'd spent weekends with his best friend's aunt and uncle. The uncle, Ellis Settle, was of Lakota and Apache ancestry. He'd been born on a wagon in Missouri during the Great Depression, and had spent part of the 1960s in the South registering black voters. After dinners on those college weekends, as Junger recounts in *Tribe*, Ellis would sit with him, drinking cold coffee and smoking Carlton ultralights and telling him stories.

"He made sense of what I was experiencing in my little suburban life," Junger said. "He made sense of why that felt so hard and wrong to me." In some ways, he said, *Tribe* was actually an elaboration of what Ellis had told him. "I was really confused by why I lived such a privileged life that felt so empty and felt so inadequate. I didn't understand."

He was a lifesaver, Junger said. "If I hadn't met him, God knows."

Listening to Junger talk, it struck me that his whole life had been about this search for deeper human connection. As an anthropologist, he'd begun thinking through this in anthropological terms, comparing modern society to more ancient Indigenous cultures. And then he'd become a war correspondent.

"After I was with the American soldiers in combat in Afghanistan, my sense of loss and sorrow after the end of that deployment really puzzled me," he said. "And I finally connected the dots. Like, 'Oh, I finally had a *community*. That's what I'm grieving—that sense of connection to other people.'

"You know, not your best friend, not your girlfriend, not your family—that's a given," he continued. "No, these are guys I didn't know six months ago. *Why do I feel so close to them, and why is it so hard to give that up?*"

The lightbulb went on for Junger during an interview, he said, when a reporter asked him why veterans were so messed up when they came home. "I took offense to it a little bit, and I said, 'Maybe *we're* messed up,'" Junger recalled. "'Maybe what's hard for them isn't that they're returning with problems. It's that they are returning knowing the solution and it's not to be found here. Maybe that's actually what's going on. Maybe they are returning to a messed-up society with actually something resembling a healthy state of mind, because of their experience together.' It just came out of me in the interview. And after I said that, I thought, *Oh shit, that's it!*"

War, of course, as he writes in *Tribe*, throws soldiers back into a tribal way of life. Danger drives them to live together in small units, do everything with one another, from eating to sleeping. They might not like their fellow soldiers, but they'd fight to the death to protect them. This deep loyalty, collectivity, brotherhood—where race and class fall away—is emotionally gratifying, and immensely healing. And very difficult to give up, once soldiers return home, greeted instead by a fractured, individualistic, and alienating society.

Since *Tribe* had come out several years before, Junger told me, he'd heard from many veterans who'd shared how transformative the book had been for them. One soldier, who'd been very depressed, had shot himself in the head. He'd survived, and was living with his parents, broke. But after reading Junger's book, he sent him a Facebook message saying it had proven to be his lifesaver. It had finally explained, on a deep level, what he'd been experiencing. What was wrong. This man, Junger said, now gave *Tribe* to all the veterans he knew, hoping to save them the same suffering.

For a writer, even one as accomplished as Junger, who'd won National Magazine and Peabody Awards, topped the *New York Times* bestseller list, seen his book *The Perfect Storm* turned into a film and been nominated for an Oscar for his first feature-length documentary, *Restrepo*—this was an incredibly powerful experience. "Everyone wants to be needed," Junger said. "That's how I can be needed in my life, in this world."

He wasn't a firefighter and he didn't fight in a war, he said. But he did feel, now, like he'd been able to help people, to serve. "It made me feel, maybe for the first time in my life, really part of this nation," he continued. "Because I was contributing to it."

Before we left, I asked Junger if he'd ever felt, again, the intense communal spirit he'd experienced during war. He emailed me the next day to say that in fact he had, at the boxing gym he worked out at. There, inner-city kids sparred with Wall Street suits on their lunch breaks. Everyone was equal in standing.

"You are judged for how respectful you are of other athletes and how hard you train—that's it," he wrote me. "And sparring is extremely intimidating to everyone and so there is that element of fear or stress that help[s] people connect with each other. Muhammad Ali said he started boxing because he liked the idea that in the ring everyone is equal—there's no race, no rich or poor, nothing."

I thought again of something Junger had said at the Gansevoort. He had stressed that for tribe-building to be effective, it had to be organic and communal. It couldn't be limited to narrow definitions of a group, based on narrow affiliations or interests. It had to include everybody.

"When people say, 'I've got to find my tribe'—if you're looking for your tribe, you'll never find one," he'd said. "It's around you. If it's not around you, in your neighborhood, you don't have one."

Later, on Lexington Avenue, leaving a coffee shop to head back to my hotel, thunder rumbled overhead and the streets flooded with rain. I made it a few blocks until, soaked, I was forced to huddle with businessmen next to a building and wait out the downpour. There was a crazy sort of exhilaration to the moment, and in my drenched sandals and jeans, my soaking-wet new blouse, I found myself laughing out loud, glad to be there, in that moment, in that city, alive.

Standing there, I felt the opposite of alone. I thought of

Zadie Smith, whom I'd interviewed that day, and a *New York Review of Books* essay of hers that I'd just read. In "Under the Banner of New York," she reflects on the city's elasticity, how the banner of New York is flexible enough to include people from radically different backgrounds. She reflects, too, on the city's many acts of kindness, the daily, tiny rescues that people perform for each other. The ways in which they come together to help a mother with a broken stroller over the curb, or an elderly woman who has fallen. Smith celebrates New York in its "everyday mode . . . in which bonds gather and dissipate with a dizzying fluidity and yet, for the brief duration that they are in place, can display a mighty strength." Quoting a line from her poet husband, she marvels at "this city's brute capacity for gathering."

As the rain hammered down, as we all gathered to take shelter from it, I fell in love with this city—with the whole idea of "the city"—all over again. With all of us, living our little human lives, trying to be together as best we could. Trying to not be irrelevant. Trying to believe that there was meaning to this universe. That what we chose to say or do mattered, and mattered cosmically.

How I loved us for that.

I went back to the newsroom. Of course I did. I probably was never not going to. It was, after all, a time in which America had lost 45 percent of its newspaper journalists. Anand Giridharadas was warning the tech elite that a future with no journalists was not inconceivable. Countries all over the world were desperately lacking local reporting, drowning in mindless clickbait and fake Facebook news. Our democracies were in peril.

The world, it seemed, probably didn't need another person who lived simply on B.C.'s Gulf Islands and Instagrammed Mary Oliver poems, lovely as that would be ("Listen, are you breathing just a little, and calling it a life?"). Just like it didn't need another self-help book on how to find nirvana through cold showers and bulletproof coffee. Sigh.

What the world did need, quite urgently, was journalists. And that, in the end, was what I was.

Being back in the newsroom felt electric—walking through that vibrating hub of activity, giant clocks on the wall counting down the seconds to airtime. Talking to reporters, radio hosts, fellow producers, laughing. Excited to sit in those meetings again, debating the big ideas of our time. Excited to pick up that phone again and listen. *Tell us your story, tell us your story. Tell the city your story.*

Back to Toronto, then. My city, my story.

I arrived on June 17, 2019, emerging from the depths of Union Station, and was met with a sea of people dressed in red, stretching out in every conceivable direction. The Raptors had won the NBA championship and parade-goers flooded the streets, now impassable by car, streetcar, bus. Impassable, even, by foot. As I made my way slowly through the crowds, heading toward the CBC, children with balloons scampered by, fathers in turbans pushed strollers, women in hijabs posed for selfies. Caribbean grandmothers fanned themselves from the heat; white Bay Street power brokers in crisp shirts grinned unabashedly, looking like the boys they once were. In the windows of the office towers above, faces were smiling, hands waving. A parked SUV nearby blasted Prince's "I Wanna Be Your Lover" from giant speakers. "I ain't got no money," the late music legend sang, and then, "I need your love . . ." A man on a microphone somewhere called out to us, "The greatest city in the world—Toronto, baby!"

Picture this: Everything had come to a standstill. Businesses shuttered, cars banished, the rush of commerce abandoned. It was, on this random Monday morning, only about the people. About togetherness. In the midst of these multitudes, I saw faces of every hue, heard languages from every corner of the world, watched strangers from every walk of life join in.

I let myself cry, then, there, among all of those people. Among all of you.

And I cried more as I sat, astonished, in CBC Toronto's lobby with my friend Jayne, watching the coverage on massive screens, watching more than a million people commune with one another. Watching old women smiling in pride; muscled young men on the parade route breaking down in tears as the players' bus rolled by; reporters I knew gleefully bearing witness. Marveling at aerial shots of the streets, the sheer mass of humanity coming together. Drake taking the stage at Nathan Phillips Square, asking all to turn to a stranger and embrace them.

Later, the international press drew the same conclusions as many of us in the street. Toronto was a remarkably diverse city, a city that welcomed immigrants, people of every faith and race and nationality and sexual orientation and gender identity and political and economic circumstance. It was a city of extremely different people living out their individual lives, together. Attending each other's weddings and learning about each other's gods; reading each other's books and eating each other's food. Dancing to each other's music. Toronto was a city of people who were learning, in the words of a recent Zadie Smith short story, to enter each other's stories.

We were all participating in a unique social experiment, collectively imagining what the city of the future might look like, rewriting the global script. And the Raptors—bless them—showed us, showed the world, that it was working.

It was far from perfect, of course, as the day's shooting attested. But in some crucial way, it was *working*.

The intensity of closeness we all felt that day, the joy, was an affirmation of the beauty that persists in modern life, in spite of all.

It reminded me in a strange way of another moment, across the country, on the ocean, the summer before. I was visiting remote Quadra Island for a travel story, out for a morning paddle with the owner of the local kayak company, an energetic outdoorsman who entertained me with tales of adventure, encounters with dolphins, wolves, grizzly cubs.

As we dipped our oars into the Pacific, heading toward

the vastness beyond the bay, scanning the horizon for whales, we were delighted to see, miles in the distance, spouts from three different pods of humpbacks. I laughed at our luck, and then, as we rounded a small island to go ashore and unpack for lunch, my guide stopped me. What are those black fins over there, he wondered. Hugging the curve of that island, we suddenly found ourselves surrounded by a pod of orcas.

I was afraid as they drew near, but my guide calmed me. Pulled my kayak to his, allowed me to hold on to his arm. *Relax,* he told me, *be still. We are safe.* And then those great dancing bodies reached the waters directly beside us, carving their ancient arcs. I heard the rhythmic lull of their breath, felt their quiet intelligence, their gentle presence. I knew, then, that all was not lost. That there was still much to love about our broken world, much to find hope in.

Right before the Iraq War, I interviewed the Brooklyn rapper El-P, who'd then just recorded an album about 9/11. As I meditated on connection, on the Raptors parade and the whales, his long-ago comments floated back to me.

"I think that we are headed toward the inevitable destruction of our society, period. Roman Empire–style," he'd told me, voicing a sentiment I'd heard from so many in our generation, then and since.

"But what can you do?" he went on. "That is a lot of what my record is about. I am just trying to enjoy the same rites of passage that people before me did. I am trying to grow up, I am trying to fall in love, I am trying to build something for myself. I am trying to figure out how to exist—and I don't want that to be interrupted. It's not fair. Unfortunately, that selfish desire and the reality of what's happening are conflicting. I don't know what to do. I'll be honest with you—I really don't know what to do.

"But I'm not here to bludgeon people with negativity," he continued. "I see hope and I see beauty. That's the whole point of the album *Fantastic Damage*. Out of these things—out of the damage—comes this inspiration. On the one hand, I want to present you with all of my horrible, negative fear. And on the other hand, I want to present the reason why the fear of destruction is there. Why else would you fear it unless there were these things that were beautiful? I see a lot of power and a lot of excitement and energy and beauty in our generation."

Tell us your story, tell us your story. Tell the city your story.

And my story? Mine is that I continued to live frugally so I could take time off from the newsroom when I needed to, thereby protecting my health and well-being. I continued to bike and walk and take transit and use car sharing, to eat at home more often than not. This, to be able to stay in my profession and also stay healthy. To have the time and energy to prepare nourishing food, and sleep, and exercise, and volunteer—maybe even go curling with friends, just for a lark. To connect. To read widely and think deeply. To be quiet sometimes. Turn off my phone. Dance in my kitchen. Enjoy being alive. Being human.

In the end, I applied all I'd learned to staying in the game. To survive our crazy world, I had to reject its most crazy-making elements. I leaned out from the culture of overwork, always-on devices, social media, consumerism. In service of leaning further in to my city, my community. And to all those things that make life worth living.

Radical Homemaking author Shannon Hayes once told me that when she traveled the States, chronicling the lives of women resisting modern life, she'd noticed that their narratives tended to have three phases. The first phase was renouncing the current economy. Then, she said, these women moved on to reclaiming the skills needed to rely less on it. Finally came the last stage, which was turning out to the world and rebuilding an economy that actually worked.

This last stage was the most critical one, she said. If you didn't turn outward, you suffered.

"What I found when you looked at [these women] over the course of a lifetime—and [what] I have found in my own life—is that you go back and forth between these phases," Hayes went on. "An economy that works allows every person to do that. We all have families. It's not just women. We *all* have families. We all need to retreat from income earning to take care of loved ones. To take care of ourselves. To go back, to reinvent. It is not a single trajectory. It's a circle, and we're all moving around it all the time."

This story, then—my story—is not a neat narrative, not a tidy line to a fixed destination. Not a linear trajectory. What I am living through, what most of us are now living through, is something much more fluid.

Make no mistake, though. If I had the choice, I would prefer a straighter shot, a simpler story. Solidity, at least some small measure of permanence, somewhere. I would, like most people, prefer contributing to society *and* having financial security. It'd be nice to have stable housing. I wouldn't be mad at the ability to set aside money for retirement. A glam night out now and then wouldn't hurt, either.

My story, then, is still shaped by the failed public policy of our era. I am still a woman who paid off enormous student debt (and an enormous interest bill to big banks), who worked untold hours in overtime, and whose health suffered for it, and who now has no financial security. I am still living in one of the most expensive cities in the world, which systematically failed to protect its citizens from a massive influx of global capital. I am still working in an industry disrupted by largely unregulated tech giants, trying to manage anxiety, the illness of our age, often linked to the products of those selfsame tech giants. I am still a woman without assets, property, investments, pensions, savings.

But I am not a woman without opportunity. I am not without a tribe. I am not without hope, or a deep faith in humanity. And I will not squander these things. I will not stop telling the stories of our time.

Acknowledgments

When I was in my twenties in grad school, after I returned from Southeast Asia, I lived in a heritage walk-up in Kitsilano, probably my favorite neighborhood on the planet. It was a nice life; the problem was that I did not seem to fit in it. Nothing came easy, and nothing seemed to work. I perpetually felt as if I was shouting across an ever-widening chasm, and nobody on the other side could make out my message. I had emerged from the cancer and the travel shaken awake by the world—attuned, now, to its immense suffering, but also its radiant beauty—and I had nowhere to go with this experience. Certainly, few people with whom to share it.

I had the strong feeling, then, of being out of place. And so I was constantly casting about, searching for a life that might make more sense. What this looked like, in practice, was drinking pot after pot of coffee, and listening to very loud hip-hop, and reading for hours at a time. I read essay collections edited by young female writers in Manhattan. I read magazines (Zadie Smith's *Vibe* interview with Eminem; Elliott Wilson's editorials at *XXL*; anything by Kris Ex). I read newspapers (Sloane Crosley and Elizabeth Méndez Berry and Greg Tate and Ta-Nehisi Coates in *The Village Voice*; Touré and Kelefa Sanneh in the *New York Times*; plus, Jelani Cobb, Neil Drumming).

I read novels (Danyel Smith's *Bliss*; Danzy Senna's *Caucasia*; Adam Mansbach's *Angry Black White Boy*). I read memoirs (Rebecca Walker's *Black White and Jewish*) and nonfiction titles (Bakari Kitwana's *The Hip-Hop Generation*; Jeff Chang's *Can't Stop Won't Stop*; Joan Morgan's *When Chickenheads Come Home to Roost*). Gathering these books to me, I constructed maps in my mind, complex webs of connections between the writers I admired, most of whom were my age and living in New York City. In this way, I was able to see, feel on an almost visceral level, how one might go about building a writing life. Poring over the books' acknowledgments sections, I found a place for myself. Met my fellow writers on the page.

At a young age, then, I knew that writing—what appears the most solitary of professions—was actually an expression of community, of togetherness. Ultimately, of love. Any success that you enjoyed as a writer, I could see, had as much to do with the souls you were lucky enough to be surrounded by as with the beauty or wisdom of your words.

I offer this blueprint of my own modest success as a writer, then, to all the remarkable people I've encountered, in gratitude. Also: to any young writer now reading this.

Thank you, Charlie Smith and Mike Usinger at the *Georgia Straight*, for giving the gift of rigorous editing, and at the most formative of times. Thank you, Charlie Demers, for the idea to write for newspapers in the first place. Thank you to my cohort at *The Peak* at Simon Fraser University. Thank you, Sheila Delany, for your confidence.

Thank you, William Gibson, for advice and encouragement at a pivotal moment.

Thank you, Elliott Wilson, for your brilliance and your generosity, and for building a crew of insanely smart, savvy, raucous writers at *XXL Blogs* and inviting me to be a part of it. Thank you, too, for being one of the first in hip-hop to say that its sexism was indefensible. Thank you to the *XXL* readers, some of whom became writers themselves. You will all remember: there was, at that moment in blogs' infancy, a feeling of taking part in a vital, game-changing conversation. It was exhilarating. And I don't think it's an exaggeration to say its impact is still felt in hip-hop today.

Thank you, Celine Wong and Rodrigo Bascuñàn. Thank you, Kris Ex.

Thank you, New York City, for introducing me to myself. Thank you, hip-hop. I used to love you, and I love you still.

Thank you, Toronto, for all the ways that you've surprised me, and sustained me.

Thank you to everyone from *Hello!*, especially Mike Killingsworth, Liza Cooperman, Jayme Poisson, Peter Bregg and Joanna Wood. Thank you, Alison Eastwood.

Thank you to my talented, tenacious colleagues all across the country at the CBC, who inspire me every single day. Thank you, Shiral Tobin in Vancouver, who showed me tremendous kindness during a difficult time (and encouraged me to take lunch breaks). Thank you, Theresa Duvall, for welcoming me back into the fold. Thank you to Stephen Quinn and the team at *The Early Edition*, especially Catherine Rolfsen. Thank you to Gloria Macarenko and everyone at *On the Coast*, especially Manusha Janakiram and Jeremy Allingham.

Thank you to the inimitable Carla Turner at CBC Toronto. Thank you to Matt Galloway and the team at *Metro Morning*—the beating heart of the city—where I began thinking through a lot of the ideas in this book. Thank you, Manjula Selvarajah. Thank you, Morgan Passi. Thank you to the late Ing Wong-Ward, a force (in fabulous boots). Thank you, Gill Deacon and the team at *Here and Now*, especially Danielle Grogan. Tanya Springer at *The Doc Project*. Karen Levine at *The Sunday Edition*. A big thank you, too, to Strombo and everyone from *George Stroumboulopoulos Tonight*.

Thank you to all the writers I interviewed for this book. Especially Johann Hari, Sebastian Junger, Shannon Hayes, Mark Boyle, Charles Montgomery, Darren McGarvey and Shaka Senghor, all of whom were so very generous with their time and insights.

Thank you for a grant from the BC Arts Council, without which this book would not have been started, and a grant from the Writers' Trust of Canada's Woodcock Fund, without which it could not have been finished. Thank you, Charlie Demers and Lisa Gabriel, for support. Thank you to the Access Copyright Foundation and the Marian Hebb Research Grant, which enabled me to include so many more voices in the book.

Thank you, Michael O'Shea.

Thank you to the Topanga Café, and the Zallen family. Thank you, Andrew Pyatt.

Thank you, Mutang Tu'o and the Penan.

Thank you, Ian Brett, for coming with me to Borneo.

Thank you, Thom Henley, Wade Davis and Doug Ragan,

for reading and commenting on the Borneo essay that later became a chapter here.

Thank you, Deborah Dundas at the *Toronto Star*, for your excellent taste in books, and for allowing me to write on so many of the topics I was mulling over for this book. Thank you to the paper, too, for allowing me to reprint portions of several pieces here.

Thank you, Katie Nanton, for your dynamism, and for assigning me so many amazing author interviews. And to Claudia Cusano and *NUVO* for permission to reprint the Sunshine Coast story here.

Thank you, Domini Clark at the *Globe and Mail*, for being your hilarious, smart, skeptical self. And for allowing me to work out my relationship to Salt Spring Island on the page, and then use it here.

Thank you, Jessica Johnson at *The Walrus*, for your dazzling editorial insights and for helping me grow immeasurably as a writer. Thank you, Lauren McKeon, for wrangling the Borneo essay into shape. Thank you, *The Walrus*, for giving me a place to begin the writing of this book.

Thank you, Portia Corman and everyone at CBC Life. And to CBC Licensing, for granting me permission to reprint parts of my early retirement article.

Thank you, Leslie Hurtig, for book chats when I most needed a break. Thank you, Julia Thiessen. Thank you to the wonderful team at JJ Bean in Cambie Village in Vancouver, where the bulk of this book was written. Thank you, Andrea Blair, Rona Herzog, Lee Holt, Micaillah Skillin, Analynn Remigio.

Thank you, Take a Hike Foundation, and all the students I had the privilege of spending time with there. You all impress me, all the time.

Thank you, Chris Arends and Kassy Radis at Quadra Island Kayaks.

Thank you to the Environmental Youth Alliance.

Thank you, Kari Bergrud.

Thank you, Carollyne Conlinn.

Thank you, Essential Impact.

Thank you, Barbara Madani.

Thank you, Katie Leah.

Thank you, Shallun Pierre.

Thank you, Heather McGillivray, for sending me on that life-changing trip to the Sunshine Coast. Thank you, Powell River Sea Kayak and the Cabana Desolation Eco Resort. Thank you, West Coast Wilderness Lodge.

Thank you, Wanderung.

Thank you, Hassan Khan.

You know what's crazy about writing a book? You're by yourself with the pages, for years—a freaking lifetime, it feels like—and then, with just a single phone call, you are no longer alone. (Thank you one more time, Charlie.) You were pushing a rock up a hill on your own, and then suddenly there are many more sets of hands pushing too. Remarkable. Thank you to my fantastic, fantastic duo of agents, John Pearce and Chris Casuccio at Westwood Creative Artists, who championed the book and whose sterling insights helped shape it in critical ways. Thank you for all the talks, in Vancouver and Toronto, and down long-distance lines.

Thank you, Robert McCullough, publisher extraordinaire, for cookbooks that feed my body and food writers that feed my soul (especially Ruth Reichl). And for the honor of appearing on the same shelves as such authors. Thank you for believing in this book.

Thank you to my wonderful, wise, witty, worldly editor Bhavna Chauhan. You are truly the best. You are such good company, on the page and in person, and the book is immeasurably better for your exquisite edits. (And Solange song references.)

Thank you to everyone at Appetite.

Thank you to the publicity team at Penguin Random House, who helped get this book out into the world, and into your hands. Especially my publicist Debby de Groot in Toronto, and Laura Cameron, an early backer, in Vancouver. Thank you to Erin Kern for diligent copy-editing, and for catching so many things that I never would have. And to Melanie Little, for a stellar proofread.

Thank you to friends, fellow journalists and experts who generously reviewed parts of this manuscript to help ensure accuracy: Manjula Selvarajah, Derrick O'Keefe, Josh Gordon, Stephen Hui, Charlene Lo, Paola Perin, James Hallett and Celine Wong. Thank you to my brother, mother and sister-in-law for feedback and facts.

Thank you to the ever-thorough Allison Baker, producer at Mi'kmaq Matters and fact-checking champ, for help with fact-checking during crunch time, and Lindsay Vermeulen at Appetite, a total star who painstakingly went through the entire document. Hooray for facts!

Thank you to friend and fellow writer, Vancouver photographer Rebecca Blissett, for my author photo. And to Aísling Conway for doing my makeup.

Thanks to the following friends who offered coffee talks, seawall walks, sunset beach barbecues, cycle-touring trips, guest rooms, dim sum dates, dinners, garden-grown arugula, pub quiz nights—and even much-needed visits with dogs and small children—at key points during this writing. In Vancouver: Nicole, Mike, Isola, Imogen and Emerson Ricci-Stiles and the Ricci family, Patty Deol, Paola Perin, Stephen Hui, Jen Monahan, Jayne Trimble, Karly Thorleifson, Tara Kutlesa, Melissa Jang, Binh Hoang, Scott Proudfoot, Estella Lum, Camilla Jeffries-Chung, Kevin Smith, Niall Feeney, Yasira Vawda, Charlene Lo, Fiona Mowatt, Sasha Tymkiw, Andrea Wadman, Kathy Wyder, and James Hallett. In Toronto: Janela Jovellano and Matt, Maddy and Xavier Lyon, Carla Turner, Jacinta Kuznetsov, Phil Leung and Ananda Fahey, Helena Cotter, Bruce Geddes and Gena Piliotis, Amy Cormier, Marnie Robinson and Mike Fitzgerald, Anuja and David Pereira, Josh Henk and Jane Forbes, Adam Nicholls, Arwen Humphreys.

Lastly, a lifetime of hugs and home-cooked meals are due to my family, in Toronto and Dublin. To Ann and the entire Mitchell family. To my kindred spirit cousin Sandy, and Dwayne, Brandon and Tyler. To my wonderful aunt Vicki and uncle Bill. To my sister-in-law Catherine, for your energy, for going on a wild adventure with me and for always being up for a good gab. To little Nathan Carter, glee personified (and Jay-Z namesake). To Aísling, bright star that you are, you are so special. To my brother Rob, for your strength and fierce loyalty and sharp intellect— and your jokes, obviously. I admire you so. And to my brave, brilliant mother Joy, without whose immense love and generosity I would be lost. I love you all.

Author Note

This is a work of memoir that also happens to be packed with information, a tricky thing to navigate. Please know that I have taken some liberties with the timeline for the sake of narrative arc; not everything here is in the order that it happened. And, when I am writing about things that happened long ago, I have done my best to reconstitute memories. Having said that, though, I do not believe in a post-truth era, obviously, so we have fact-checked this book rigorously and provided sources to ensure accuracy. Errors are, of course, entirely my own, and for any and all, I fully expect to be hung out to dry on Twitter.

Notes on Sources

This chapter covers a lot of ground, spanning from the summer of 2001 to the end of 2015, and my entire life and work in the media in between. So, no big deal.

Thankfully, a lot of my earliest newspaper articles are not available online, sparing me endless embarrassment. A lot of my *XXL* columns are still on the now-defunct magazine's website, preserved for posterity (but stripped of bylines and, sadly, links to other writers and to comments sections, where so much of the ongoing conversation played out). You can download my master's thesis from Simon Fraser University's library, although I sincerely wish you wouldn't.

2   *after completing a master's degree, I was $60,000 in debt* I've written several times about my student loan debt. The first piece was for the *Georgia Straight*, "To Outthink the Red Ink," and was published February 17, 2005: https://www.straight.com /article/to-outthink-red-ink. I remember how horrified I was even saying the number out loud, let alone printing it. But of course my editors made a good argument for why it should be in the piece, and so we ran it. Looking at it now, I still cringe. $60,000!

4   *wrote my story on anti-war hip-hop* "A New Game: Hip-Hop Takes a Political Turn in NYC" was published in the *Georgia Straight*, March 15, 2003.

5   *I scored bylines in newspapers like the Globe and Mail and The Guardian* My first piece for the *Globe*, "Assuming the Lotusland Position," in October of 2004, captures the supreme frustration I was feeling with the West Coast at the time. And you can still read my *Guardian* piece from that time, "The

Black Panther Rap," published August 28, 2003: https://www
.theguardian.com/theguardian/2003/aug/28/features11.g21

6   *Somali drivers with their heads hung out the window, K'naan's
     "Soobax" blaring from the radio* K'naan's "Soobax," a direct
     address to Somali warlords, was an epic song. I once saw
     him perform it at Black Sunday, a community gathering in
     Soweto, South Africa. What a day that was. You can read my
     first interview with K'naan here: https://www.straight.com
     /article/knaan-reps-african-hip-hop. I love "Soobax," but I
     think the song of his that stands out most to me is "Strugglin',"
     with its moody poetry: "And mostly I'm up and stressing
     when other folks sleep / Believe me, I know struggle and
     struggle knows me / My life owes me, like an overdose I'm
     slowly / Drifting into the arms of trouble, then trouble holds
     me." Super moving. If you feel like having a good cry, you
     should definitely take a listen.

6   *my life feeling like an early Margaret Atwood novel* I was think-
     ing, here, about Atwood's *The Edible Woman* (McClelland &
     Stewart, 1969). I seem to remember there being bacon break-
     fasts in it, and chilly Toronto streets. Though I haven't gone
     back and re-read it recently, so I may be imaging that.

6   *and I landed a staff writer job at a women's magazine* It was
     Hello! Canada.

7   *it was a city where you might plausibly spot Matt Damon and his
     wife at a film screening. . .* These things all happened. Every
     one of them.

7   *ushered into midnight parties in Tribeca, hosted by iconic pop stars
     and their rapper husbands* Beyoncé and Jay-Z. I know, right?

8   *the feeling of jet lag was with me always, bleeding into my days
     and nights* I only recently read Pico Iyer's mesmerizing *The
     Global Soul: Jet Lag, Shopping Malls, and the Search for Home*
     (Vintage, 2001), while preparing to write a profile of him. I wish
     I had read it when I was writing this chapter.

11   *and proceeded to spend the day baking lemon squares and watch-
     ing the first snowfall of the season* I'm pretty sure it was some
     version of these lemon bars: https://www.chatelaine.com

/recipe/quick-and-easy/lemon-coconut-shortbread-squares/.
I was listening to this melancholic Drake album at the
time, which I'm actually still listening to all the time today:
https://www.straight.com/article-330269/vancouver/drake
-justifies-hype-thank-me-later

11   *and doormen who stood in for family* Shout out to Shallun
Pierre.

13   *there was nothing more satisfying than walking purposefully
through its impressive atrium every morning* Seriously, just
thinking about CBC Toronto's lobby makes me emotional.

14   *I mourned each new closing of a shop in my neighborhood* RIP,
Yorkville Espresso Bar. RIP, The Cookbook Store. What an
amazing place that was. If you want to understand just
how foundational it was for Toronto food culture, read this:
https://www.macleans.ca/culture/books/saying-goodbye-to
-torontos-cookbook-store/. I could see this store from my
bedroom window! Before the demolition, that is.

15   *and Tinder culture* https://torontolife.com/city/life/bay-street
-tinder-diaries-dating-age-internet-hookup/ (Hilarious!)

15   *of the populist mayor Rob Ford getting caught smoking crack*
https://www.thestar.com/news/gta/2014/02/01/crazy_town_
the_rob_ford_story_exclusive_excerpt_of_robyn_doolittles_
book.html (Not funny at all.)

16   *these were the days when we started talking a lot about mental
illness in the city, later found to afflict one in every two workers
in our city* This *Metro Morning* segment on mental illness rates
aired after I moved to Vancouver, and I remember sitting
on my couch listening to it, missing the team, and suddenly
being hit by the full weight of these stats. https://www.cbc.ca
/news/canada/toronto/programs/metromorning/civicaction
-mental-health-toronto-hamilton-1.3540757

18   *I was reading, not surprisingly, Joan Didion's farewell to New
York City, "Goodbye to All That," and imagining writing my
own melancholic love letter to big-city life* I was certainly not
the first one to have this idea, and will not be the last. https:
//www.nytimes.com/2013/11/24/fashion/From-Joan-Didion-to

-Andrew-Sullivan-some-writers-leave-behind-letters-when
-they-leave-new-york-city.html

CHAPTER ONE: **The Modern City**

Vancouver has been blessed with some seriously dogged reporters, writers and academics, whose work I have drawn on here. I'm talking about Kerry Gold and Kathy Tomlinson at the *Globe and Mail*; Sam Cooper at Global; Ian Young at the *South China Morning Post*; Andy Yan and Josh Gordon at SFU; and, more recently, Natalie Obiko Pearson at Bloomberg. And of course, everyone at CBC Vancouver, including Stephen Quinn and all who put together the podcast series *Sold!* Also, you're going to want to watch the documentary *Vancouver: No Fixed Address* (which I'm pretty sure you can stream for free on the Knowledge Network site). You should know that this story and its data are constantly evolving. If you want the most up-to-date numbers, check out the Twitter feeds of the reporters above, and read their most recent work.

21 *where I camped out at the Plaza Athénée in a sprawling suite with a grand piano, overlooking the Eiffel Tower* If you are wondering if I made this up, I did not. You can read about this charmed hotel stay, in my review of it here: https://www.theglobeand mail.com/life/travel/destinations/the-plaza-athenee-a-parisian -bastion-of-old-world-elegance/article28715749/

23 *"Dear Vancouver" breakup letters circulated regularly on social media* This one, of all of the Dear Vancouver breakup letters, got me the most. In part because it was so well-written and in part because Jessica Barrett was, as she pointed out, the defi-nition of a Vancouver success story. And she *still* could not stay. https://thetyee.ca/Opinion/2017/10/30/I-Left-Vancouver/

24 *anyone could see that much of the money was coming from China* The definitive article on the impact of Chinese capital, emailed to me from friends all around the world, ended up being by Bloomberg. https://www.bloomberg.com/news/features /2018-10-20/vancouver-is-drowning-in-chinese-money

25 *the mayor objected to housing crisis research, claiming it had "rac-ist tones"* I'm referring here to Gregor Robertson's criticism of

urban planner Andy Yan, now the director of the City Program at Simon Fraser University. https://vancouversun.com/news /staff-blogs/nothing-racist-about-metro-housing-study-experts -say This is the study that the mayor took issue with: http:// www.vancouversun.com/business/bank+mortgages+bags+cas h+behind+chinese+home+buys+vancouver/11485324/story.html

25   *then premier Christy Clark insisted foreign investment was play-ing a negligible role* Christy Clark's courting of foreign capital is documented here: https://vancouversun.com/news/local -news/clark-wat-met-hong-kong-developers-while-foreign -investor-debate-roiled-b-c

25   *with one report finding that $5 billion had been laundered in B.C.'s real estate sector in a single year* https://vancouversun. com/news/politics/money-laundering-hikes-b-c-real-estate -prices-report. And here's a timeline of the scandal, which was all going on as I wrote this book: https://vancouversun.com /news/local-news/money-laundering-in-b-c-timeline-of-how -we-got-here

25   *In 2016, government data showed that in one five-week period, close to $1 billion in foreign money had poured into Metro Vancouver's real estate market* https://thewalrus.ca/vancouvers -flimsy-foreign-tax/

25   *like Simon Fraser University's Andy Yan, who maintained that speaking out against the destructive impact of foreign capital was not synonymous with anti-immigrant bigotry, and that that charge was, in fact, being used to silence the conversation around housing affordability* He says this explicitly in this *Maclean's* piece, and it's worth quoting him in full: "So you had these whispers about racism being used to shut down a dialogue about afford-ability and the kind of city we want to build here. It's a kind of moral signalling to camouflage immoral actions. It's oppor-tunism, and it's a cover for the tremendous injustices that are emerging in the City of Vancouver and across the region. It's a weird Vancouver thing. It's very annoying. It's kale in the smoothies or something." https://www.macleans.ca/economy /realestateeconomy/andy-yan-the-analyst-who-exposed -vancouvers-real-estate-disaster/

(As an aside, Yan is a highly quotable individual: https://
thetyee.ca/Culture/2019/04/02/Tao-of-Andy-Yan/)

Here's an overview piece on this local dynamic, which *The
Guardian* describes as "a very Canadian discomfort with
talking about race": https://www.theguardian.com/cities
/2016/jul/07/vancouver-chinese-city-racism-meets-real-estate
-british-columbia

26   *never mind that the average one-bedroom in Vancouver rented
for more than $2,000 a month* This number fluctuates a lot but
seems to stay around the $2,000 mark: https://vancouversun.
com/news/local-news/vancouvers-average-rental-price-for
-one-bedroom-apartment-jumps-to-2100

27   *meanwhile, Hootsuite's CEO, Ryan Holmes, penned an impassioned op-ed in the paper saying he couldn't recruit, or retain,
talent in a city where nobody could afford to rent, let alone
own:* https://theprovince.com/news/local-news/ryan-holmes
-hootsuite-ceo-without-affordable-housing-vancouver-risks
-becoming-an-economic-ghost-town

27   *As writer Michael Kluckner put it in Caroline Adderson's edited
collection* You can find that quote in *Vancouver Vanishes:
Narratives of Demolition and Revival* by Caroline Adderson
(Anvil, 2015).

27   *real estate reporter Kerry Gold's Walrus cover story* The May
2016 issue: https://thewalrus.ca/the-highest-bidder/

27   *Sam Cooper went even further, arguing that the social contract
in the city had been broken* He said this in the documentary
Vancouver: No Fixed Address: https://www.knowledge.ca
/program/vancouver-no-fixed-address

28   *a church in Kitsilano was put up for sale, evicting dozens of
community groups and shuttering an emergency cold shelter
for homeless men* https://www.straight.com/life/991306/homeless
-vancouver-kitsilano-has-lost-its-only-emergency-mens-homeless
-shelter

28   *after forty years, a meditation center was forced to find a new
venue* https://vancouver.shambhala.org/community/location/

28 *crushed by soaring property taxes, small businesses closed their doors* https://thetyee.ca/News/2019/01/22/Save-BC-Small-Businesses-Property-Tax/

28 *struggled to find minimum-wage staff, who could no longer afford to rent apartments here* https://www.theglobeandmail.com/business/commentary/article-affordable-rental-housing-is-nearly-nonexistent-for-minimum-wage/

30 *data had been published revealing that Shaughnessy was one of the lowest-income neighborhoods in the city* https://vancouversun.com/news/staff-blogs/thousands-of-metro-vancouver-mansion-owners-avoiding-taxes

30 *the federal government had released studies to show that refugees earned more income than those who arrived through Canada's controversial investor immigration program* https://www.cbc.ca/news/business/refugees-pay-more-income-tax-than-millionaire-investor-immigrants-1.2984982

30 *in an opinion piece for the Vancouver Sun, SFU professor Josh Gordon pointed out* https://vancouversun.com/opinion/op-ed/opinion-surtax-needed-to-bring-fairness-to-vancouver-real-estate. And also read this: https://vancouversun.com/opinion/op-ed/josh-gordon-speculation-tax-is-essential-for-housing-affordability

32 *in the novel, Gibson coins a term, "soul lag," for the surreal sensation that accompanies international jet travel* I am referring to *Pattern Recognition* by William Gibson (Berkley, 2005). I love this novel so much that I will quote the passage I'm thinking of in full: "She knows, now, absolutely, hearing the white noise that is London, that Damien's theory of jet lag is correct: that her mortal soul is leagues behind her, being reeled in on some ghostly umbilical down the vanished wake of the plane that brought her here, hundreds of thousands of feet above the Atlantic. Souls can't move that quickly, and are left behind, and must be awaited, upon arrival, like lost luggage." Good god, he can write.

33 *the forty-seat eatery* Some memories of the Topanga Café: https://www.straight.com/food/1099686/mark-leiren-young-memories-topanga-cafe

34   *a painter, had a boyfriend, Iain, in a punk rock band called Curious*
     George https://www.youtube.com/watch?v=m28LCTyULuA

34   *Iain worked at the Topanga Café* He also worked at CBC
     Radio, as a producer on *The Early Edition* and *On the Coast*,
     two shows I've also worked for.

35   *the Cole Porter tribute Red Hot + Blue* What an album: https://
     www.youtube.com/playlist?list=PL681ACF45BFED2663

36   *he loaned me Anthony Bourdain's Kitchen Confidential* I thought
     of Tom when I got the great privilege of interviewing Anthony
     Bourdain, for his *Medium Raw* book in 2010. Tom would have
     loved him. As everyone who met Bourdain did. What a beau-
     tiful soul he was.

37   *informing me that Topanga was on fire* You can read about it
     here: https://vancouversun.com/news/local-news/firefighters
     -battle-blaze-at-kitsilano-restaurant

38   *surrounded by aging boomers with their flowing tunics and New*
     Yorker canvas tote bags On the topic of aging West Side
     boomer hippies, I recall once going to a party in a 1970s-style
     mansion owned by the parents of a classmate, and taking a
     local female rapper with me. Once inside, she looked around,
     and said, "Oh, okay, I get it—rootsy with loot."

39   *I'd hoped the cross-country move would cure my burnout*
     Burnout is nothing to play with: https://www.cnn.com
     /2019/05/27/health/who-burnout-disease-trnd/index.html

39   *in his essay collection The Horrors, Vancouver writer Charles*
     Demers writes about our need for narrative arcs This is in Z
     chapter of *The Horrors: An A to Z of Funny Thoughts on Awful*
     Things by Charles Demers (Douglas & McIntyre, 2015).

39   *and quotes Douglas Coupland, that as the twenty-first century*
     unspools, "it will become harder to view your life as 'a story'" This
     is from "A Radical Pessimist's Guide to the Next Ten Years"
     by Douglas Coupland, published in the *Globe and Mail*,
     October 8, 2010. The full thought was: "The way we define
     our sense of self will continue to morph via new ways of
     socializing. The notion of your life needing to be a story will
     seem slightly corny and dated. Your life becomes however

many friends you have online." Also of relevance here: "You've become a notch in the Internet's belt. Don't try to delude yourself that you're a romantic lone individual. To the new order, you're just a node. There is no escape." https://www .theglobeandmail.com/news/national/a-radical-pessimists -guide-to-the-next-10-years/article1321040/. You can listen to his related CBC Massey Lectures here: https://www.cbc.ca/radio /ideas/the-2010-cbc-massey-lectures-player-one-what-is-to -become-of-us-1.2946885

CHAPTER TWO: **The Woods**

The opening to this chapter is an extended version of a travel story I was lucky enough to write for *NUVO*. You can read it here: https://nuvomagazine.com/travel/exploring-the-sunshine-coast -bc. You can also read about the region here:

https://sunshinecoastcanada.com/things-to-do/hidden-gems /princess-louisa-inlet/ and

here: https://www.princesslouisa.bc.ca. One of the most magical places on Earth.

41   *on the sheltered Princess Louisa Inlet* This area made head-lines after I had finished the book, when a crowdsourcing campaign raised the three million dollars the BC Parks Foundation needed to purchase part of the land and protect it from logging, preserving close to two thousand acres for generations to come. https://www.nytimes.com/2019/09/10/world /americas/princess-louisa-inlet-crowdfunding.html

44   *I disappeared into Grant Lawrence's* memoir I'm talking about *Adventures in Solitude: What Not to Wear to a Nude Potluck and Other Stories from Desolation Sound* by Grant Lawrence (Harbour, 2010).

47   *my parents lived in Project One, an intentional community in San Francisco* There's apparently a documentary about Project One (1972, Optic Nerve) out there: https://archive.org/details /cbpf_000052. And my mother sent me this link to a fascinat-ing *San Francisco Chronicle* article from 1972: http://www .alangrinberg.com/one/Albright/Albright1.html. You'll notice that the rent there was twenty-three dollars a month.

47   *they lost an acquaintance's sister in the anti-war protest at Kent State* This was Allison Krause, the 19-year-old who was one of four students shot by the National Guard in 1970 on Kent State University grounds. Allison's sister was friends with a roommate in the communal house, dubbed The Ivey League, that my parents lived in in Pittsburg.

47   *they lived on a commune, the secluded Primal Point on Galiano Island* Some of the local history is chronicled here http://www.galianoclub.org/2012/09/daystar-market-adventures-in-the-west-coast-whole-foods-movement-conversations-with-lony-rockafella-by-akasha-forest/

48   *to the draft-dodger haven of Salt Spring* You can read a bit about Salt Spring's past here: https://www.saltspringtourism.com/history/

50   *I felt raw and utterly defenseless* Of course what I'm describing here is anxiety. To read a better description of anxiety, read the pocket essay *Exposure* by Olivia Sudjic (Peninsula, 2018).

53   *the Japanese practice of shinrin-yoku, or forest bathing* Some links if you're interested in reading more on forest bathing: https://time.com/4718318/spring-exercise-workout-outside/

       https://time.com/5259602/japanese-forest-bathing/

       https://davidsuzuki.org/story/nature-calms-the-brain-and-heals-the-body/

       https://www.cbc.ca/news/health/nature-health-1.5128482

       https://www.frontiersin.org/articles/10.3389/fpsyg.2019.00305/full

56   *attention distraction can lead to high stress and bad moods* https://www.nytimes.com/2013/05/05/opinion/sunday/a-focus-on-distraction.html and

       https://www.nytimes.com/roomfordebate/2014/11/24/you-wont-believe-what-these-people-say-about-click-bait/click-bait-is-a-distracting-affront-to-our-focus

56   *boasting about the "996"* https://www.reuters.com/article/us-china-tech-labour/opting-out-some-of-chinas-996-tech-tribe-quit-seek-less-stress-idUSKCN1SM0HX

57   *there was a treasure trove of data amassing* You can read
     highlights here: https://www.cbc.ca/life/wellness/can-hitting
     -snooze-and-taking-a-long-lunch-be-the-real-keys-to-success
     -1.4127784

57   *perusing photos of the Sunshine Coast Trail* See Stephen Hui in
     the *Georgia Straight*: https://www.straight.com/blogra/530376
     /10-amazing-sights-awaiting-hikers-sunshine-coast-trail-bc and

     https://www.straight.com/blogra/505591/10-things-hikers-can
     -expect-see-north-coast-trail-bc

58   *McGarvey's prize-winning book* That's *Poverty Safari: Under-
     standing the Anger of Britain's Underclass by Darren McGarvey*
     (Luath, 2017).

59   *what's called the ACE questionnaire* Collected info on the
     ACE: https://www.cdc.gov/violenceprevention/childabuseand
     neglect/acestudy/index.html

59   *higher scores being correlated with higher levels of not just mental
     illness but also physical illness throughout life* Vancouver-born
     Dr. Nadine Burke Harris has a good talk about that here:
     https://www.ted.com/talks/nadine_burke_harris_how_
     childhood_trauma_affects_health_across_a_lifetime/discussion

60   *"the Glasgow Effect" [report]* Coverage of that can be found
     here: https://www.theguardian.com/cities/2016/jun/10/glasgow
     -effect-die-young-high-risk-premature-death

60   *study commissioned by a think tank in Britain, the Mental
     Health Foundation* You can read about that here: https://
     www.theguardian.com/society/2018/may/14/three-in-four
     -britons-felt-overwhelmed-by-stress-survey-reveals

60   *in the U.S., three out of four people report having experienced at
     least one stress symptom in the past month* https://www.apa
     .org/monitor/2017/12/numbers *workplace stress costs the economy*
     https://hbr.org/2016/06/battling-the-physical-symptoms-of-stress

61   *in Canada, 73 percent of adults report feeling stressed* https://
     globalnews.ca/news/4138006/stress-causes-today/

63   *Kristin Kimball, a Manhattan writer* Her book is *The Dirty
     Life: A Memoir of Farming, Food, and Love* (Scribner, 2011).

63   *Hollywood film executive Gesine Bullock-Prado* Her book is *My Life From Scratch: A Sweet Journey of Starting Over, One Cake at a Time* (Broadway Books, 2010).

63   *there was the Marie Claire editor Helen Russell* She wrote *The Year of Living Danishly: Uncovering the Secrets of the World's Happiest Country* by Helen Russell (Icon, 2015).

63   *Canadian journalist Naomi Klein* I'm referring to *This Changes Everything: Capitalism vs. the Climate* by Naomi Klein (Knopf, 2014). And Klein's comments can be found in this *Vancouver Sun* article: http://www.vancouversun.com/health/naomi+klein+seeks+solace+sunshine+coast/10313913/story.html.

64   *Dee Williams, too, whose heart problems had forced her to retire* Her book is *The Big Tiny: A Built-It-Myself Memoir* by Dee Williams (Blue Rider, 2014).

64   *One of her fans, Tammy Strobel, wrote her own book* And that is *You Can Buy Happiness (and It's Cheap): How One Woman Radically Simplified Her Life and How You Can Too* (New World Library, 2014).

64   *the Minimalists, a pair of male bloggers* I'm referring to *Everything That Remains: A Memoir by the Minimalists* by Joshua Fields Millburn and Ryan Nicodemus (Asymmetrical, 2014).

64   *living in a van on his Duke University campus* That's *Walden on Wheels: On the Open Road from Debt to Freedom* by Ken Ilgunas (New Harvest, 2013).

64   *writing books from a homemade houseboat in the waters off Tofino* The most recent one is *Wild Fierce Life: Dangerous Moments on the Outer Coast* by Joanna Streetly (Caitlin, 2018).

64   *who took ten months out to cycle 10,000 miles* I'm talking about the blockbuster book *Lands of Lost Borders: Out of Bounds on the Silk Road* by Kate Harris (Knopf, 2018).

65   *on a bike, you're so exposed to the world* These comments of Kate Harris's are from a June 9, 2018, feature I did for the *Toronto Star* on the recent wave of books from female adventure writers.

67   *exquisitely articulated by the New Yorker's Jia Tolentino* In *Trick Mirror: Reflections on Self-Delusion* (Random House, 2019).

70   *as Hayes puts it in her book of essays* That's *Homespun Mom Comes Unraveled—And Other Adventures from the Radical Homemaking Frontier* by Shannon Hayes (Left to Write, 2014).

71   *nonfiction titles about their movement* Like *Radical Homemakers: Reclaiming Domesticity from a Consumer Culture* by Shannon Hayes (Left to Write, 2010).

CHAPTER THREE: **The Plate**

The opening to this chapter comes from a travel feature I did for the *Globe and Mail* on October 10, 2016: https://www.theglobe andmail.com/life/travel/activities-and-interests/salt-spring-island -perfect-for-travellers-on-a-restricted-diet/article32314573/

And the diet? True story. Shout-out to Katie Leah.

76   *but which, amazingly, got my asthma under control to the point that I no longer required daily doses of steroids, or even an inhaler* I have a lot of doctor friends. They would like me to remind you that at the same time as I changed my diet, I also moved to a city with better air quality, reduced stress and increased sleep and exercise. So, it's impossible to know what factor— or combination of factors—improved the asthma.

77   *I stumbled into Morningside Organic Bakery Café and Bookstore in Fulford Village* I highly recommend paying Morningside a visit.

80   *journalist Michael Pollan spent years unpacking the forces* For *In Defense of Food: An Eater's Manifesto* (Penguin, 2009). I interviewed Pollan for this book, but sadly, I long ago lost that transcript.

80   *he describes how he tracked the rise of "nutritionism"* For this whole section, I'm quoting from Pollan's UCSB talk. You can watch it here: https://www.youtube.com/watch?v=sBr_iimH_o8

83   *my grandmother gave me the Better Homes and Gardens New Junior Cook Book* I just bought my little niece a similar

cookbook and, in Ireland, cooked pancakes and cupcakes and cookies with her.

85   *she told me, too, about the day of the Queen's coronation* Footage of a street party to celebrate the Queen's coronation: https://www.youtube.com/watch?v=df7Mn2E8eg4

86   *Madeleine L'Engle's magical marine tale* That is *A Ring of Endless Light* (Farrar, Straus and Giroux, 1980).

91   *all pleasure, no pointless deprivation* See *French Women Don't Get Fat: The Secret of Eating for Pleasure* by Mireille Guiliano (Knopf, 2004).

92   *on opposite coasts, we slow-roasted tomatoes* Oh, how I love Molly Wizenberg's writing. And recipes. Do yourself a favour and make these: http://orangette.net/2005/08/better -living-through-slow-roasting/

92   *baking brownies* You're also going to want to try Ruth Reichl's brownies. For real. http://ruthreichl.com/2015/05/the-best-brownie -ever.html/

96   *feeding myself as I would a small child* Read *French Kids Eat Everything (And Yours Can, Too)* by Karen Le Billon (Collins, 2012).

97   *yeast dressing* You can find it here: *Hollyhock Cooks: Food to Nourish Body, Mind, and Soil* by Moreka Jolar and Linda Solomon (New Society Publishers, 2003). Be sure to make the Best Ever Cornbread recipe too. It's no joke.

97   *hilariously named vegan "Glory Bowls"* Found here: *Whitewater Cooks: Pure, Simple and Real Creations from the Fresh Tracks Café* by Shelley Adams (Whitecap, 2011). The Glory Bowl recipe is also posted online here: https://whitewatercooks .com/portfolio_page/glory-bowl/

97   *a simple tomato sauce* David Rocco has been generous enough to post the recipe here: https://davidrocco.com/2017/03/23 /tomato-sauce/

98   *traces the origins of many of today's food fads* Read *Hippie Food: How Back-to-the-Landers, Longhairs, and Revolutionaries Changed the Way We* Eat by Jonathan Kauffman (William

Morrow, 2018) and particularly the brown rice chapter, which is eye-opening to say the least.

CHAPTER FOUR: **The Pocketbook**

Well, this is fun. Who wants to talk about money—specifically, about how broke you are? Pretty much no one. But nevertheless, here we are.

103 *I knew this might not be the case if I had been raised in privilege* Or not. Everyone is different.

105 *as I mulled this all over* This is adapted from a piece I wrote for the *Toronto Star*, published November 11, 2017, and aptly headed "A Sad Story." If you Google it, you should be able to find a Pressreader version, but there's no link, unfortunately.

106 *according to the Writers' Union of Canada* The most recent Canadian writer income stats are here: https://www.thestar .com/entertainment/books/2018/10/22/canadian-writers -make-on-average-just-9380-a-year-survey-finds.html, while the U.S. stats are here: https://www.authorsguild.org/industry -advocacy/six-takeaways-from-the-authors-guild-2018 -authors-income-survey/. Feel free to weep into your coffee.

107 *in 1992, David Sedaris was working* I learned these David Sedaris factoids reading his *Theft by Finding: Diaries 1977–2002*, and interviewing him for this *NUVO* feature: https:// nuvomagazine.com/magazine/autumn-2017/david-sedaris

107 *take the case of another boomer luminary* See *Where the Past Begins: A Writer's Memoir* by Amy Tan (Ecco, 2017).

108 *in a 2014 online essay* Here's Emily Gould's piece: https:// humanparts.medium.com/how-much-my-novel-cost-me -35d7c8aec846

108 *wrote a similar piece for Marie Claire* And Merritt Tierce's: https://www.marieclaire.com/career-advice/a22573/merritt -tierce-love-me-back-writing-and-money/

108 *including a leading literary critic, John Freeman* I'm referring to *Tales of Two Americas: Stories of Inequality in a Divided Nation*, ed. John Freeman (Penguin, 2017).

110   *another anthology editor* I'm talking about *Scratch: Writers, Money, and the Art of Making a Living* by Manjula Martin (Simon & Schuster, 2017).

114   *such lessons were easily lost in the urgency of Vancouver's housing crisis* This section is adapted from a piece I wrote for *The Walrus*: https://thewalrus.ca/meet-the-frugal-millennials -planning-for-decades-of-retirement/

117   *the blockbuster blogger known as Mr. Money Mustache* The Pete Adeney comments in this story are from a *CBC Life* article I wrote (along with quotes from Kristy Shen and Bryce Leung), and are gratefully used with permission from CBC Licensing. I've also quoted unpublished comments from my email correspondence with Adeney, used with permission from him. And have added details from Shen established via email in the fact-checking process. https://www.cbc.ca/life/work-money /six-surprising-lessons-we-can-all-learn-from-early-retirement -gurus-1.4736770

117   *a decades-old personal finance book* This is *Your Money or Your Life: 9 Steps to Transforming Your Relationship with Money and Achieving Financial Independence* by Vicki Robin and Joe Dominguez (Penguin, 1992).

117   *he was still kind of pissed about a Rubik's Cube he bought for his son in 2015 that broke* That detail is from this feature: https:// www.newyorker.com/magazine/2016/02/29/mr-money -mustache-the-frugal-guru

119   *back in uber-expensive Vancouver* This section is also adapted from the *Walrus* piece.

121   *the wry logic of a recent Guardian article* Here it is: https:// www.theguardian.com/commentisfree/2016/oct/17/baby -boomers-have-already-taken-all-the-houses-now-theyre -coming-for-our-brunch

122   *or lipstick, for that matter* This detail is in *Meet the Frugalwoods: Achieving Financial Independence through Simple Living* by Elizabeth Willard Thames (HarperBusiness, 2018).

CHAPTER FIVE: **The Internet**

Another super popular topic, no? Everyone loves to hear from people who hate technology.

128   *in Squamish, British Columbia, as friends and I hiked the Chief* Question: Is social media ruining hiking? Answer: Sure is. https://www.cbc.ca/news/canada/british-columbia/social -media-hiking-1.3755738

129   *there's a moment at which it dawns on us Gen-Xers* This is from *My Misspent Youth: Essays* by Meghan Daum (Picador, 2014).

130   *we listened for the call of the peregrine falcon* You can read about the falcons here: https://www.cbc.ca/news/canada /british-columbia/peregrine-falcon-stawamus-chief-1.5190034

133   *I left that day and started one* I'm talking about *Global Beat: The Hip-Hop Diaries*. The blog is now defunct, but you can access it through the Wayback Machine online archive: https://archive.org/web/

135   *if I posted a critical review* This is the review of Jerry Heller's book: https://www.straight.com/article-74977/ruthless-a-memoir. I think there was one for *XXL* as well, but it's no longer online.

135   *down visiting friends at the Brooklyn Hip-Hop Festival* Shout-out to Greg Trani, co-founder of the festival.

135   *our exceptional editor-in-chief* G.O.A.T. editor-in-chief Elliott Wilson.

136   *I came out swinging* The whole back-and-forth is still on the site. You'll forgive me if I don't link to it.

139   *collection of essays* I'm referring to *Never Drank the Kool-Aid* by Touré (Picador, 2006).

139   *the Internet was responsible for my career* That, and Elliott Wilson.

141   *before leaving Toronto, I made a radio documentary* The CBC radio documentary is called "Thirty-Nine," and it's about being single and childless and baffled by my life. Still sitting on the Internet for every guy I ever date to Google. Good times. https://www

.cbc.ca/radio/thesundayedition/justice-or-vengeance-presidential
-hopefuls-at-the-starting-line-women-turning-39-israel-may-not
-survive-1.3393989/thirty-nine-female-crazy-job-no-partner
-no-kids-aaaaaaaaahhhhh-1.3394084

142   *she'd recently published her first novel* This is *Sympathy* by
Olivia Sudjic (Houghton Mifflin Harcourt, 2017).

142   *the twenty-nine-year-old wrote a new one* This is *Exposure* by
Olvia Sudjic (Peninsula Press, 2018).

143   *when I called her in London* This interview is from a piece I
did for the *Toronto Star*, published December 21, 2018: https://
www.thestar.com/entertainment/books/2018/12/21/how-the
-internet-shaped-british-author-olivia-sudjics-writing.html

144   *paints a picture of social media as a large-scale behavior-modification apparatus* Please read *Ten Arguments for Deleting Your
Social Media Accounts Right Now* by Jaron Lanier (Henry Holt
and Co., 2018). This is adapted from my review of the book for
the *Toronto Star*, published July 27, 2018: https://www.thestar
.com/entertainment/books/reviews/2018/07/27/tech-guru-says
-delete-your-social-media-now.html

147   *this journey led me back online* Here's what Mark Boyle learned
from living without money: https://www.theguardian.com
/environment/2015/sep/15/living-without-money-what-i
-learned. And here's his TED Talk: https://www.youtube.com
/watch?v=-PuyYVVVkIM

147   *"the consequences of this ever-intensifying industrialism"* I'm
quoting from his column in *The Guardian*, published March
19, 2008: https://www.theguardian.com/commentisfree/2018
/mar/19/a-year-without-tech-debt-gadgets-reconnect-nature

CHAPTER SIX: **The Void**

In the words of all my favorite rappers (and rap bloggers): s**t
is about to get real.

153   *the British journalist Johann Hari found himself in Hanoi* This
story is from *Lost Connections: Uncovering the Real Causes*

of Depression—and the Unexpected Solutions by Johann Hari (Bloomsbury, 2018).

155 *profile of the late American novelist Madeleine L'Engle* The *New Yorker* piece can be found here: https://www.newyorker. com/magazine/2004/04/12/the-storyteller-cynthia-zarin

155 *I was among those who did* This chapter is adapted from a web essay I wrote for *The Walrus*, published March 28, 2018: https://thewalrus.ca/madeleine-lengle-taught-me-the-universe -has-meaning/

156 *the novel follows Vicky Austin* The book is *A Ring of Endless Light* by Madeleine L'Engle (Farrar, Straus and Giroux, 1980). Easily my favourite L'Engle novel.

158 *the men were on the Voices for the Borneo Rainforest world tour* You can read a newspaper that the Western Canada Wilderness Committee produced about the tour here: https:// www.wildernesscommittee.org/sites/all/files/publications /1990%2010%20Help%20the%20Penan.pdf

159 *we both joined a delegation of young environmentalists* The retreat followed the model of Rediscovery International, which Thom Henley founded with First Nations elders in 1978 in Haida Gwaii: https://rediscovery.org

161 *I had a dream. I was in Borneo, with a friend, in a longboat on the river* For a quick visual of what Sarawak looks like, watch the first 1.5 minutes of this Raphael Treza documentary: https://www.youtube.com/watch?v=TiQBTesZUJQ

167 *I happened upon some words from Frank Church* The quote is from *Love, Medicine and Miracles* by Bernie Siegel (Harper Perennial, 1998).

168 *a tourist family takes a bird-watching boat trip on a river* This short story is in *Bluebeard's Egg: Stories* by Margaret Atwood (McClelland & Stewart, 1983).

170 *we settled into our hostel, run by a Thai family* If you get a chance, Google Image Sukıı Hostel in Bangkok. What a magical place it was. Shout-out to Anil Yossundara and family.

171 *environmentalist Thom Henley's eco resort* The Dawn of Happiness resort in Krabi. Henley is no relation.

171   *Thom gave me a book he'd written about the Penan* That book
is *A Seed of Hope* by Thom Henley (2000).

173   *L'Engle once wrote* In *The Rock That Is Higher: Story as Truth*
by Madeleine L'Engle (Harold Shaw, 1993).

173   *the feeling of the moment* This is the song that was playing in my
mind at the time: https://www.youtube.com/watch?v=pYzZLnIj85I

177   *as the former war correspondent Sebastian Junger writes* In *Tribe:
On Homecoming and Belonging* (Harper Perennial, 2016). You
can read the May 2015 *Vanity Fair* article the book is based on
here: https://www.vanityfair.com/news/2015/05/ptsd-war-home
-sebastian-junger

179   *multimillionaires flooded the streets to protest minuscule property tax increases* This forum on the property tax increase was
infamous in Vancouver:

https://www.cbc.ca/news/canada/british-columbia/david-eby
-school-tax-town-hall-1.4680358

CHAPTER SEVEN: **The Tribe**

In which I attempt to break out of my isolation, and overcome
my aversion to sharing circles. And spend time all over my hometown, searching for community.

185   *finally helped me see that my longing for more closeness* I'm
referring to the book *Lost Connections: Uncovering the Real
Causes of Depression—and the Unexpected Solutions* by Johann
Hari (Bloomsbury, 2018).

187   *recently spoke with a yoga critic* His book is *Practice and All Is
Coming: Abuse, Cult Dynamics and Healing in Yoga and Beyond*
by Matthew Remski (Embodied Wisdom, 2019). You can read
his *Walrus* piece on yoga and sexual abuse here: https://the
walrus.ca/yogas-culture-of-sexual-abuse-nine-women-tell-their
-stories/

188   *her company's three-day workshop on non-directive coaching*
My friend's company is Essential Impact.

194 *I started posting cycling trips on the group email list* Shout-out to Wanderung.

196 *went to dim sum for Chinese New Year* If you're looking to sample some of the best dim sum in the world (in my opinion), may I recommend Sun Sui Wah and Kirin in Vancouver?

197 *Bob told me he had an article in Megaphone* Bob Dennis's article is in the *Megaphone* issue that came out in January 2019.

198 *a local alternative high school for vulnerable youth* Take a Hike is one of the most impressive organizations I've ever come across.

199 *Harris is the Vancouver-born founder and CEO of the Center for Youth Wellness in San Francisco* Her book is *The Deepest Well: Healing the Long-Term Effects of Childhood* Adversity by Nadine Burke Harris, M.D. (Houghton Mifflin Harcourt, 2018).

200 *it reminded me of a story* I learned about South African psychiatrist Derek Summerfield's research in Johann Hari's book *Lost Connections*, in the context of a passage about the introduction of antidepressants to Cambodia. My intention in quoting it here is not to wade into the medication debate, but simply to underscore how important it is to build community and address the concrete conditions of people's lives.

202 *I went to see the attorney, author, TV host and former presidential advisor Van Jones speak* You can watch the February 28, 2018, SFU Public Square event with Van Jones and Anne-Marie Slaughter here: https://www.youtube.com/watch?v=tBTiu8C9qvI. My colleague, the CBC's Laura Lynch, did a brilliant job moderating.

204 *I read his New York Times–bestselling autobiography Writing My Wrongs: Life, Death, and Redemption in an American Prison* by Shaka Senghor (Drop a Gem Publishing, 2019).

204 *watched his TED Talk* And here's Senghor's TED Talk: https://www.ted.com/talks/shaka_senghor_why_your_worst_deeds_don_t_define_you?language=en

204 *streamed his Oprah interview* And his conversation with Oprah Winfrey: http://www.oprah.com/own-super-soul-sunday

/full-episode-oprah-and-criminal-justice-activist-shaka
-senghor

204   *where Senghor now lives and writes* He's now focusing on his
writing career, working on a new book and a one-man show,
and writing for TV and film.

210   *Senghor eventually wrote the man he'd killed a letter* Senghor
reprints this letter in full in his book.

214   *seeking out deeper human connection* I would be remiss here if I
didn't point out how funny Senghor is, too. If you've read this
far, you know I'm a technophobe, so you probably won't be
surprised to hear that I taped our interview on an iPhone 5s.
When I turned off the recording, he looked at me, cocked an
eyebrow and said, "So, what, they just stopped making iPhones
in Canada? Or did you just give up? What happened there?"

CHAPTER EIGHT: **The Home**

The globe-trotting continues as I head to Ireland to track down a
dude who lives in the middle of nowhere without any technology
whatsoever. Should be pretty straightforward, right?

220   *the concept of home is a tricky one in the twenty-first century*
Once again, I wish I'd read Pico Iyer's brilliant book *The
Global Soul: Jet Lag, Shopping Malls, and the Search for Home*
(Vintage, 2001) when I was writing this chapter.

222   *Mark Boyle, the Guardian columnist* You can read his archive of
articles here: https://www.theguardian.com/profile/mark-boyle

222   *I had checked one of Boyle's books out of the library some five
years before* This is *The Moneyless Man: A Year of Freeconomic
Living* by Mark Boyle (Oneworld, 2011).

223   *in a TED Talk* You can watch that talk here:

https://www.youtube.com/watch?v=-PuyYVVVkIM

225   *a cob-and-cordwood hostel, the Happy Pig* There's a piece about
the hostel here:

https://www.permaculture.co.uk/articles/tales-happy-pig
-mark-boyles-free-pub

226 *he was just putting finishing touches on some work for his new book* That book is *The Way Home: Tales from a Life Without Technology* by Mark Boyle (Oneworld, 2019).

228 *in the past forty years, 60 percent of wildlife had disappeared* I think this is the report he was referring to: https://www .cbc.ca/news/technology/living-plant-wwf-2018-1.4882819

228 *recent book he'd read from British author Robert Macfarlane* You can read a review of *Landmarks* here: https://www .theguardian.com/books/2015/mar/08/landmarks-review-robert -macfarlane

228 *it wasn't yet out* I'm referring to *The Age of Surveillance Capitalism: The Fight for a Human Future at the New Frontier of Power* by Shoshana Zuboff (PublicAffairs, Hachette, 2019).

230 *Parry had just made a film about the Penan* You can read about it here: https://www.theguardian.com/environment/2017/sep /29/bruce-parry-interview-borneo-penan-documentary

231 *juice windows where you could share the intimate details of your biology* The juice bar was located in the Ace Hotel in Shoreditch. You may have guessed by now that this is my favorite hotel chain.

232 *George Monbiot's famed essay in The Guardian proclaiming our era the age of loneliness* Found here: https://www.theguardian .com/commentisfree/2014/oct/14/age-of-loneliness-killing-us

234 *interviewing leading experts and examining data-driven research* You can listen to all the research interviews Hari did for his book here: https://thelostconnections.com/the-interviews/

CHAPTER NINE: **The Commons**

Back in my hometown, I think through urbanism, income inequality and the cult of overwork.

239 *as a society, we were at our worst* The summer after I finished the book, I contributed to a month-long series on the state of the Downtown Eastside for CBC Radio Vancouver's *The Early Edition*, diving into this topic in detail.

239   *in walked Charles Montgomery, author* His book is *Happy City: Transforming Our Lives Through Urban Design* (Anchor Canada, 2013).

240   *tattooed men served up miso barley bowls* Montgomery introduced me to the miso barley bowl at The Birds & the Beets—"I'm having one, and so should you"—and now I am straight-up addicted.

241   *as he detailed in a later TED Talk* You can watch it here: https://www.ted.com/talks/enrique_penalosa_why_buses_represent_democracy_in_action?language=en

241   *in his talk, he noted that ten thousand kids were killed every year worldwide by cars* We were not able to independently confirm this fact. We do know that, according to the World Health Organization, from data published in 2013 (the year Peñalosa gave his TED Talk), 1.24 million road traffic deaths occur each year. A more recent report by WHO, published in 2018, says that, worldwide, road traffic injuries are the leading cause of death of children and young adults between the ages of 5-29.

241   *he reduced rush hour traffic by 40 percent, and planted a hundred thousand trees* You can read more about Peñalosa's work here: https://www.pps.org/article/epenalosa-2 and in Montgomery's blog for the World Urban Forum: https://thetyee.ca/Views/2006/06/23/Mayor/

242   *the annual car-free day in the Colombian capital* And, since the 70s, every Sunday has been a cycling day in the capital. You can read about the Ciclovía's history here: https://www.nationalgeographic.com/environment/2019/03/bogota-colombia-ciclovia-bans-cars-on-roads-each-sunday/ and here: https://www.citylab.com/transportation/2018/10/how-bogotas-cycling-superhighway-shaped-a-generation/571900/

243   *a study has determined is the optimal commute time* See the "perfect commute" section: https://www.regus.com/work-us/why-the-key-to-happiness-is-a-16-minute-commute/

244   *a large chunk of 2019's infrastructure budget was going toward repairing the Gardiner Expressway* We had initially thought

this number was roughly half, and reached out to the City of Toronto to confirm this. Ellen Leesti, Strategic Communications, emailed: "Of the approx. $590 M to be spent on rehabilitating and improving transportation infrastructure, approx. $200 M is for the FG Gardiner. That works out to closer to one-third rather than one-half. The percentage is even less if you add in other City infrastructure—such as water infrastructure."

244 *a staggering 1.7 million passenger trips per weekday* You can find TTC ridership data here: https://www.ttc.ca/About_the_ TTC/Operating_Statistics/2017/section_one.jsp

245 *analysts reviewed the data and found that foreign owners had captured $75 billion of the Metro Vancouver real estate market* https://vancouversun.com/news/local-news/dan-fumano-a -75-billion-snapshot-of-foreign-owned-vancouver-real-estate

247 *couples who had a forty-minute commute* I think this is the Swedish study he's referencing: https://journals.sagepub.com /doi/abs/10.1177/0042098013498280. And here's more info on the perils of commuting: https://slate.com/business/2011/05/long -commutes-cause-obesity-neck-pain-loneliness-divorce-stress -and-insomnia.html

247 *driving in traffic can have a greater effect on stress levels than being a riot cop in a protest* https://www.theguardian.com /uk/2004/nov/30/research.transport

248 *studies showed that people who live in cohousing report paying $1,500 less a month in childcare* We were not able to independently confirm this fact.

250 *Bernie Sanders penned an op-ed for the Wall Street Journal* Here's PolitiFact at the Poynter Institute, fact-checking Bernie Sanders' claims: https://www.politifact.com/truth-o-meter /statements/2019/jul/03/bernie-sanders/bernie-sanders-target -saying-3-richest-have-much-w/

250 *"the three richest men in America—Bill Gates, Jeff Bezos and Warren Buffett—now owned more wealth than the bottom half of the American population."* https://www.theguardian.com /global-development/2017/jan/16/worlds-eight-richest-people -have-same-wealth-as-poorest-50

251   *Oxfam also reported that 82 percent of the global wealth gener-ated in 2017 had gone directly to the one percent* https://www.oxfam.org/en/pressroom/press-releases/2018-01-22/richest-1-percent-bagged-82-percent-wealth-created-last-year

251   *Income Inequality: The Canadian Story* You can find that here:

      https://irpp.org/research/income-inequality-the-canadian-story/

251   *told the podcast Policy Options* The podcast can be found here: https://policyoptions.irpp.org/2016/02/23/po-podcast-5-inequality/

252   *Wilkinson stressed in a TED Talk* All of his quotes in this section are from this talk, as is all of the research he cites: https://www.ted.com/talks/richard_wilkinson.htmlminute6/discussion

254   *a Dutch historian and writer for The Correspondent who rose to prominence* His book, of course, is *Utopia for Realists: How We Can Build the Ideal World* by Rutger Bregman (Back Bay/Little, Brown and Company, 2014).

255   *stood at a podium at the Aspen Institute's Action Forum* His Aspen talk is online: https://www.aspeninstitute.org/videos/anand-giridharadas-thriving-world-wilting-world-you/

256   *subsequent book* I'm referring to *Winners Take All: The Elite Charade of Changing the World* by Anand Giridharadas (Knopf, 2019).

259   *Productivity, in fact, has risen more than 70 percent since the 1970s* https://www.epi.org/productivity-pay-gap/

262   *she wrote in an op-ed* Eliza Khuner's piece for *Wired* is here: https://www.wired.com/story/i-am-a-data-scientist-and-mom-but-facebook-made-me-choose/

263   *a Lean In devotee-turned-critic, wrote in an essay* Katherine Goldstein's essay for *Vox*: https://www.vox.com/first-person/2018/12/6/18128838/michelle-obama-lean-in-sheryl-sandberg

265   *Basecamp founders Jason Fried and David Heinemeier Hansson published a book* And that book is *It Doesn't Have to Be Crazy at Work* (HarperBusiness, 2018).

265 *a think piece on what it called "performative workaholism"* Erin Griffith's *New York Times* think piece: https://www.nytimes .com/2019/01/26/business/against-hustle-culture-rise-and-grind -tgim.html

266 *Marissa Mayer, then the CEO of Yahoo!, claimed to have worked 130 hours a week building Google* Marissa Mayer's nonsense: https://www.businessinsider.com/yahoo-ceo-marissa-mayer -on-130-hour-work-weeks-2016-8

EPILOGUE: **The Adventure**

In which I dance to rap songs in a number of different cities and contexts. And somehow find a way to link the Raptors, whales and a Brooklyn emcee. Ha!

269 *in the wake of his now-famous speech* Rutger Bregman in Davos: https://www.theguardian.com/business/video/2019/jan/30 /this-is-not-rocket-science-rutger-bregman-tells-davos-to-talk -about-tax-video

270 *when Republicans dismissed her environmentalism as elitist, delivering a scorching speech* AOC on quality of life: https:// www.youtube.com/watch?v=m5M8vvEhCFI

270 *London's National Portrait Gallery was turning down a million-pound donation from the billionaire Sackler family* https:// www.theguardian.com/artanddesign/2019/mar/19/national -portrait-gallery-turns-down-grant-from-sackler-family -oxycontin

270 *Transparency International Canada was releasing a new report revealing the extent of money laundering in Toronto real estate* http://www.transparencycanada.ca/news/billions-unknown -funds-flow-toronto-real-estate/

272 *The rapper in a hotel restaurant, after a global hip-hop summit on healthcare, freedom, food, giving me a message for the rest of the world* My Venezuela story from eons ago: https://www .straight.com/article/its-bigger-than-hip-hop

274 *the mournful, melodic Rihanna chorus of Drake's "Take Care" filled the room* Too many Drake references for one book? Too bad.

277   *he'd heard from many veterans who'd shared how transforma-*
      tive the book had been for them Reading *Tribe* proved a pivotal
      moment in my journey here in this book, too. And I have
      also given copies of it to many people.

279   *a New York Review of Books essay of hers that I'd just read*
      Zadie Smith's essay "Under the Banner of New York" for the
      New York Review of Books, November 4, 2017: https://www
      .nybooks.com/daily/2017/11/04/under-the-banner-of-new-york/

279   *with all of us, living our little human lives* This of course refers
      back to the Madeleine L'Engle quote that I opened the book
      with.

279   *America had lost 45 percent of its newspaper journalists* Stats on
      decline in newspaper reporters: https://www.pewresearch.
      org/fact-tank/2019/07/09/u-s-newsroom-employment-has
      -dropped-by-a-quarter-since-2008/ft_18-07-30_newspaper
      decline_newspaper-newsroom-employees/

279   *Anand Giridharadas was warning the tech elite that a future*
      with no journalists was not inconceivable Here's his talk at
      Google: https://www.youtube.com/watch?v=d_zt3kGW1NM

281   *Drake taking the stage at Nathan Phillips Square, asking all to*
      turn to a stranger and embrace them Here's Drake's speech:
      https://www.youtube.com/watch?v=eUnr2BVs9cw. Perhaps
      you didn't quite gather that I am a Drake fan? Just in case.

282   *in the words of a recent Zadie Smith short story, to enter each*
      other's stories You can find that in *Grand Union: Stories* by
      Zadie Smith (Penguin, 2019).

283   *right before the Iraq War, I interviewed the Brooklyn rapper El-P*
      That article was "A New Game: Hip-Hop Takes a Political Turn
      in NYC," published in the *Georgia Straight*, March 15, 2003.

      Judging from the looks of this notes section, I spend way too
      much time reading. I need to get out more. For real.